GOVERNING GREATER STOCKHOLM

A publication of the
Franklin K. Lane Memorial Fund,
Institute of Governmental Studies,
University of California, Berkeley

The Franklin K. Lane Memorial Fund takes its name from Franklin Knight Lane (1864–1921), a distinguished Californian who was successively New York correspondent for the San Francisco *Chronicle,* City and County Attorney of San Francisco, member and later chairman of the United States Interstate Commerce Commission, and Secretary of the Interior in the cabinet of President Woodrow Wilson.

The general purposes of the endowment are to promote "better understanding of the nature and working of the American system of democratic government, particularly in its political, economic and social aspects," and the "study and development of the most suitable methods for its improvement in the light of experience."

12.75

GOVERNING GREATER STOCKHOLM

A STUDY OF
POLICY DEVELOPMENT AND
SYSTEM CHANGE

By THOMAS J. ANTON

Published for the
INSTITUTE OF GOVERNMENTAL STUDIES

UNIVERSITY OF CALIFORNIA PRESS
Berkeley • Los Angeles • London

JS
6272
.A84

University of California Press
Berkeley and Los Angeles, California

University of California Press, Ltd.
London, England

Copyright © 1975, by
The Regents of the University of California

ISBN 0–520–02718–3

Library of Congress Catalog Card Number: 73–94447

Printed in the United States of America

*To the doctors and nurses of St. Göran's,
for whom Lynn was more than just
another patient*

CONTENTS

TABLES

MAPS

CHARTS

FOREWORD

"WE SHALL NOT repeat America's mistakes," proclaimed Hjalmar Mehr, Stockholm's socialist leader in the municipal campaign of 1958 (pp. 67–68). He was especially concerned with housing, transportation, and city development. By then all of these matters were recognized by Stockholm's leaders as clearly metropolitan in scope and incidence. Among American "mistakes" was a failure fully to comprehend that in metropolitan communities no part, not even a huge central city, can be truly self-sufficient, autonomous, and independent.

Hjalmar Mehr and his colleagues in the city recognized that the issues of housing, transportation, medical care, and education could be moved from a local to a metropolitan agenda only by organizing the metropolis to articulate and administer the agenda. Certainly they must have noted, as one of "America's mistakes," our difficulty in deciding how to elevate matters of metropolitan import to broader levels of concern, debate, planning, decision, and administration. In any event, within eight years of his statement a Greater Stockholm County had been created, and another five years later it went into full operation.

Professor Anton would probably object to our emphasis on the personal role of Hjalmar Mehr. A major mode of Anton's analysis is to place individual acts, influence, and even orientation, in the conditioning context of organization and culture. One of the strengths of Anton's study is that the personality of individual leaders comes through distinctly even when their behavior is presented as manifestations of collegial decision making according to long-standing cultural patterns. Thus Anton speaks of Mehr's "constant repetition of the Greater County Council idea, at a time when no one else seemed to care about it," and refers to this as "a classic example" of an act of political will by which influential individuals can define is-

sues, problems, and solutions. Mehr's activity was instrumental in
helping define the Stockholm solution that has since been adopted.

It is too early to tell whether the new regional government meets
the expectations of its proponents or justifies the fears of its opponents. But Professor Anton's analytical reconstruction of the politics
of intergovernmental relations, and of the processes through which
they were redesigned and reorganized in the period between 1946
and 1970, is a fascinating chronicle. The story is instructive for North
Americans, and for people in all other parts of the world who are
struggling with ways to establish or maintain effective and acceptable
governance of metropolitan communities.

Anton's study must first be viewed as an account of the behavior
of the ruling elite of one of the world's great cities, regions, and nations. Here the telling of the tale itself justifies the narrative. The
case study method is the only form of expression used by social sci-
entists that can recount a network of actors, situations, objectives,
and institutions moving and changing over time.

Anton has carefully reconstructed and told this story for English-
language readers. Without it only a few of us could have penetrated
the language barrier and peered into a society so similar to ours and
yet so different.

The author is more than a historian of two decades of Stockholm
and its region. As a political scientist he reviews events analytically.
This has enabled him to refine and extend concepts and schemes of
political decision making. He moves us from a cross-sectional analysis
of specific events at given times to a longitudinal analysis of the seam-
less web of politics. In doing so he has made the case study a more
useful vehicle for political analysis.

He reviews in detail policymaking in three cases to illustrate the
actions required to generate new institutional forms. There must be
some common understanding of need such as was developed in the
Stockholm area through regional planning. Also, new institutional
capacity must be developed. This is seen in Anton's case study of
housing. Finally, there must be a new level of integration of previously disparate structures. In Stockholm this occurred almost simultaneously with the development of a regional transportation policy.

Neither an isolated event nor even several related episodes are
adequate in themselves to explain complex institutional change. The
complex meaning of policy can only be captured by focusing on sequences of decisions over a long time. Anton demonstrates this by a
description of the simultaneous dynamic development over time of

institutions, and of "solutions" to problems. He combines two perspectives—each of which has been pursued by other scholars—into
a unified analysis. As a result we see how the system shapes policy
while policy is shaping the system. Anton thus enriches the concept
of decision making and makes it much more useful for analyzing organizations, whether it be metropolitan, industrial, ecclesiastic, or a
national government.

As one reads this study of how the political system of Stockholm
and its municipal neighbors changed while it was producing decisions about the development of the metropolis, one recalls *Governing New York City* by Wallace Sayre and Herbert Kaufman. Whatever else may or may not be transferable from a study of the politics
of another culture, Anton, using similar but not identical analytical
categories, makes one wish that Sayre and Kaufman had stopped for
a moment at any one of innumerable places in their rich physiologi-
cal anatomy of the political system of New York City to show us how
the system operates *as a system.*

Professor Anton makes no effort to hide his normative concerns
over the quality of urban life in America and the "failure of existing
mechanisms of social power to cope effectively with the problems of
our cities." He specifically rejects any kind of determinism as an explanation.

He characteristically ties his normative concerns and judgments to
the analysis of the constant and reciprocal interplay between policy
development and institutional change. Moreover, he emphasizes that
the way problems are solved is closely dependent on the culture's
problem-solving procedures. Even so, he does suggest, from time to
time, things that we can learn from Swedish experiences.

Thus the development of complex relationships encompassing the
metropolitan region of Stockholm may comfort citizens of the United
States who find their governments and officials similarly entangled. It
is somehow reassuring to find these relationships occasionally taking
similar patterns in nonfederal and parliamentary countries, as well
as in the United States.

The most pervasive form of metropolitan governance in the United
States today is the voluntary regional council. It is almost ubiquitous
in metropolitan areas, largely because of the intervention of the
national government. Councils of governments (COGs) are certainly
weak confederational forms of metropolitan government. They represent, however, more commitment and more participation by city
and county governments in regional affairs than anyone would have

dreamed, much less predict, a decade ago. Are they primarily defensive associations of local officials? Are they adequate and effective
means of coordinating a multitude of disparate agencies operating in
metropolitan areas? Are they forerunners of more powerful metropolitan governments? Will they be transformed into "genuine" metropolitan governments? These questions are suggested by apparent
similarities in the development of metropolitan institutional forms
in the United States and Stockholm.

The answer to each of these questions seems to be yes—in some
instances. In the Minneapolis-St. Paul, Atlanta, and Portland (Ore-
gon) metropolitan areas, confederal advisory regional planning commissions or councils of governments have been replaced with more
authoritative regional agencies. In the San Francisco region, the Association of Bay Area Governments has repeatedly requested since 1967
that the State Legislature transform it into, or replace it with, a mandatory, independently financed regional planning agency with authority to require that cities, counties, and special districts conform
to the regional plan. In each of these four instances, experiences with
one or more confederal regional bodies played a role in developing
proposals for a more authoritative agency.

The U.S. Advisory Commission on Intergovernmental Relations
has gone almost but not quite this far in recommendations that fed-
erated COGs be created in all metropolitan areas, with mandatory
membership, and with carefully qualified powers to enforce the regional plan.[1]

Similarly the development of the Greater Stockholm County Council emerged after substantial experience with voluntary and advisory
regional agencies for planning, allocation of housing units, and transportation. These experiences extended over more than two decades,
beginning with the creation of an advisory regional planning body
in 1949. For a time the city and the suburbs were in conflict over the
division of membership between city and suburbs. By 1952 a compromise had been negotiated and a director hired.

[In 1953] representatives of the suburbs had asserted a responsibility for
a non-local problem [housing production]. For the first time, too, the suburbs had asserted a responsibility for action to resolve the problem, rather
than mere participation in "studies." Either way, the suburban response
marked an obvious departure from earlier attitudes. (p. 52)

1. Advisory Commission on Intergovernmental Relations, *Regional Decision
Making: New Strategies for Substate Districts* (Washington, D.C.: U.S. Government Printing Office, 1973), pp. 353–355, 363.

It is significant that, as Anton notes, there was a softening of attitudes of the city and suburbs toward each other. This change took place "largely through the vehicle of a regional planning agency and the opportunities it provided for reaching common understanding." He noted that "the situation seemed ripe for further institutional development" (p. 52).

The next institutional development was the creation of the office of a new Stockholm commissioner in charge of city-suburban relations. Whether this device be copied or not, certainly central cities in America would be well advised to organize their own agencies to deal with the suburbs. These relationships can be handled bilaterally, between the central city and the suburbs; they can be organized in COGs and other regional agencies; or the relationships and issues can be dealt with by state and national legislatures and executive agencies. Suburbs are *not* fading away—instead the proportion of suburban population grows and that of central cities declines.

In 1957 a new joint city-suburban authority, the Greater Stockholm Planning Board, was created to administer a metropolitan housing program. "The political foundations" of the new agency

were fragile to the point of delicacy. . . . The planning board was an agency for "voluntary cooperation" between two "equal" partners, whose decisions could only "influence," not bind, the various member communes. As if to underline this delicate relationship, two chairmen of the board were to be elected, one by city members, the other by suburban members, and leadership was to be shared on a rotating basis. (p. 60)

Anton concludes that not much in the way of concrete accomplishment had been achieved during the 1950s. But this is not the whole story:

If one views the events of this decade from a process rather than a structure point of view, however, it seems clear that, despite an absence of accomplishment, something very important was going on. Intellectually, a common understanding of the problems of the region, together with an appreciation of the steps required to solve them, was being spread among an ever widening set of officials. (p. 62)

Equally important in the social learning of city and suburban officials was the effort to develop and administer a *voluntary* metropolitan housing placement service. Finally in 1968, under threat of national intervention, a centralized metropolitan housing exchange was created. "Many local officials undoubtedly saw national intervention in this matter as a 'failure.' From an analytical point of view, however, it surely makes sense to view that intervention as an additional demonstration of system capacity" (p. 95).

Hjalmar Mehr and his colleagues were able during the 1960s to turn the development of a regional transportation policy into an opportunity to create a Greater Stockholm County Council. This provided a two-tier system but with members of the regional County Council directly elected. The new metropolitan government does not, therefore, provide for municipal representation. Nevertheless, the social learning acquired in two decades of experience with confederal regional agencies was an important stage in the movement toward the Greater Stockholm County Council.

In the United States we are now going through a stage in which two essential elements of the Stockholm story are present in indigenous form: widespread use of voluntary, advisory confederal councils of governments, and more or less ambiguous leadership of the national government. A reading of Anton would suggest that we use our native institutional and policy developments to prepare ourselves to consider whether and how our local governments, and indeed our state and national governments, can become organized into effective and acceptable agencies of metropolitan governance.

In this endeavor, careful analytical case studies can facilitate better understanding of what we are doing, by helping us see more clearly what appear to be analogous processes, not gimmicks, in other urban regions and other cultures. Anton's highly sophisticated Stockholm study helps us to see the urban governance processes in different planes of generalization, at different levels of reality. Each of them is valid in the sense of being useful: of helping to understand what is going on and how it came about. Thus the "what-makes-Stockholm-tick" analysis ends initially by emphasizing those characteristics— even peculiarities—of political and institutional character and personality that help answer the question "why did this happen in Stockholm, and why did it happen now?" But then Anton backs further away from the action, and one begins to see more clearly how these are virtually universal experiences and forces, working through the Stockholm context and cast of characters.

The issues of housing, congestion, open space, and growth are familiar in San Francisco, Toronto, London, and Stockholm. The demand for better performance, and a slow, fumbling, persistent search for it is evident everywhere. So are the slogans of civic frustration and demand that may help grease the wheels of change. "Tear Skärholmen Down!" "Tear Down the Embarcadero!" "Stop Spadina!"

the "green wave," and "Save the Green Foothills," "Save the Coast," "the Battle of the Elms," "People's Park" and "Zero Population Growth." Such phrases echo concerns with environmental degradation, growth, over-building, autos, pollution, congestion, and squalor —as opposed to open space, blue water, green foothills, good transit, housing, amenities, and "people" programs. These are concerns with too much and too many: too little and too late. They are eloquent protests—and often effective ones—against bureaucracies seen as unresponsive.

Anton helps us see how, even in a small country, with a comparatively unitary "system" and what was thought to be a passive citizenry, the process of adaptation is both frustratingly and richly complicated. Moreover, the result is not creation of a "device," but the working and modification of a process, a process that is still going on and will persist and will continue to change as long as there is a Stockholm, a Toronto, a London, or a San Francisco.

It is Anton's gift of large perspective, while looking at a small country, that makes the Stockholm story and its interpretation so fruitful and so challenging. Perspective and ways of looking at things can be so important, controlling—blinding or enlightening. Viewing a "foreign" system carefully can aid, by both comparison and contrast, in achieving a better understanding of one's own domestic homeplace.

Again, perspective in terms of knowing the kinds of measures other systems have found workable, or unworkable, can help clarify the more generic nature of what may seem like ad hoc or opportunistic experimentation. For example, Anton comments on the traditional and well-known reluctance of U.S. institutions and leaders to utilize public agencies to solve problems:

Limitations on the housing responsibilities of public authorities reflect the general American reluctance to seek public solutions to problems if there is any possibility for private solutions. Put another way, the scope of governmental activity accepted as legitimate is distinctly broader in Sweden and Stockholm than it is in the United States. Whereas public policy imagery in Sweden has come to emphasize community-defined living standards, guaranteed for all citizens, American imagery continues to stress freedom from community standards, individual initiative, and the chance to "strike it rich." (p. 192)

Yet Anton suggests that, as things become more complicated, this may change:

. . . as urban regions continue to expand, and as social relations within them continue to become more complex, expansion of public authority seems unavoidable. Will Americans find some ingenious way to avoid the "unavoidable"? Or will we move toward a more active governmental role in our urban regions, and if so, how? These are real issues. . . . (p. 193)

Anton's Stockholm analysis and some of his conclusions thus help us to comprehend analogous processes that we should be watching for at home: what shape will they take, and how will they proceed? Indeed they are already at work in many forms. Perhaps the United States is now learning from its own failures, just as did Sweden and Hjalmar Mehr, whose comment on our "mistakes" introduced this Foreword.

We can build on Anton's perspective by shifting the focus from Stockholm to the San Francisco Bay Area. We seem to be witnessing in the nine-county San Francisco region a major and long-term phenomenon wherein governmental and non-governmental leaders are thinking and experimenting, largely on a trial-and-error basis, with new integrative mechanisms for governing the metropolis, and for resolving issues and implementing policies. Similar events seem to be taking place in other metropolitan areas.

Paralleling these institutional developments are new philosophies on the governance of regional functions, new attitudes on environmental and social control, and a willingness to contemplate remarkable shifts in what is considered appropriate and workable in public-private sector relationships. The result of both experimentation and hard thinking, these new attitudes and views have a substantial empirical basis. Or perhaps one could say that the emerging views grow out of experience with conflicts between new urban realities and demands, and an earlier and widely accepted ethic, referred to by Anton above.

To oversimplify, the older ethic is represented by (1) "local home rule," "states rights," and independent governmental action, (2) heavy reliance on the private sector, and (3) conviction that many functions (especially transportation) should be financed by market-like mechanisms (the "highway users" tax, and the fare box).

The emerging new ethic seems to be characterized by (1) a realization that local home rule and states rights alone are unworkable, that effective urban and metro policies must be intergovernmental and interlevel to a degree that most Americans had not previously realized; (2) acceptance of much stronger controls than formerly over the private sector, ranging even to reasonably radical new views on the basic nature of property rights (for example land ownership being viewed much more as constructive custodianship or responsible tenancy, rather than unrestricted power to exploit or dispose of a commodity); and (3) acceptance of a stronger public-sector role in financing certain functions, and acceptance of a much wider variety of sources of financing. For example, extensive acquisition of public ownership or easements over open space has strong support; "subsidized" public transit now seems almost universally accepted among Bay Area and other leaders, and "free" transit no longer is viewed as an absurd heresy; moreover use of gas tax money for public transit is now widely held to be not only appropriate but desirable, and the use of bridge tolls and sales taxes to support transit is a reality.

These comments represent a great oversimplification of intricate governmental phenomena and changes in public attitudes, but we hope they serve to emphasize the complexity of what we have referred to as "new developments in regional governance." What once seemed to be viewed as primarily a need for "a regional government" is now seen as far more complicated than simple establishment of such an integrative organization, although such arrangements are clearly still an important *part* of many solutions. Anton's analytical case study makes it clear how complicated these processes are.

It appears that, among metropolitan regions in the United States, the San Francisco Bay region is in the forefront in this process: many consider that the environmentalist movement had some of its early origins and successes here; the nation's first freeway revolt occurred in San Francisco; the Bay Conservation and Development Commission (BCDC) was created here, another national first; the Metropolitan Transportation Commission is still another national precedent; the coast commissions were in large part an outgrowth of the perceived effectiveness of BCDC; the Bay Area Comprehensive Health Planning Council considers itself something of a national model; and the Association of Bay Area Governments was the first council of governments to request the legislature to convert it into a limited multiple purpose metropolitan government. Thus rightly or wrongly many Bay Area observers consider the region "out in front" in exploring new processes of governance.

But a lot of experimentation is going on elsewhere, aided and encouraged by federal programs, as well as by programs and initiatives at the state governmental level. Anton emphasizes the crucial role of upper level governments in working out processes of governance. This applies in the United States with a vengeance, given our national government with many interested agencies, plus the fifty states and *their* agencies. All are increasingly concerned with urban governance. Complexity is the watchword, with a respectable admixture of confusion. But things are happening, alternatives are being explored, and recommendations are being issued. These emanate from many sources, perhaps most important is the persistent and continuing work of the Advisory Commission on Intergovernmental Relations.

Anton helps us understand these efforts as organized, purposive processes of political compromise and deliberate, thoughtful design. Achieving changes in governance is not "automatic" but results from acts of will and judgment. Governmental reforms are human and intellectual enterprises, as well as the consequence of strategy and jockeying.

. . . considerations suggest a far more active role for political leaders than is implied by conventional analytic modes. Indeed, they suggest that much of what is recognized, after the fact, as part of a political environment has achieved that status through acts of political will: issues and problems, it turns out, have to be *defined* by someone. (One might add here that solutions, too, have to be defined. Hjalmar Mehr's constant repetition of the Greater County Council idea, at a time when no one else seemed to care about it, is a classic example.) (p. 200)

Stockholm's accomplishment thus stands as both a promise and a challenge to others. In Anton's closing words:

To citizens of San Francisco, Toronto, Detroit or London . . . , Stockholm represents performance, no less than promise. To them, the continuing experiment that is Stockholm contains a message of first importance: mid-twentieth century cities need not be dangerous and decaying relics of a former age; efficient function need not destroy beauty and liveability; in this age, on this earth, a group of men entrusted with the future of their urban environment have behaved responsibly, and with a measure of success that the rest of the world can envy, if not emulate. (p. 208)

Stanley Scott
Editor, Lane Fund
Publications

Victor Jones
Coeditor, Lane Studies in
Regional Government

Berkeley, California
May, 1974

PREFACE

THIS IS an inquiry into the conditions under which processes of urban growth can be harnessed for the public benefit rather than for the private advantage of various interests that make up a modern metropolis. It is at the same time an inquiry into the conditions under which systems that exert control over growth processes are themselves changed by their efforts to exert control. The locale is Stockholm, Sweden, though the approach is meant to be applicable to any urban political system seeking solutions to the problems raised by rapid development. To the extent that the study succeeds, it should help us to understand and deal more effectively with the politics of urban problem-solving.

No study of this kind would be possible without assistance of many kinds, from many sources. My greatest debt is to the John Simon Guggenheim Memorial Foundation, whose generosity made it possible for me to spend a year (1967–68) in Stockholm learning the difference between questions that could be asked and questions that could be answered. In that year, and later, my relationship with the United States Educational Commission in Sweden (the Fulbright Commission) proved invaluable, as did my relationships with the students, faculty, and administration of the University of Stockholm. Neither the United States National Science Foundation nor the Bank of Sweden Tercentenary Fund were directly involved in funding this study, but both organizations provided support that indirectly assisted in its completion. Finally, both the Department of Political Science and the Institute of Public Policy Studies of The University of Michigan have provided several kinds of support as well as a very special kind of indulgence. I am extraordinarily grateful to each of these organizations and to the people acting in their behalf who have been so very kind to me.

My colleagues in the Department of Political Science of the University of Stockholm, particularly Hans Meijer, Olof Ruin, Elias Berg, and Thomas Hammar, seem to me to have borne the brunt of a foreigner's ignorance with remarkable humor; they were mentors and have become friends. Among the scores of Stockholm city officials who provided assistance, two went to special lengths to educate me: Commissioner Joakim Garpe and Direktör Karl-Gustaf Paulsson. I hope that neither will be offended at the result of their considerable efforts on my behalf. Oliver P. Williams of the University of Pennsylvania will appreciate how much he has contributed to this study and why I value that contribution above all others. Stephanie Cameron offered intelligent and helpful comments at an opportune moment, as did Victor Jones, Stanley Scott, and Francine Rabinovitz. Roland Artle made a very special, and I hope successful, effort to improve the quality of this study. Since I know that all of these people disagree with me on a variety of points of fact or interpretation, none of them should be blamed for deficiencies in the following chapters. All of them contributed something to my thinking about this material, however, and they thus deserve a portion of the credit for whatever merit the study may have.

As much as I have learned from all of these good people, I have learned even more from Barbara, Lynn, Leslie, and Tom. They have borne an unusual burden with unusual good will. Fortunately, I can offer them affection, as well as gratitude.

POLITICS AND URBAN GROWTH

FOR CITIES in Western Europe and the United States, the period since 1945 has been one of rapid social and structural change, marked especially by the development of new settlements outside of existing city boundaries. The quantitative significance of such settlements already has changed the way we think: instead of "cities," we now speak of "metropolitan areas," "Greater London," or "Greater Stockholm," in order to express conceptually the ties between cities and their outlying areas that recently have become political and economic facts. Hundreds of thousands of people now live in settlements that did not exist as recently as twenty or thirty years ago and whose chief reason for being is proximity to a large city. Armies of architects, financiers, politicians, engineers, developers, and planners have created these settlements and, for the foreseeable future at least, those armies will continue to grow as even more new settlements are developed to meet a continued demand. To inquire into the patterns of behavior through which such settlements are created is thus to inquire into a range of activities that has been, and will continue to be, of great importance to modern societies.

Urban growth, of course, can hardly be said to be a "new" phenomenon—indeed, it is as old as urbanization itself. But a number of developments of the past two decades have underlined the significance of urban growth as a "problem" for citizen and scholar alike. Residents of American urban areas, observing the rash of disturbances that swept such areas after the mid-1960s and the general ineffectiveness of later efforts to deal with the causes of such disturbances, surely have cause to wonder about the continued viability of American cities as places to live and work. Residents of the expanding urban areas of Western Europe may not have experienced such drama, but they,

1

too, have witnessed problems of dislocation, disruption, and aliena-
tion, and they, too, recently have come to question the viability of
the city as an urban form. However different American and European cities may be, then, they have recently presented their citizens
with similar difficulties, and citizens in both appear to be drawing
remarkably similar conclusions.[1]

To scholars, the "problem" now raised by urban growth is somewhat different. Largely as a result of recent scholarship, students of
urbanization no longer assume city formation and growth to be beyond human influence. Whereas an older view attributed urban
development to technological and economic capacity, constrained by
geographic barriers,[2] modern scholars recognize that technology no
longer commands either location or size. Where human settlements
are located, how large they become, and how they function are now
recognized to be malleable issues, in a world subject to considerable
human intervention. Indeed, as more is learned about the impact of
human intervention on city form and function, it becomes increasingly clear that the older deterministic view is outmoded. In the
United States, for example, we have come to understand that national and state legislation, bureaucratic procedures, political ideologies, and a variety of other "human" factors have affected the development of our urban areas.[3]

Inevitably, this understanding has led scholars to the realization
that urban growth must be considered as a policy problem: if human
intervention shapes urban patterns, then we cannot avoid asking the
question, Are present modes of intervention adequate, and if not,
what alternatives should we pursue? Thus, while scholars may—and
probably do—share with citizens an uncertainty about the future of
urban settlements, they also carry a special burden, for they know that
the present urban pattern can be changed. To them falls the peculiar
responsibility of discovering and stating the conditions under which
various urban patterns, judged good or bad, occur. To them, too, falls
the difficult responsibility of using that knowledge to assess the consequences of existing and prospective policy programs.

It seems plausible to assume that the burden of these several re-

1. For evidence, see below, Chapter VII.
2. A good expression of this view is Raymond Vernon, *The Myth and Reality
of Our Urban Problems* (Cambridge: Joint Center for Urban Studies, 1962), pp.
2–13.
3. See National Commission on Urban Problems, *Building the American City*
(Washington: GPO, 1968), Part II, chs. 1, 2.

sponsibilities accounts for the energy with which academics have debated the "planning" issue. Two generations ago that issue separated socialists from liberals and conservatives, but in the 1950s and 1960s it came to represent a division between urbanists and all others, precisely because of the widespread notion among "urbanists" that the fundamental defect of American urban areas was their "chaotic" or "unplanned" character.[4] As the pattern of postwar urban growth took shape, academics joined forces with journalists and a growing body of professional planners to develop what has since come to be known as the "planning critique." [5] Over time, frequent condemnations of "sprawl" or "ticky-tacky houses" became as standardized— or stereotyped—as the mass-produced suburbs that were the principal targets of planners and academics. And always, in addition to the critique, there was the proffered solution: more planning and more planners. By now, of course, events in the real world have outrun this critique, and with it earlier notions about the quality of plans and the business of planners. To believe that the issue of "planned or unplanned suburbs" is a more important issue than racial hostility, mass violence, environmental destruction, or governmental incompetence is no longer possible for most of us, just as it is no longer possible to believe that larger numbers of trained planners are likely to have a decisive impact on our collective urban future.

But the planning issue will not go away, because it cannot go away so long as human intervention is both unavoidable and questionable. It is therefore imperative that we clarify its meaning. The major diagnostic error made by the urbanists of the 1950s and 1960s, it now seems clear, was to mistake the absence of planning for the absence of order. Although it was and is true that American urban regions are generally "chaotic" in a physical sense, it was not and is not the case that these urban regions are unstructured. By focusing so much attention on the physical appearance of urban regions, however, earlier critics diverted attention away from the social structures responsible for urban form. Solutions derived from the planning critique were often intellectually satisfying, but seldom effective, for they

4. For a review of the evolution of planning ideologies see Henry Fagin, "The Evolving Philosophy of Urban Planning," in Leo F. Schnore and Henry Fagin, eds., *Urban Research and Policy Planning* (Beverly Hills, California: Sage Publications, Inc., 1967), pp. 309–328.

5. A skeptical view of this critique is found in Edward P. Eichler and Marshall Kaplan, *The Community Builders* (Berkeley and Los Angeles: University of California Press, 1967), ch. 1.

uniformly avoided structural analysis and thus the problem of implementation. Indeed, if there is one image that characterizes the 1950s
and 1960s for academic urbanists, it is the failure of planning as a
guide to policy intervention.

Gradually, urbanists have come to recognize the significance of the
implementation problem and have shifted their foci accordingly. Instead of bemoaning the absence of a single authoritative source of
urban rationality, we have begun to appreciate the fact of urban diversity and to discover ways of accommodating "planning" to that
diversity; instead of physical plans, we have begun to think seriously
about the needs of people; instead of techniques such as zoning maps
or cluster development, we have begun to devote some attention to
ways of *coordinating institutions* to achieve politically acceptable
goals; instead of "physical planning" we are now talking more about
"policy planning," or "social planning." [6] In short, we have come to
realize that "planning" is not simply an intellectual issue, but a
structural issue as well. It is no longer satisfying to propose a plan
without also addressing the question of how that plan is to be implemented, through what structures, with what resources.

STUDYING STOCKHOLM

These shifting public and scholarly concerns help to define the
significance of Stockholm as a source of instruction to those concerned about the causes and consequences of urban growth. Population growth averaging close to 20,000 persons per year after 1945,
combined with large-scale redevelopment of the core city in the 1950s
and 1960s, produced a variety of growth-related problems in the
Stockholm region: population dislocation, a severe housing shortage,
inadequate mass transportation, inadequate service delivery, un-
coordinated service delivery in new housing areas, and so forth. Although these problems were similar to those faced by a number of
European and North American cities during the same postwar period, the Stockholm response has been acclaimed by professional organizations around the world as a superior example of imaginative
and well-executed development planning.[7] Since 1945 the downtown

6. See Fagin, *loc. cit.*
7. In 1961, for example, the International Union of Architects awarded the
Abercrombie prize to Stockholm for its "foresight in land policy and intelligent
co-ordination of the many problems confronting the modern city." Cited in
Yngve Larsson, "Building a City and a Metropolis," *Journal of the American
Institute of Planners,* Vol. XXVIII (1962). See below for more about Yngve
Larsson.

core, once a depressing slum, has been totally renewed; a new subway system has been built and even now is being extended; many new suburban communities have been built, providing new housing for hundreds of thousands of Stockholmers, with easy access to the core city via subway. Less widely acclaimed, but of equal significance here, are the structural changes induced by these development policies. Those changes include the creation of a new metropolitan government for the Greater Stockholm area on January 1, 1971. Surely this experience, involving both planning success and structural change, can tell us something about the interrelationships between planning and social structure.

American observers, of course, will be particularly interested in the Stockholm experience, if only because similarities between Sweden and the United States are so pronounced. These similarities extend well beyond the fact that both countries share a common "western" heritage, or that they are both leading examples of the "new industrial state," [8] in which private enterprise and massive welfare programs coexist somewhat uneasily, under the tutelage of new managerial and technocratic elites. What is even more relevant here is that, since 1945, the response to pressures of urbanization has been channeled through very similar governmental structures. Local governments have been the front line of public response to urban pressures in both countries, popular support for local government is strong in both, and the higher authority of the state intrudes into, and frequently controls, local actions in both. To be sure, the Stockholm region has only recently begun to experience the racial hostility that has characterized so many American cities. That important difference aside, however, it remains true that similar growth pressures and a similar structure of public response have produced what many professionals believe to be a strikingly "better" set of outcomes. Why? And how? Good answers to these questions may provide help, as well as enlightenment.

SOME CONCEPTUAL AND METHODOLOGICAL PROBLEMS

If the preceding argument is sound, developing good answers to these questions will require a conceptual focus capable of dealing with the problem of metropolitan social structure, as well as an analytic scheme capable of illuminating the issue of "planning." Fortunately, an appropriate focus has been available since at least 1954,

8. The phrase, of course, comes from John Kenneth Galbraith, *The New Industrial State* (Boston: Houghton Mifflin Company, 1967).

when William H. Form published a conception of the metropolitan area as an "ecological order," in which a variety of activities—commercial, industrial, residential—are conducted, maintained, and changed by a number of separate but interacting organizations. Since, in his view, all of these activities were bound to and shaped by physical location, land use was the fundamental datum for the analysis of metropolitan structure, and *land use change* the fundamental indicator of urban growth. These ideas had been familiar among geographers and demographers for years, but Form's insight was to link land use to organizational structure, thus offering the possibility of a sociological explanation of urban growth. To Form, explanations for land use patterns had to be sought in the operations of the metropolitan land market, but he rejected conventional economic images of the "market." "Obviously," he wrote,

the image of a free and unorganized market in which individuals compete impersonally for land must be abandoned. The reason for this is that the land market is highly organized and dominated by a number of interacting organizations. Most of the latter are formally organized, highly self-conscious, and purposeful in character. Although at times their values and interests are conflicting, they are often overlapping and harmonious. That is, their relationships tend to become structured over a period of time. From a study of this emerging structure one obtains a picture of the parameters of ecological behavior, the pattern of land use change, and the institutional pressures which maintain the ecological order.[9]

This was and remains a persuasive formulation but, curiously, few scholars have attempted to apply it in examining urban growth. In the United States, disciplinary preferences for a focus on "public" rather than private organizations have discouraged political researchers from investigating the banks, real estate developers, contractors, and other private-sector organizations that are deeply involved in shaping urban development. Disciplinary preference aside, however, *access* to such private-sector organizations is extraordinarily difficult to achieve. Organizations seeking to obtain large enough blocks of land to generate development profits can hardly be expected to publicize their activities, particularly when such publicity can affect profitability. Scholars are not totally precluded from entering this world, but the terms of entry are strict and seldom permit anything more than distant analysis of past events.

9. William H. Form, "The Place of Social Structure in the Determination of Land Use: Some Implications for a Theory of Urban Ecology," *Social Forces*, Vol. 32 (1954), p. 317.

Nevertheless, two decades of research on other aspects of the metropolitan order have produced widespread acceptance of imagery similar to Form's early conception. Political researchers in particular have repeatedly discovered that extraordinarily few members of the metropolitan mass public participate in political affairs, that "self-conscious and purposeful" organizations therefore constitute the bedrock of urban politics, and that the interests of urban organizations are indeed often "overlapping and harmonious"—although it must be added that *the extent to which* such interests are harmonious has been a much-debated question.[10] Clearly, following these views means directing our attention to *the behavior of those organizational elites whose interactions determine the use of urban land.*

How, then, do we discover which organizations determine land use in any given environment and, having discovered the appropriate organizations, what behavior do we investigate? Here again, the concept of "planning" is a poor guide. The American experience suggests that the activities posited by an analytic definition of the term may not in fact exist in the real world. On the other hand, studying the activities of agencies officially charged with "planning" responsibilities would beg the fundamental question of whether such activities actually had an effect on the course of urban development.

The more sensible course is to assume that land use determinations result from a process of choice. Using this assumption, we can retrospectively identify major changes in land use, identify the organizational actors involved, and investigate the criteria used by such actors to make their choices. Examination of a sufficient number of such choices would permit identification of a "structure" of organizational relationships, as well as the purposes pursued by organizational actors. Extended over time, this kind of analysis would permit us to draw conclusions about the processes involved in choice behavior. We might, for example, conclude that these processes resembled "planning," but we might also reach quite different conclusions. Finally, of course, this assumption would permit us to take advantage of a conceptual scheme that has achieved some analytic popularity in recent years: the concept of decision-making.

To use the concept of decision-making as a research tool, however,

10. One of the earliest, and still best, statements of the significance of organizations in urban politics is Edward C. Banfield, *Political Influence* (New York: The Free Press of Glencoe, 1962). A good review of the community power structure debate can be found in Michael Aiken and Paul E. Mott, eds., *The Structure of Community Power* (New York: Random House, Inc., 1970).

some considerable reformulation will be required. Consider, to begin with, the very concept of "decision" itself. In an effort to give this concept some analytical precision, early scholars of decision-making adopted the view that "decision" (or "choice") referred to some observable or knowable event that took place at a single point in time. By treating that single event as though it could be isolated from its social and structural context, and by gathering exhaustive information about the motivations and actions of the person or persons involved in the event, these scholars argued that such events could be "explained," and that such explanations would gradually produce a body of generalizations about decision-making behavior. Structural factors, when they were taken into account, generally fell under such a rubric as "organizational competence," but sometimes were included under a term such as "situation"—a congeries of events, rumors, history, and motivations to which the decision-makers were presumed to be oriented. Underlying much of this work was an essentially simple analytic scheme: *actors,* oriented to a *situation,* having *goals* with regard to that situation, and taking *action* to produce a *decision* that presumably resolved the situation.[11]

Exceedingly few studies have been attempted which follow the more elaborate formulations of this scheme, and earlier hopes for the development of well-supported generalizations have been largely abandoned. At the same time, a considerable body of literature focusing on the study of one or more decisions has grown up in the field of community politics research.[12] Indeed, enough of this literature has appeared to suggest the serious limitations of the decision-making approach. Studying a single decision at a single point in time, or even several decisions at a single point in time, obviously inhibits our ability to say very much about social change or the dynamics-of-change processes, particularly when the choice of which decisions to study is so largely determined by the prejudices of the observer, which in practice has meant the prejudices of the elites that typically

11. This formulation oversimplifies a vast body of research referred to in Richard C. Snyder, "A Decision-Making Approach to the Study of Political Phenomena," in Roland Young, ed., *Approaches to the Study of Politics* (Evanston, Illinois: Northwestern University Press, 1958), pp. 3–38.

12. A useful bibliography of this work is available in Charles M. Bonjean, Terry N. Clark, and Robert L. Lineberry, eds., *Community Politics: A Behavioral Approach* (New York: The Free Press, 1971), pp. 373–387. For a study of a decision in a Swedish suburban municipality, see my "Politics and Planning in a Swedish Suburb," *Journal of the American Institute of Planners,* Vol. XXXV (1969), pp. 253–263.

are the focus of inquiry. Quite apart from the biased assumptions implicit in this approach, however, it now seems evident that the scheme itself does not raise questions capable of producing answers with much theoretical payoff, for the focus on "decision" is a focus on an analytic abstraction that seldom corresponds to real-world conditions.

This conclusion becomes clear when we consider the results achieved by the best of these studies, which have repeatedly demonstrated that major public policies more often than not result from an accumulation of past commitments, rather than a "choice" made at time X. Or, decision-makers are shown to be continuously influenced by culturally derived preferences, by the networks of contextual relationships they maintain with other actors, and even by constraints of bureaucratic routine. Failure to take account of such factors often leads the analyst of public choice to impose an intellectual pattern on processes which may have little or nothing to do with intellect. This intellectual pattern involves not only the notion of actors "solving problems" through "goal-seeking," but also the notion that the problems "solved" by a decision are solved once and for all. Raymond Bauer, among others, has pointed out recently that concepts such as decision-making

imply a discrete sequence of events with a single definite point of termination. Serious policy-making does not involve such decisive resolutions of a problem. A Supreme Court ruling of 1954 did not abolish segregation in public education, nor did the Civil Rights Act of 1965 eliminate discrimination in politics. Each of these events redefined the terms in which an ongoing struggle was conducted. The experienced policy maker knows that as he resolves issues he is posing others. He realizes that he is frequently not settling an issue but redefining the rules of the game and if, in any meaningful sense, he has been "victorious," he hedges his victory to give himself room for maneuver in the future.[13]

The realities of social choice are thus considerably more complex than the simple language of "actor-goal-situation-decision" would suggest. To understand what Bauer would call "serious policy-making" in urban development, we clearly need to shift our attention away from the single choice, considered at a single point in time, and away from our present overly intellectual emphasis on the "reasons for" a particular choice. Just as clearly, we need to find some way

13. Raymond A. Bauer, "The Study of Policy Formation: An Introduction," in Raymond A. Bauer and Kenneth J. Gergen, eds., *The Study of Policy Formation* (New York: The Free Press, 1968), p. 18.

to analyze decision-making behavior that recognizes the continuity of social structure over time, and the "ongoing struggles" built into that structure.

In what follows, four simple devices are used to respond to these needs. First, the analysis is extended over a twenty-five year period, roughly 1945–1970. Second, instead of "a decision," the focus is on sequences of decisions in three areas of significance to land use: planning, housing, and transportation. Third, enough strategic and behavioral detail is provided to permit some analytical conclusions regarding both the content of the ongoing struggle (i.e., what the struggle is about) and the manner in which issues "resolved" become issues "posed." Finally, individual action is explicitly placed within a context of organizational and cultural constraints, imposed through discoverable patterns of interaction. Ultimately, these devices prompt a reconsideration of the decision-making schema, as well as a suggestion for alternative concepts more appropriate to the analysis of a larger idea: public policy-making.

PLAN OF THE STUDY

The following chapters are divided into four parts. In Part One, Chapter I introduces the reader to the environment within which urban development policies have been shaped. Structurally, that environment includes national-local relations as well as the variety of organizations involved in more strictly local interactions. Culturally, it includes the orientations of elites and masses toward the substance of politics. In dealing with these aspects of the environment, Chapter I will provide a set of intellectual "bench marks" for use in interpreting the material in succeeding chapters.

Part Two, "Patterns of Choice," describes the development of a series of separate, but overlapping, policies of major significance. Chapter II traces out the gradual emergence of a common understanding of metropolitan problems among relevant organizational actors. Chapter III describes the development of capacity for joint action by area politicians, focusing on the problem of housing. And Chapter IV examines the strategies employed by leading organizational actors to convert housing success into, first, a new transportation system and, second, a new metropolitan government structure. Throughout Part Two, then, the focus is on the action of organizational elites, in an effort to reveal patterns of elite behavior.

Part Three, "Patterns of Participation," attempts a two-part explanation of the activity reported in earlier chapters. Building on the uniformities revealed in the earlier material, Chapter V offers a more systematic analysis of the structure of elite interrelationships. Here, actors are viewed as individuals seeking satisfactions (rather than pursuing goals) but constrained by both organizational commitments and other actors in their selection of appropriate action strategies. The policies described earlier are thus "explained" by showing their relationship to an organized pattern of constraints. Chapter VI takes this kind of explanation one step further by considering some obvious cultural orientations to political processes, paying particular attention to Swedish attitudes toward open conflict. In effect, this chapter "explains" aspects of the Stockholm system of guiding urban growth by showing how that system reflects norms and expectations widespread throughout the Swedish population.

Finally, in Part Four, Chapter VII attempts to draw together the various threads contained in the preceding analysis by asking what, if any, portion of the Stockholm experience might be transferable to other cultures. In attempting to answer that question, both the metropolis as "problem" and policy-making as a focus for analysis are subjected to reconsideration.

Part One

THE SETTING

CHAPTER I

THE ENVIRONMENT OF
URBAN POLITICS IN SWEDEN

OF ALL the problems social analysts must confront in studying cultures other than their own, surely the most troublesome is the constant temptation to interpret events of one culture in terms of analytic assumptions taken from another. American analysts of urban political phenomena, for example, talk a great deal about "the strength of local government" in the United States, and conduct studies based upon the assumption that, for most political purposes, local authorities in the United States are in fact independent. With that assumption in mind an American analyst might journey to Sweden, observe that Swedes, too, talk a great deal about the "strength" of local government, and begin planning studies of Swedish municipalities based on the familiar assumptions of independence.[1] In very short order, however, this observer would be confronted with an even more powerful observation: most of the roughly 2,500 local authorities that existed in Sweden in 1950 are being eliminated; as of 1974 only 274 municipalities remained![2] Noting that the process of reducing the number of municipalities has been controlled by the national government, the American observer might well wonder whether he

1. Mark Kesselman has noted the incongruence of the assumption of independence in a foreign setting in his "Research Perspectives in Comparative Local Politics: Pitfalls and Prospects," *Comparative Urban Research*, Vol. 1 (Spring 1972), pp. 10–13.
2. A brief but useful treatment of the process of municipal consolidation is available in Terrance Sandalow, "Local Government in Sweden," *The American Journal of Comparative Law*, Vol. XIX (Fall 1971), pp. 770–774. See also Donald R. Niemi, "Sweden's Municipal Consolidation Reforms" (unpublished Ph.D. dissertation, University of Chicago, 1966).

and his Swedish colleagues have the same things in mind when they talk about local government "strength."

The answer, of course, is that they do not have the same things in mind at all. Different historical experiences, interpreted through different cultural lenses, have produced institutions and processes that are very different, even if the words used to refer to them are similar. While hardly surprising, this discovery imposes a special burden on students of policy-making behavior. If we cannot assume that superficially similar institutions and processes will "mean" the same thing from one culture to the next, then we clearly cannot impute motivations on the basis of institutional similarity alone. We must first come to grips with the meanings attached to institutions in a specific cultural context. Put differently, before we can hope to understand what the players are doing, we must know what the game is, and how score is kept.

To that end I begin here with some observations about two aspects of the Swedish political system that are especially significant for policy-making activities that take place in Swedish metropolitan areas. The first might be called the "framework of understanding," by which I mean the ideas that Swedes use to organize their perceptions and evaluations of government, including local government. The second can be thought of as the "framework of behavior," by which I mean the patterns of interaction that appear repeatedly in Swedish public decision-making. One framework will be recognized as an aspect of Swedish political culture;[3] the other as an aspect of Swedish political structure.[4] Both should be thought of as important elements of the "environment" within which Stockholm's politics of growth has taken place. Having discussed these general frameworks, I conclude this chapter by noting some more specific characteristics of the Stockholm setting that will be relevant to the chapters that follow.

3. For an examination of general aspects of Swedish political culture, see my "Policy-Making and Political Culture in Sweden," *Scandinavian Political Studies*, Vol. 4 (1969), pp. 88–102.

4. Structure seen from a local perspective is analyzed in my "politics and planning in a Swedish Suburb," *Journal of the American Institute of Planners*, Vol. XXXV (July 1969), pp. 253–263. A useful analysis of national structures is provided in Nils Stjernquist, "Sweden: Stability or Deadlock?," in Robert A. Dahl, ed., *Political Oppositions in Western Democracies* (New Haven and London: Yale University Press, 1966), pp. 116–146. A somewhat revised version of the following material is available in my "The Pursuit of Efficiency: Values and Structure in the Changing Politics of Swedish Municipalities," in Terry N. Clark, ed., *Comparative Community Politics* (Beverly Hills, California, 1974).

A FRAMEWORK OF UNDERSTANDING

Let us begin by noting the more obvious consequences of the rapid urbanization Sweden has experienced during the past three decades.[5] At an individual level, thousands of people have been leaving small towns and moving to the largest cities, where jobs in industry, commerce, and government increasingly have been concentrated. At the government level—and largely *because of* this massive shift in population—more than two thousand municipalities have been eliminated and replaced by totally new units, created by combining several of the older units into "Kommunblocks." Individuals have left their former places of residence in search of work and enjoyment, while officials formerly holding public office have voluntarily agreed to changes which have eliminated both their municipalities and the offices they held in those municipalities.[6]

LOW SALIENCE OF COMMUNITY

The voluntary nature of these individual and official decisions suggests that Swedes do not attach much significance to local boundaries. Though a number of traditional "company towns" still exist in areas far from the largest cities, many have disappeared as factories or lumber mills have shut down, thus reducing the importance of the municipality as a source of work. Nor is the municipality an important source of social status: only a handful of visibly upper-class communities exist, and some of those have been absorbed into larger units in the process of structural reform.[7] Largely divorced from important social values, the local community is not highly valued in Sweden.

The consequences of this low affective investment in community are clearly visible in the Stockholm area where—again with the exception of two or three upper-class suburban municipalities—identification with or commitment to municipal units seems almost non-

5. For a survey, see Ella Ödmann and Gun-Britt Dahlberg, *Urbanization in Sweden* (Stockholm: Government Publishing House, 1970).

6. Niemi, *op. cit.*, reports that plans for the consolidation legislation of 1952 and 1962 were circulated among all localities for comment. Of the communes that reacted to the government's proposals, only 15 per cent were clearly opposed to the first and only 27 per cent were clearly opposed to the second reform, with opposition heavily concentrated among the smallest communes on both occasions. The figures are on pages 41 and 163 of his study.

7. Danderyd and Djursholm, two of the most obviously upper-class residential suburbs north of Stockholm, were joined together on January 1, 1971.

existent. Residential turnover in the new suburbs that have been developed during the past two decades is high,[8] while studies of residential satisfaction have repeatedly shown that place of residence is of minimal interest to Swedes.[9] What counts most is convenience—that is, access to work and entertainment—and quality of housing—that is, modernity, time-saving household equipment, and size.[10]

Given a choice between poor and high quality housing, Swedes move from wherever they are located to another location. And, given a choice between high quality but poor convenience and poor quality but high convenience, Swedes prefer convenience. Many Stockholmers, for example, would happily exchange an apartment in a modern, well-planned suburb for an apartment in the middle of their beautiful but noisy city—provided, of course, that their workplace was in the city. Most Stockholmers, it should be added, do not have such choices to make. With 185,000 persons registered in the housing queue (1971 figures) and six years as the average waiting period for an offer of an apartment, Stockholmers often are forced to choose between accepting an apartment in an inconvenient location or remaining in an apartment whose inconvenience or inadequacy was the principal cause of their becoming registered in the first place.[11] This, too, hinders municipal identification in the new suburbs, most of whose residents arrived there less by choice than by compulsion.

Swedish official policy-makers have demonstrated a similar lack

8. During the 1960s one new suburb was adding roughly 3,000 inhabitants per year to its population. At the same time, some 3,000 people were leaving the commune each year, producing a turnover of some 6,000 persons every year. See Anton, "Politics and Planning . . . ," loc. cit., for a review of the development of this suburb.

9. Bengt Owe Birgersson, Sören Häggroth and Gunnar Wallin, Att leva i Salemstaden (Stockholm: Statens institut för byggnadsforskning, 1973), pp. 3, 141.

10. Ibid. For additional evidence, see Torsten Åstrom, "En sociologisk undersökning av fem glesbygdsområden," Statens offentliga utredningar 1970:14 (Stockholm: Inrikesdepartementet, 1970), Bilaga 3. Hereafter these reports of Swedish Royal Commissions will be cited in abbreviated form, i.e., SOU 1970:14.

11. It should be added here that Swedes include "high cost" in their definition of inconvenience and are thus unwilling to expend a very high proportion of their income on housing. Despite the thousands in the queue, for example, some 2,000 two-bedroom apartments were without tenants in 1968, many of them in Skärholmen, the "new town," where rentals ranged from $160 to $180 per month. In 1970 such apartments were available in distant suburbs for $100 to $120 per month, but many were nevertheless empty. A similar situation prevailed in Gothenburg, Eskiltuna, Köping, and other cities. See Dagens Nyheter, August 29, 1970.

of commitment to existing municipalities. For them, the Swedish "tradition" of strong local government has required that most such governments be eliminated, precisely because most localities had become incapable of providing the services that officials felt were minimally necessary. Among officials, then, the Swedish tradition has emphasized "strong" rather than "local." This emphasis has led to changes based upon careful calculations of the minimum population and tax base necessary to support decent housing, schools, and commercial services.[12]

The reader should note the significance of an ideology of equal opportunity that has prevailed among representatives of the governing Social Democratic party. According to this ideology, no child should be penalized—in terms of inadequate schools or career possibilities—simply because of the accident of being born in an area that has lost population and resources to the more fortunate portions of the country. To maintain equal opportunity the government has shaped tools to equalize local financial resources and job opportunities, as well as restructuring local governments into administrative units with sufficient strength to properly use these tools.[13]

COMPETENCE AND SERVICE V. PARTICIPATION

A citizenry without powerful, affective attachments to municipalities *per se,* in short, has been governed by officials with equally weak commitments to existing boundaries but with powerful ideological interest in reducing disparities in life changes arising from rapid ubanization. For both of these groups municipalities have not been appraised in terms of what they are (or have been) but in terms of what they can do: their administrative and financial competence. Those whose competence has been found wanting have been eliminated, with few strong voices of protest to be heard. Those that remain after 1975 will be large and well-financed units, staffed with large numbers of administrators to meet the convenience and service demands of the citizenry. In Sweden's "service democracy," to borrow

---

12. In answer to the question, "How can communal democracy be encouraged?" Prime Minister Palme recently responded as follows: "A major issue for communal democracy . . . is our capacity to create communes that are sufficiently strong to meet popular demand for better conditions." *Kommunal Tidskrift,* Nr 14 (September 1970), p. 814. For a good review of the rationale behind municipal consolidation, see Niemi, *op. cit.,* pp. 135–159.

13. Niemi, *op. cit.,* reviews this ideology and its application.

a phrase from Professor Jörgen Westerståhl,[14] municipalities have become predominantly service-oriented organizations.

But just as "strong" has been more important than "local" in Swedish thinking, "service" has been far more important than "democracy." The preceding discussion should have made clear that the value of "democratic participation" has not been given much weight in the reorganization of Swedish municipalities, whose affairs will increasingly come to be dominated by the appointed administrators who replace elected officials. Understanding this general disinterest in participation is always confused by Sweden's well-publicized record of extraordinarily high turnout in general elections. This record is clear and impressive,[15] but it conceals the fact that Swedes have virtually no opportunities to participate in public decision-making apart from voting.

At the municipal level, for example, there is no opportunity for referenda on important issues, and no tradition of public hearings on controversial (or noncontroversial) matters to gather impressions of public opinion. Nor is there a very strong tradition of citizen pressure groups, organized around specific issues or outside regular party or other organizational channels, to protest or support public decisions.[16] Indeed, it is virtually impossible for such groups to form except in an *ad hoc* way, for local decision-making takes place in the various committees established by the local council, and the meetings of these committees are not open to the public. Protests do occur, of course, but they are seldom effective in changing decisions already made and, over time, such protests seem only to reinforce prevailing patterns of citizen apathy.[17]

14. *Dagens Nyheter,* August 4, 1956.
15. Since WW II, turnout in Swedish parliamentary elections has ranged from 77.4 per cent (1958) to 89.3 per cent (1968). Turnout in local elections has ranged from 72 per cent (1946) to 88.1 per cent (1970). For the figures, see the useful volume by Stig Hadenius, Björn Molin, and Hans Wieslander, *Sverige efter 1900* (Stockholm: Bokförlaget Aldus/Bonniers, 1972), pp. 292, 293.
16. Sven-Runo Bergquist, "Kommunerna och Organizationerna" (unpublished Ph.D. dissertation, Uppsala University, 1969), pp. 108–112, shows activity by *ad hoc* groups in a sample of 36 municipalities to be insignificant.
17. The possibility that such protests have become more significant is discussed below, Chapter VII.

HIGH LEVEL OF SATISFACTION

Some portion of this general nonparticipatory orientation is probably due to a reasonably high level of satisfaction among Swedes with the level and quality of the services they receive. By any standard, these services must be judged to be very high, particularly by a population which includes so many persons over the age of 50.[18] Such persons are in a position to recall how poor Sweden was thirty to forty years ago and to know by their own experience the extent of the progress made since then. Beyond satisfaction, however, it remains true that most Swedes do not see the work of government as something in which they either can or should be involved. The popular conception of government as an "expert" undertaking emphasizes knowledge or special information as the principal criterion of legitimate public participation at the same time that it dampens the expression of opinion not grounded on fact. There seems to be, in addition, the feeling that citizens are busy enough with their own problems and interests—earning a living or enjoying their free-time activities—to devote much time to politics. Swedish citizens live in a highly organized society, but they are highly privatized as individuals. Finally, when it comes to local politics in particular, Swedes tend to believe that activities at this level are far less interesting and significant than national politics.

LOW INTEREST IN LOCAL AFFAIRS

Fortunately, there is now a fair amount of evidence to support these conclusions. Recent surveys in thirty-six Swedish communes of three size classes (0–8,000, 8–30,000 and 30,000+), for example, revealed that an average of only 38 per cent of the respondents indicated a "high interest" in politics.[19] Since those reported as having "high interest" include both a small proportion who indicated that they were "very interested" and a larger proportion who said they were "quite interested," this average of "high interest" persons probably overstates the level of interest considerably. It certainly overstates the level of interest in communal politics for, according to the same study, an average of only 22 per cent of the respondents indicated a "high interest" in local, as opposed to national, politics.[20]

18. For figures showing the increasing proportion of older persons in the Swedish population, see Hadenius, Molin, and Wieslander, *op. cit.*, p. 316.
19. Claes Örtendahl, "Politisk Kommunikation—Politisk Information" (unpublished Ph.D. dissertation, Uppsala University, 1969), p. 84.
20. *Ibid.*, p. 85.

What even this figure can mean may be judged by what these respondents know and what they do. Though they get a fair amount of information about politics, most of it concerns national rather than local politics, and they thus have considerable difficulty on local questions. An average of only 10 per cent of respondents in these communes correctly identified the local tax rate, only 8 per cent could name a local issue in the 1966 campaign, and less than 3 per cent, on the average, could identify a local issue put forward by at least two parties in that campaign.[21] Moreover, while 15.5 per cent said they were members of a political organization and 59 per cent indicated membership in some nonpolitical organization, only 4.1 per cent remembered being present at a party meeting where local issues were discussed, and only 6.5 per cent were in organizations that discussed local questions.[22] When they discussed such questions at all, they did so in the home (75.5 per cent), among friends (64 per cent), or at the place of work (73 per cent). These latter figures are almost certainly misleading, however, since the great majority of respondents were unable to name even one local issue that had been discussed among family, relatives, and work-comrades.[23]

These figures portray a population with not much interest in politics, with more interest in national than in local politics, and with little political connection to either political parties or the organizations for which Sweden is so well known. Additional support for such conclusions may be drawn from a recent study of 647 officials in the Swedish cities of Norrköping, Karlskoga, and Skellefteå. Four hundred sixty-four of these officials were members of the Swedish Association of Industries and 183 were associated with the Swedish Municipal Employees Association. The purpose of the study was to compare the political activity of the two groups and to identify the factors contributing to or preventing such activity. All of these individuals are middle class, and the industrial officials especially make up a group whose political participation in local affairs has been the subject of so much American speculation.

Consider, now, some conclusions drawn from this work. Among the 464 industrial officials, 8.6 per cent indicated that they were or had been members of "some political organization" in the preceding three-year period, and 3 per cent indicated that they were or had been members of "some state or local agency" during the same period. Among the local employees, the respective figures were some-

---

21. *Ibid.*, pp. 155, 118.   22. *Ibid.*, pp. 42–45.   23. *Ibid.*, pp. 63–67.

what higher—12.6 per cent and 11.5 per cent—though not spectacularly so, considering their employment.[24] Asked to indicate the most significant hindrances to greater political activity, 40.5 per cent of the industrial officials and 31.1 per cent of local officials named "other vocation interests," followed by "job responsibilities" (15.7 per cent, 17.5 per cent), "family requirements" (5.6 per cent, 7.1 per cent) or some combination of these (26.3 per cent, 26.9 per cent).[25] Clearly enough, neither of these groups participated very much, and both placed a higher value on more privatized nonpolitical action. To repeat, these were white-collar officials, with time to participate if they had the desire. Participation rates among the more hard-pressed members of the working classes in each town presumably were even worse.

What emerges is a portrait of a people who have little attachment to locality, little interest in politics, and even less interest or participation in local politics. The municipality is viewed primarily as a provider of convenience (i.e., access to job) and service, and evaluated in terms of its ability to provide both. Without either or both of these provisions Swedes willingly abandon one locality for another if they can. If they cannot move, they are most likely to suffer or complain privately, for they are not easily mobilized for collective action outside of established party and organization structures. In any case, they are far more interested in privatized activities than in collective action. For most Swedes, influencing public decisions is either impossible, because they do not think of themselves as competent, or unnecessary, because they believe public matters are being handled well enough by those whose job it is to look after the public interest.

A FRAMEWORK OF BEHAVIOR

Orientations of the kind discussed above may be more or less temporary, particularly in a society that is changing so rapidly. Moreover, the more lasting kinds of orientations do not simply exist, as though permanently fixed, in mid-air. They are maintained by persons acting out political-institutional roles which reinforce some patterns of action, while denying legitimacy to others. I want, now, to examine some of these patterns and draw out some of their implications for local politics in Sweden.

24. Tomas Bolmgren, "Industritjänstemännens faktiska samhällsengagemang 1969" (unpublished seminar paper, Stockholm University, 1970), p. 25.
25. *Ibid.*, p. 27.

The obvious point of departure here is the party system, whose major participants during the last several decades have been five party organizations. On the left, the Social Democratic party has been consistently supported by 45 to 50 per cent of the electorate, while the Communist party has typically been able to draw the support of 4 to 6 per cent of the electorate. The right, or "bourgeois," vote has been divided between the centrist Liberal and Center (formerly agrarian) parties and the more openly conservative Moderate (formerly "Right") party.[26] This pattern of support has enabled the Social Democrats to retain power continuously since 1932, giving them a powerful hold on the machinery of government.[27]

LOCAL ISSUES SUBMERGED

Of more significance for my purposes, however, is the fact that all of these parties are national parties, built up from local party organizations which carry the same names and which follow policies determined by the national leadership. Thus the same organizations that compete for national electoral support also compete for support from the various local electorates. From time to time, specifically "local" parties appear, usually organized around some special local interest, but these are few, short-lived, and seldom significant. The result, not unexpectedly, is that local issues tend to be submerged in political conflict that focuses on issues of national significance. This result will be even more pronounced in the future because of the constitutional change initiated in September 1970. Beginning with the election held at that time, and continuing in the future, elections to national and local offices are to be held on the same day, at three-year intervals.[28]

This is not to say that local issues are insignificant, or that they are handled the same way in every commune. Such issues are extremely important to the daily welfare of Swedish citizens, and they are handled differently if only because Social Democratic control of

26. For useful analyses of Swedish electoral behavior, see Bo Särlvik, "Political Stability and Change in the Swedish Electorate," *Scandinavian Political Studies,* Vol. 1 (1966), pp. 188–222, and Bo Särlvik, "Voting Behavior in Shifting 'Election Winds': An Overview of the Swedish Elections 1964–1968," *Scandinavian Political Studies,* Vol. 5 (1970), pp. 241–283.

27. Stjernquist, *loc. cit.*

28. It should also be noted that the *Riksdag* became a unicameral parliament in 1971, thus eliminating the ability of county councils to elect members to one house. For a brief discussion of the *Riksdag,* in English, see Torsten Bjerlöw, *Sweden's Riksdag* (Stockholm: The Riksdag's Administrative Board, 1971).

the national government has not been matched by similar local power. A great many communes have been, and are, led by bourgeois coalitions, though of course such power may be more difficult for the bourgeois parties to win under the new electoral system.[29]

NATIONALIZED PARTY SYSTEM

Two consequences of this nationalized party system are extremely important for local politics. One is that such issues of local significance as may exist are difficult, if not impossible, to perceive by average citizens.[30] A major obstacle to clear perception is the practice of giving proportional representation to all local party groups in committees of the local councils, where decisions are actually made. Thus a Social Democratic voter in a commune controlled by the bourgeois parties may dislike a public decision, but if he pursues the matter (recall that committee meetings are not open to the public), he will discover that members of his own party participated in making that decision. Unless the decision has strong ideological overtones, his party representatives will not have opposed it and will not be likely to agitate the decision into an "issue." Local decisions thus appear to citizens as products of unanimity among local politicians, despite the supposedly different points of view represented by local parties.

The second consequence, following from the first, is that a great deal of citizen sophistication is required to act upon issues that have been determined to be locally significant. The Social Democratic voter in the above case might, as a consequence of his dissatisfaction, decide to vote for the communist or one of the bourgeois parties in the next local election. He might still want to cast his ballot for Social Democracy at a higher level, however. Conceivably this would be a

29. Since 1945 control of local councils has been relatively evenly divided between bourgeois and socialist coalitions. After the 1966 elections, however, bourgeois party coalitions had a majority of council seats in 542 municipalities, as opposed to socialist majorities in 292 units. See Joseph B. Board, Jr., *The Government and Politics of Sweden* (Boston: Houghton Mifflin Co., 1970), pp. 223–224, and M. Donald Hancock, *Sweden: The Politics of Postindustrial Change* (Hinsdale, Illinois: The Dryden Press, Inc., 1972), pp. 96–98.

30. In the six groups of communes, of different size classes, examined by Örtendahl, the average percentage of respondents who could identify a local issue in the 1966 campaign were as follows: 0.0, 3.2, 3.5, 6.3, 7.9 and 12.6. Another survey of the same respondents taken around the time of election day revealed that these percentages increased somewhat, although in one case the percentage actually declined, from 7.9 to 6.3. Örtendahl, *op. cit.*, p. 119.

"sophisticated" response, but the evidence is that very few Swedes vote this way.[31] Since they do not, local issues are seldom decisive in deciding local electoral outcomes.

Operating in environments where citizen knowledge, interest, and participation is low, and where it is difficult or impossible to identify or act upon "local" issues, communal political elites are relatively free from constraints that might be imposed by the local citizenry. They are, on the other hand, severely constrained by the necessity of securing approval and/or assistance from other elites in a complex, but well-integrated, structure of national organizations.

THE NATIONAL GOVERNMENT

The first such organization is the national government itself, which exerts commanding influence over both what localities do and the resources available for local actions. Detailed national legislation obliges municipalities to carry out certain responsibilities (education, social service, housing and planning, etc.) in specified ways. And, in keeping with the national policy of equalized opportunities, the national government grants general financial assistance to communes with inadequate tax resources as well as categorized assistance for special programs. The effect of these obligations and contributions is to remove much discretionary power from local authorities: more than 80 per cent of the average local budget is devoted to these obligatory programs.[32]

Municipalities are, of course, free to act in any area that is not regulated by national legislation. They can, for example, own and operate utility or transportation companies, housing and land development companies, recreation facilities, municipal theatres, and so on. Moreover, the national government has no formal authority to interfere with local tax rates, which are set independently by each com-

31. Niemi, *op. cit.*, pp. 90–91, examined the relationship between percentage of votes cast for the Social Democratic party in local and national elections in 20 communes over the period 1936–1962. Six pairs of elections were used, producing the following coefficients of correlation: .977, .981, .996, .989, .986, and .996. More recent evidence of the predominant role of national, rather than local, party identification can be found in Lennart Månsson, "Rikspolitiska Attityder —Kommunalpolitik" (unpublished Ph.D. dissertation, Gothenburg University, 1968), esp. p. 123.

32. A useful introduction to some of these relationships, in English, is Per Langenfelt, *Local Government in Sweden* (Stockholm: The Swedish Institute, 1964).

mune.[33] Clearly, wealthier municipalities are in a position to exercise a great deal of discretionary power by offering a wide variety of services supported through public taxes. Even here, however, national influence is felt, for major discretionary programs often require heavy capital investments, and borrowing by public agencies is subject to national review. For this purpose, as well as to supervise obligatory programs, a representative of the national government is located in each county and provided a staff capable of reviewing the actions taken by local governments in the area.[34] In practice, then, no major action can be taken by a local government without the knowledge, and in most cases the explicit approval, of the national government.

OTHER NATIONAL STRUCTURES

Other national structures focus less on supervision than on the provision of technical and financial assistance to municipalities. The League of Cities (*Kommunförbundet*) maintains a large staff, operates a well-known school for local officials, and publishes a magazine to keep local officials up to date on new legislative and judicial requirements. The League is also an important participant in national policy determination as well as an easily available source of technical assistance to communes with difficult problems to solve.[35] Two large cooperative housing organizations, HSB and Svenska Riksbyggen, account for roughly a third of all new housing construction in Sweden, maintaining large central staffs that work closely with local officials —in one case (HSB) through local affiliates of the national organization.[36] Locally controlled public housing companies account for an-

---

33. The rate referred to is an income tax rate, since local property taxes are insignificant in Sweden. The local rate applies uniformly to all local residents who earn income that is taxable. For most Swedish communes, the 1971 local tax rate was between 20 and 25 crowns per hundred crowns of taxable income. See Sandalow, *loc. cit.*, pp. 781–784, for a helpful discussion.

34. This official is called the Landshövding, or County Governor, and the office is one of the most prestigious in Sweden. The amount of prestige attached to the office may be gleaned from a recent appointee who, in accepting appointment, experienced an income reduction of more than 250,000 crowns. Hancock, *op. cit.*, p. 96, presents information about the persons appointed to these positions since 1945.

35. The League, in fact, operates a consultant organization with offices in major cities around Sweden.

36. Svenska Riksbyggen was formed by construction unions in order to stabilize employment, as well as provide housing. HSB is an association of individ-

other third of new construction, and they, too, operate with the assistance of a national organization.[37]

Salary scales for local workers are set in national negotiations between the central labor organization (LO) and the central employer's organization, while salary scales for public officials are set in national negotiations between the central white-collar unions (TCO, SACO) and the national government.[38] Money to finance the large building projects undertaken by so many Swedish communes recently is provided by the few large national banks or, increasingly, from the burgeoning general pension fund created a decade ago[39]—all according to detailed regulations laid down by the State but administered by the communes.

Merely to recite this very partial list of national organizations that are necessarily and continuously involved in the work of local units should be enough to indicate how extraordinarily limited in descriptive significance the word "local" is in Sweden. Constraints arising from a localized electorate may be relatively insignificant, but the constraints arising from the need to secure consent or cooperation from a variety of nationally organized structures are very powerful indeed, and in some cases (i.e., wage negotiations), totally beyond local influence.

SOURCES OF CITIZEN APATHY

Perhaps it is now possible to understand, however imperfectly, some of the structural sources of citizen apathy. The costs of learning about local activities, in an environment where elections are dominated by national issues, are extremely high. Even when successful, such efforts to find out what is going on are likely to produce little reinforcement, since what is "learned" will consist of knowledge

---

uals who, through savings deposited in an HSB organization, create the financial conditions necessary to provide them with housing administered through a cooperative organization.

37. SABO, the national organization, had about 300 local affiliates in 1968. In fact, these public housing companies have been increasing their share of new construction over the past decade. See Ödmann and Dahlberg, *op. cit.*, pp. 185–186.

38. TCO is the central organization of white-collar workers. SACO is the central organization of academically trained workers. For a useful discussion of interest organizations in Sweden, see Hancock, *op. cit.*, pp. 146–169.

39. The rapid growth of the General Pension Fund (APF) and the increasing application of the Fund to housing loans has been sketched out recently in Magnus Roos, "Allmänna Pensionsfonden och Obligationsmarknaden" (unpublished seminar paper, Stockholm University, 1970). Mimeographed.

about the extraordinary number of organizations, including national organizations, directly involved in local affairs, the complexity of the negotiations required to bring about local action, and the difficulty of establishing responsibility for actions taken in so many different settings, by so many different actors. And if, as will surely be the case, discovering who is responsible is discovering that some national bureaucrat, labor official, or bank president made the decision or decisions, the citizen will have some reason to throw up his hands in frustration, for how can he, as a local citizen, influence such actions? The same question will present itself if a local official is discovered to be responsible, for the only weapon available to citizens—the vote— will have little impact on that official. From a citizen point of view, certainly, attempts to influence local decisions will be very much like punching a ball of dough: the system absorbs every blow without ever changing its character.

HOW THE SYSTEM WORKS: ELITE INTERACTION

But what, in fact, is its "character"? How does a system composed of so many public, semipublic, and private actors, at all levels of authority, manage to work? One answer, of course, is that sometimes it doesn't work. A new suburb (or new town) is built for 40,000 people, but contains no fire station: the result is a $10 million loss in Scandinavia's largest furniture store.[40]

A four-lane superhighway connector is built to relieve pressure on the streets of central Stockholm, but the only exit from the highway is a single traffic lane leading onto an already overburdened city street. Two giant hospitals are planned for essentially the same location. One is begun but the other, after an expenditure of $10 million for land clearance, is halted.[41] This sort of list could be expanded, but it would prove little, except that Swedes are like other people. For in spite of examples such as these, the system functions well enough. How?

That the system, of necessity, works slowly should be obvious. Though mobilization for quick action sometimes occurs, the need to secure agreement among large numbers of officials for any major action typically requires a good deal of time for, first, lengthy informal negotiations leading to an acceptable proposal; second, official studies of the proposal; and, third, more discussion leading to acceptance of

40. *Dagens Nyheter*, September 8, 1970.
41. *Dagens Nyheter*, September–December, 1970.

the proposal or some modified version of it. Swedes themselves often complain about the slowness of policy-making, but the process has at least this great virtue: by the time a decision is made, most conceivable objections or alternatives have been so well aired that implementation of the decision finally reached becomes noncontroversial.[42]

It should also be emphasized that the system is one of elite interaction. While the number of elite participants for any given decision is likely to be large, neither participants nor common citizens expect any interference from outside citizen groups. A wide range of potential uncertainty is thereby eliminated, leaving the more manageable problem, for officials, of learning which people, in what agencies or firms, have what authority or resources to help resolve what range of problems. Such learning naturally takes time, but top-level government personnel change slowly ("expertise" cannot be developed overnight) and local officials also tend to have long tenure.[43] Even longer tenure can be expected as the new communes create more full-time positions to manage their increasing work load. Thus, over time, local officials develop clear solutions to the problem "whom to see about what," and use that information to structure regularized channels of interaction between themselves and their organizational counterparts at the national level.

"AVOIDANCE STRUCTURES"

Part of what officials learn in this process is that some problems simply have no shortcuts, that some red tape is too entrenched to cut. Perhaps it is such knowledge that has led so many communes to establish "avoidance structures," that is, organizations created outside of the existing organizational system to solve problems that have no solution within it. One problem that has been especially onerous to the more rapidly urbanizing communes has been the necessity to secure national government approval for loans to support heavy capital investment in housing, land, etc. To avoid this difficulty a great many communes—including virtually all suburban communes around Stockholm—have created private stock companies, particularly for housing. All of the shares in such companies are held by the commune, and all board members are local officials, but these com-

---

42. See Anton, "Policy-Making and Political Culture in Sweden," *loc. cit.*, for a more general discussion of this point.

43. Between 1950 and 1966 there was no change in political control in sixteen of the twenty-eight Stockholm-area municipalities. In five others, there was only one change during that period.

panies are legally private and thus may borrow large sums from banks without securing national approval.[44]

Another problem for such communes arises from the Swedish Constitution, which requires that records of all public transactions be made immediately available for public inspection.[45] This requirement applies not only to official directives or minutes of meetings, but also to transactions such as correspondence between officials. The obstacles thus created for localities anxious to buy land for new housing, industrial parks, or recreation areas can easily be imagined. Once again, the common technique for overcoming them has been the creation of private stock companies, whose transactions need be reported only in the form of annual reports. Unquestionably the most significant company of this type is the City of Stockholm's land acquisition company, AB STRADA. Created in 1954, this company began slowly, but in the period 1960–67 alone, it purchased 77,500 acres of land in and around Stockholm. This was 21,500 acres more than the city had purchased in the preceding 55 years, when AB STRADA did not exist. As we shall see, purchases of this magnitude have enabled Stockholm to exert strong control over urban growth as well as to earn substantial sums of money through land and apartment rentals. City officials now take considerable pride in their successes as land speculators. There is little doubt that Stockholm's success has contributed to the spread of such companies to other localities.[46]

Note that such organizations are not designed to hide anything from other members of the governing elite. Indeed, for reasons to be discussed shortly, they could not hide very much from other elite representatives. Such organizations do, however, permit local officials to hide their activities from citizen scrutiny, particularly in those cases where citizens may own desirable property which local officials wish to buy. Above all, however, they are designed to permit public au-

44. There is no good study of such organizations, but numerous examples of how they work can be found in Anders Jonason, *Byggherrarna* (Stockholm; Wahlström & Widstrand, 1970).

45. Pierre Vinde, *The Swedish Civil Service* (Stockholm: The Ministry of Finance, 1967), p. 26, discusses this provision.

46. Speculation, of course, often involves concealment of true motives. Stockholm officials have been both adept at this form of activity and proud of it. Hjalmar Mehr, a leader in these activities, has been quoted as follows: "Thus, we buy earth. That's one of the biggest political tricks that's been done. We don't say what and where. We talk about recreation uses and we've bought land at recreation prices." See Shirley S. Passow, "Land Reserves and Teamwork in Planning Stockholm," *Journal of the American Institute of Planners,* Vol. XXXVI (1970), p. 184.

thorities to get around systematic restrictions on their behavior built into the existing organizational structure. Similarly *ad hoc* organizations are created for other purposes as well: a special company may be created to avoid State salary limitations, a nonprofit foundation may be created as still another way of avoiding borrowing limitations, and so on. Proliferation of such organizations must constitute a further note of confusion for citizens, while also aggravating the problem of coordination among more and more organizational elites—or so it would seem.

ELITES: OVERLAPPING AND CIRCULATION

For officials, at least, these appearances are deceptive, due to an extraordinary degree of overlapping among elites. It is well known, of course, that many local officials sit in the Riksdag,[47] but that is only one form of overlapping. One Stockholm Social Democrat was for years an elected member of the City Council, member of the Council's Executive Board, Managing Director of the largest Stockholm housing company, member of the Finance Committee of the new Greater Stockholm Council, and regular participant in the various study commissions appointed by the national government to research policy proposals in housing and urban problems.[48] A suburban politician was an elected member of the communal council, the county council, and the Riksdag, while serving as local school superintendent. Another was vice-chairman of the local building board, president of the local HSB organization and member of the Council, while simultaneously employed full-time by a company responsible for much of the new construction in the commune.[49]

In addition to overlap, circulation among elites is common. Officials knowledgable in one area often pursue their expertise in a

47. See Hancock, *op. cit.*, p. 95, for figures on local representation in parliament.
48. American students of community politics may compare this official, Albert Aronson, to Edward Logue, as described by Robert Dahl in *Who Governs?* (New Haven: Yale University Press, 1961). Some data for such a comparison can be found in David Pass, *Vällingby and Farsta—From Idea to Reality* (Stockholm: National Swedish Building Research, 1969), pp. 218–229.
49. The holding of multiple positions is characteristic of Swedish politicians at all levels and can be carried to great extremes. For example, the first Chairman of the Finance Committee of the new metropolitan government for Stockholm is reported to have resigned eight managing directorships and more than thirty "part-time" responsibilities in order to concentrate his attentions on Metro. Even at that, he managed to retain six other positions in addition to the Finance Committee Chairmanship. See *Dagens Nyheter*, January 7, 1971.

number of organizations working in that area. An official may move from a private construction company, to a local public housing company, to the head office of HSB, to the National Building Board, and back again, in a game of musical chairs in which positions change while function remains the same. If there is anything that can be observed as a behavioral coordinating device, overlapping and circulation is it.[50]

One may question, of course, whether there is any need for an explicit coordinating device in such a system, for overlapping and circulation in effect produce a situation in which everyone more or less knows what everyone else is doing. Officials involved in activities of municipal significance come from many organizations, but they know each other and are often involved in each other's work. The official world is unlikely to be disturbed by public pressures, so officials can be confident that the only support they need is support from others like themselves. Reasonably long tenure in office provides plentiful opportunities to develop that support by developing personal relations and, once developed, such relations can structure the processes through which major local policies are developed. What is done is accomplished more through common understandings than through directives, more through the nuances and subtleties of interpersonal relations than through formal—and thus observable—procedures. Confusing and largely impenetrable from the outside, from the inside it must be regarded as a tight little world.[51]

50. I use "behavioral coordinating device" here to distinguish overlapping from the formal coordination provided by the *remiss* system. According to that system, all proposals of more than minor significance are circulated to representatives of all organizations prior to action that affects the interests of such organizations. For more discussion of this procedure, see Hancock, *op. cit.*, pp. 156–159.

51. Jonason offers a number of good examples of how this "tight little world" operates. In one of them, a small commune in the south of Sweden hired the consulting firm K-Konsult (owned by Kommunalförbundet) to help plan an area of vacation-type houses. The firm's office was in another city, which happened to be the location of all county offices (controlled by the Landshövding), which meant that the planning consultant was in very close contact with the county officials whose approval of any plan would be necessary. The builder was located in yet another city, but the builder's architect was also in close contact with the planning consultant, with whom he had worked for some time. Plans for the area were developed initially by the builder, reviewed and changed somewhat by the planning consultant, and approved by the county authorities without even being sent to the commune for which the plan was made. See Jonason, *op. cit.*, p. 71.

STOCKHOLM AS SETTING: "A SPECIAL PLACE"

Stockholm, of course, is "a special place" in Swedish social and political life. The city itself is the cultural and intellectual, no less than the political, capital of Sweden, while the metropolitan area as a whole—Greater Stockholm—has experienced a disproportionately large share of Sweden's postwar urban growth. Since 1945, an area population already distinguished by the presence of well-educated and well-paid government officials, corporate executives, journalists, artists, authors, diplomats, and the like, has been enlarged through the addition of tens of thousands of people with the talent to "make it" in the big city. Given their talents and their mobility, Stockholm area residents have been even more interested in convenience and high-quality public services than their countrymen, even less committed to municipal boundaries, and considerably more aware of local political activities—without, however, being much more interested in participation in those activities.

Stockholm is "special" in a governmental sense as well. Operating under its own law, Stockholm has possessed broader authority than other Swedish municipalities, including the authority to handle hospital and health care activities dealt with by county governments in other parts of Sweden. Formally, all city activities are directed by a 100-member City Council, assisted by a 12-member Central Board of Administration, which prepares reports and agenda for council meetings. Real control over city affairs, however, rests in the hands of another institution unique to Stockholm: The Board of Commissioners.

The Board of Commissioners was founded in 1920 to improve political and administrative coordination of city affairs. The mechanism devised to achieve this purpose was a new, full-time position called City Commissioner (borgarråd in Swedish). By giving each commissioner a number of administrative departments to supervise, coordination within a given functional area could be achieved. And by assigning these positions to leading politicians from the several local party organizations, coordination at the level of policy might be achieved. The number of commissioners has varied, depending on the division of municipal service responsibilities. At the close of WW II there were eight such positions but, as we will see below, a ninth was created in 1954 to deal with a functional problem that had come to assume major importance: coordination between the city and its surrounding suburban municipalities.[52]

52. For general background information on sociopolitical characteristics of Stockholm, see Hans Calmfors, Francine F. Rabinovitz, and Daniel J. Alesch,

Part Two

PATTERNS OF CHOICE

CHAPTER II

PLANNING: THE POLITICS OF TRUST

PERCEPTIONS

IN SWEDEN, forecasting is a national sport, and planning a national obsession. Nevertheless, plans and forecasts sometimes go astray. A national record for inaccuracy may have been established by the city of Stockholm in the period immediately preceding World War II, when city officials competed with academics for the distinction of being least prescient regarding the city's future population. As late as 1941, when the Greater Stockholm regional population stood at 770,000 persons, a distinguished scholar argued confidently that the region would come to contain no more than 900,000 people. Moreover, he asserted that the new figure would not be reached until 1970, after which the region's population would increase no more.[1] Only five years later, the Greater Stockholm population shot past 900,000, on its way to a total of some 1.3 million in 1970. Seldom has a projection on a matter of such significance been so wrong so publicly. In a city of great technical and statistical sophistication, this prediction is still remembered—with justification—as one of the major misjudgments of modern political history.

IMPACT OF THE ERROR

Had it stood by itself, a mistake of such magnitude would be worth little attention. But in fact that incorrect estimate, or something very much like it, was widely accepted by the city's political-administrative elite. Because it was so widely shared, the idea that regional

---

1. The scholar was W. William-Olsson, whose *Stockholm: Structure and Development* (Stockholm: Almqvist & Wiksell, 1961) remains a valuable analysis. His earlier mistaken projection is cited in *Stadskollediets Utlåtanden och Memorial, Bihang nr 73, år 1950*, p. 6. Hereafter cited as *Bihang nr 73, 1950*.

population would grow slowly and begin to stagnate by 1970 remained a cornerstone of official planning expectations during the early war years, as it had been for the preceding decade.[2] The result was a kind of official complacency regarding policy for future growth. Only after several years of massive wartime population increases nearly double those of any previous year did the complacency begin to dissolve. By 1950, the city's elite had begun to realize that future population growth would be of a much greater magnitude than anything previously anticipated, and that a whole range of new policy initiatives would be required.

By this time, too, city officials had concluded that effective implementation of virtually all of the new policies would require massive reorganization of the existing structure of metropolitan government.[3] This straightforward conclusion was based on the obvious contradiction between a growing need for regional solutions to problems of water supply, transportation, or housing and a governmental system that distributed public authority among twenty-eight independent suburban municipalities, in addition to Stockholm. Each of these suburbs was as jealous of its independence as was Stockholm itself. More serious, politically, was the deep hostility many suburban political leaders felt toward the big city. Before any efforts to solve problems could be attempted, something would have to be done about city-suburban antagonism.

SOURCES OF SUBURBAN ANTAGONISM

One important source of that antagonism was in fact directly traceable to the city's mistaken complacency about future growth. During the depression, leaders from several poor and hard-pressed suburbs pleaded with city authorities for annexation. If the city were willing to take over the financial burdens they were unable to meet, these suburban leaders were willing to have their municipalities annexed to their larger and wealthier neighbor. The city would have had to assume larger obligations, but in return it would have achieved substantial territorial growth.

Neither of Stockholm's two principal political party confederations—the Social Democrats and the bourgeois—was interested. Both were wary of the electoral consequences of increasing taxes to meet

2. For confirmation, see Joakim Garpe, "Stockholm at the Opening of the 1960's," *Stockholm Regional and City Planning* (Stockholm: City Planning Commission, 1964), pp. 24–25.

3. These ideas are reviewed below.

added responsibilities. And the bourgeois parties were reluctant to become too closely related to heavily working-class suburbs such as Solna or Nacka. Besides, as one official later admitted, "the forecasts for the future . . . did not suggest that Stockholm would ever need to expand beyond the then existing boundaries." [4] In short, the city had no need for additional territory, and was not interested in merely being helpful, particularly when being helpful would cost city taxpayers money.

Stockholm's less than charitable attitude toward its suburbs created deep wounds by emphasizing the inequality that existed between one large, rich, and well-equipped public authority and several that were both small and poor. As area population continued to grow rapidly during the war years, city-suburban inequities became at once more obvious and more serious. The city had a large stock of housing, whereas most of the suburbs had little to offer. The city had good streets and a well-developed mass transit system, whereas most of the suburbs were little more than country towns. The city had good schools and a fine system of hospitals, whereas the suburbs were still operating one-room schoolhouses, and very few hospitals were available. Finally, the city had a large, well-trained, and well-paid bureaucracy, whereas most of the suburban governments had yet to hire their first full-time employees.

Population increases served only to underline these inequities, both physically and psychologically. Because of the city-suburban contrast, new arrivals to the area naturally preferred to live within the city's administrative boundaries. These cumulative preferences quickly strained the city's facilities, particularly its housing stock. With no room in the city, population soon began to spill over into suburban municipalities. There, widespread resentment at the absence of space inside the city, reinforced daily by the contrast in physical surroundings, created mass anticity sentiments which reinforced the attitudes of suburban officials who had so recently been spurned by their big neighbor.[5]

---

4. Garpe, *loc. cit.*, p. 24.
5. Many of these regional inequities were summarized in the 1958 regional plan proposal. Among the more striking findings reported there was that, as of the early 1950s, some 70 per cent of the region's working population were employed in inner-city locations. See *Förslag Till Regionplan för Stockholmstrakten* (Stockholm: Stockholmstraktens Regionplanenämd, 1958), pp. 12–21.

A ROYAL COMMISSION

The predictable consequences of these deepening cleavages were serious enough to bring national government intervention. Accordingly, in 1944, a Royal Commission whose work was interrupted by the war was reorganized and instructed to examine the problem of securing better cooperation among Stockholm area municipalities. Three years later that Commission produced a report that may be regarded as a landmark, both because of its comprehensive review of alternatives and because of its discussion of a course of action that, as we shall see, ultimately was adopted.

The Commission considered two alternatives and rejected both. One was the proposal that a single communal government be created by consolidating Stockholm with its surrounding suburban neighbors. Such a solution, the Commission argued, might be adequate for administration of some programs but, considering the service problems likely to arise in an urban region much larger than its present size, it would probably not be able to give adequate consideration to peculiarities of various local areas. Above all, such a solution would destroy local self-government, replacing it with a large, less democratic, centralized administration.

An alternative solution, significantly enough favored by the two most prominent Stockholm members of the Commission, was a plan to unite the city government with the county government for the administration of regional services, while retaining the existing municipalities for the provision of more localized services. Since the county government—the "landsting"—was essentially a single-service government, with the great bulk of its budget devoted to the operation of hospitals, creation of a new unit (a "Storlandsting") could be accomplished simply by grafting appropriate city agencies together with the existing county government. But deciding *which* city functions to transfer, and *how*, together with the problem of devising mechanisms for representation that would satisfy both city and county, were difficulties the Commission was unable to resolve.

"A REGIONAL MUNICIPALITY"

Instead, the Commission proposed a totally new unit of government, between the existing municipalities and the county, to handle regional problems such as planning, housing, water, sewer systems, etc. Far from serving as a basis for political agreement, this proposal for a new "regional municipality" only intensified existing political disagreements. In keeping with Swedish political practice the proposal was sent out "on remiss," that is, for review by all affected agencies. The responses revealed that none of those agencies could accept it. Suburban governments were strongly opposed, partly on grounds that representation by population in the regional municipality's council would guarantee control by the city, and partly because the proposal dealt inadequately with what the suburbs then felt to be their most pressing need: hospital care. City officials opposed the idea because to them it seemed costly, confusing, and ultimately inefficient. And the county legislative body, on which suburban governments were well represented, rejected the proposal by a substantial majority. Both the county and the city thought the problem needed more work, and the city officially requested that further study be given to the two alternatives rejected by the Commission. Observing these local reactions, the national government decided to let the matter drop.[6]

AN ABOUT-FACE: STOCKHOLM OPTS FOR EXPANSION

Stockholm, however, was in no position to let the matter drop so easily. By the late 1940s population growth had become a pressing reality rather than an uncertain forecast. Extending that reality into the future led city officials inexorably toward one conclusion: since city land resources were quite limited, the thousands of new Stockholmers who were expected could be accommodated only in the suburbs.[7] That conclusion was the fundamental premise organizing work on the Stockholm Master Plan, begun in 1945; it motivated incorporation of two suburban municipalities into the city in 1949, as well as creation of a "long-range investment" committee in the same year; and it rationalized increased city efforts to purchase land in the suburbs during the late 1940s and early 1950s. Stockholm, in short, had committed itself to expansion, one way or another, regardless of what the suburbs thought. Almost overnight, the accepted dogma had changed from forecasts of population stagnation to forecasts of explosive growth. Suddenly the city's line changed from "Who needs the suburbs?" to "Ready or not, here we come."

Nowhere was the ideology of the new line better displayed than in a document submitted by the city to the national government on June 20, 1950. Entitled "The Greater Stockholm Problem," the

6. The alternatives were proposed in *SOU 1947:30.* Responses to these proposals are reviewed in *Bihang nr 81, 1966,* pp. 8–12.
7. *Bihang nr 73, 1950,* pp. 9–10.

document constituted a formal request by the city for another commission to consider the problem of government organization in the Stockholm area. Though not explicitly stated, it was clear from the argument that the city wanted a reorganization that would produce some form of metropolitan-wide governmental authority to deal with future growth.

As far as city officials were able to foresee, rapid growth was all but inevitable, primarily because the city continued to create large numbers of new jobs. Attempts to limit the location of new industries in Stockholm had been quite successful, but industries already in the city were expanding rapidly. Continuation of these trends implied that the region could expect, not 900,000, but closer to 1,300,000 people by 1970. Given the city's shortage of land, most of those people would have to go into the suburbs. If they did, suburban population would more than double in only twenty years. Public investment would have to rise enormously and, to avoid economic waste and administrative chaos, some means of permanent coordination of city-suburban policies would have to be found. The city stood ready to do its part in such an effort and urged the government to initiate action "as soon as possible." [8]

Stockholm's case was well argued, well documented, and, if one accepted its fundamental assumption of regional economic unity, logically unassailable. It may also have been the last straw for suburban politicians. Having experienced city incorporations of suburban territory, a city land-grab policy of large but secretive dimensions, and a well-publicized planning policy in which suburban areas were treated as merely resources, to be used as the city saw fit, suburban politicians now observed an official city proposal aimed at the very existence of their governments—and, it should be added, their jobs.

It was primarily in response to such anticipated pressures that suburban officials had come together in 1946 to form the Stockholm Suburbs Cooperative Association.[9] Though unable to prevent city annexation of Spånga and Hässelby in 1949, the Association provided a handy forum for expressing the antagonisms generated by that series of events. And, while the city was able to persuade the national government to order the creation of a Regional Planning Commis-

8. *Ibid.,* p. 26.
9. For a history of this organization, see Anders Lind, "Stockholms förortskommuner och urbaniseringen," *Kommunernas Tidskrift,* Argang 48 (1967), pp. 153–160.

sion in 1949, members of the new association found effective means of resistance to that action. In its 1950 petition to the government, the city revealed how effective suburban opposition had been, even in a matter as innocuous as an *advisory* regional planning body. "Though a year and a half has passed since the regional planning area was approved," the city complained in June 1950, "agreement has not been reached on representation of the City and the suburban communes in this agency." Continuing, the city was petulant:

The City, which represents more than three-fourths of the people and the taxing power of the region, has for its part rejected a majority in the decision-making body and has contented itself with requesting the same number of representatives as the suburbs in the regional planning board, the operating agency. The other communes, however, have argued that even this would give too much influence to Stockholm.[10]

As of the middle of 1950, then, the cleavage between Stockholm and its suburban neighbors was deep, and apparently deepening. Moreover, by the end of that year it had become clear that city efforts to form a stronger coalition with the national government would fail: though the city's petition for a new commission study was circulated and discussed, it was never acted upon by the government.[11] Solutions to the problems perceived by city officials would have to be worked out jointly by officials of the region, without national intervention. In view of the openly expansionist aims of the city, and the strong resentments generated by such aims among suburban governments, prospects for reaching solutions to Stockholm's "metropolitan problem" seemed poor.

SYSTEM

Just how poor those prospects appeared to be in 1950 can be appreciated best by recalling the character of the governmental system that structured the actions of units referred to here as "the city" and "the suburbs." Public authority in the Stockholm region was divided among twenty-nine separate local governments, ranging from the wealthy and populous giant, Stockholm, to tiny rural communes of

10. *Bihang nr 73, 1950,* p. 22.
11. The petition was dated June 20, 1950. One participant has suggested that the outbreak of war in Korea may have diverted attention from the Stockholm problem. In an interview, this participant reported that the then Prime Minister, Tage Erlander, seemed "stunned" at the news from Korea, and totally absorbed with that problem.

considerably less than 2,000 inhabitants.[12] With minor exceptions, each of these units possessed a similar range of legal powers granted by national legislation. Far more significant, each of them was heir to the powerful Swedish tradition of local independence. In contrast to nations such as the United States, local units in Sweden enjoy a *constitutional* guarantee of independence, arising from a phrase mandating local governments to "manage their own affairs." This guarantee—interpreted as authorizing local governments to undertake any activity not specifically prohibited by national law—and the broad variety of locally initiated activities it supports, has structured a politically powerful mythology of grass-roots control not unlike the "home-rule" ideology so common in the United States. However unequal the Stockholm suburbs may have been in population, wealth, or services, each was the legal and traditional equal of the big city. Moreover, the city could do very little to alter that situation.[13]

In principle, at least, it was possible to overcome this decentralization of public authority through the informal mechanism of political party control. Because most of the suburban jurisdictions were populated by workers or others from the less affluent classes, most of the suburban governments (two-thirds) were controlled by the Social Democratic party—and had been since the mid 1930s.[14] The more heterogeneous city population supported stronger opposition parties, but even here the Social Democrats were by far the largest political group. Having won the 1946 city election, in fact, the Social Democrats were in power during the very period when the city-suburban cleavage became most obvious.[15] Clearly enough, party similarity was not sufficient to produce a similarity of views on the problems of city-suburban relations. Indeed, it is more accurate to assert that, if anything, socialist control of both city and suburb during this period exaggerated existing policy differences.

These policy differences were exaggerated largely because sub-

12. For population figures for area municipalities in 1930, 1940, 1950 and 1955, see *Statistical Year-Book of Stockholm* (Stockholm: Stockholm Office of Statistics, 1956), p. 244.

13. Sandalow, *loc. cit.*, discusses the legal status of Swedish municipalities in more detail.

14. Anton, "Politics and Planning . . . ," offers a brief history of one such suburb and recent changes in its politics.

15. Strictly speaking, it was the Social Democrats *and* Communists who won in 1946, since the seventeen Communist seats were necessary to give the thirty-eight Social Democrats a majority. For statistics on the party distribution of council seats since 1910, see Hadenius, Molin and Wieslander, *op. cit.*, p. 296.

urban socialist leaders could afford to be as independent politically as they were by law and tradition. With predominantly working-class constituencies, suburban socialists could count on being reelected as often as they wished. Furthermore, national issues dominate campaigns for public office in Sweden—even local public office[16]—so that suburban leaders could count on the absence of localized policy preferences to constrain them once in office. In the absence of either localized policy constraints or national directives, the socialist leaders who were repeatedly elected to office in the suburbs were largely free to develop whatever policies toward the central city they pleased.[17] Such policies, strengthened by long tenure in office, structured an extraordinary degree of fragmentation in the metropolitan political system.

National political issues also dominated Stockholm city politics, but the consequences were somewhat different and considerably more complex than the consequences produced in the suburbs. Though local electoral constraints were traditionally weak, constraints imposed by the organizations supported by a more heterogeneous population had considerable significance. In the city the Conservative and Liberal parties gave the Social Democrats stiff competition for control of the City Council.[18] The result was not only stronger bourgeois party organizations, but also a strong, dominating bourgeois press, which generated a great deal of information about city politics and not infrequently participated in the generation and resolution of issues.[19] Moreover, because the electorate was more evenly divided in the city than in the overwhelmingly socialist suburbs, the slight shifts in national electoral patterns that made no impact on the suburbs often led to changes in government within the city. Accordingly, city politicians were in a curiously unreal position:

16. See Chapter I above, for elaboration of this point.

17. Recall, however, that national directives controlled the bulk of what the suburbs were able to do in areas defined by the national government as "essential" services.

18. Hadenius, Molin, and Wieslander, *op. cit.*, p. 296.

19. *Dagens Nyheter*, the major morning newspaper in Sweden as well as Stockholm, has historic ties to the Liberal party. *Svenska Dagbladet* is closely tied to the conservative forces in Stockholm, now represented by the Moderate party. Both have close formal and informal ties to the organs of city government: newspaper editors and reporters are frequently members of legislative or administrative bodies. *Expressen*, an afternoon tabloid, is also controlled by Liberal party interests, while *Aftonbladet*, another afternoon tabloid, is controlled by LO, the central labor organization in Sweden. Thus the Social Democrats have only one outlet among the four current newspapers.

what they did or did not do locally seldom had any impact on local electoral outcomes, yet those outcomes often led to shifts in political control that very much determined what would be done locally, and by whom. In an environment characterized by a constant search for "issues" on the part of political organizations and the mass media, these conditions imposed a peculiar kind of restraint on city politicians. From an electoral point of view there was very little they could do that could be regarded as "good" and virtually nothing that could be regarded as effective. Yet their failure to attempt "good" actions could at any moment be subjected to a barrage of criticism and publicity that would surely be considered "bad" by colleagues and constituents alike.[20]

At a later point we shall explore the structure of responses to this predicament in some detail. Here it is sufficient to note that one obvious reaction on the part of the city elite has been to withdraw behind the clear boundary separating officials from nonofficials, to conduct most serious public business in this "back-stage" area while attempting to carefully manage the "front-stage" relations with political and mass-media organizations, and of course to maintain as much confidentiality as possible concerning "back-stage" activities. A major factor contributing to the viability of this reaction has been the firm tradition of coalition government, rather than majority party rule. Thus the center of power in city politics, the Board of Commissioners, grants representation in proportion to party voting strength, which means that leaders from minority as well as majority parties are always represented. The necessity for close collaboration in day-to-day work encourages—indeed requires—a level of cohesion among commissioners which not only helps to maintain a psychological separation from outsiders but also virtually eliminates serious partisan disagreements. Regardless of whether socialists or bourgeois parties are in power, therefore, the views and policies emanating from City Hall are likely to be very much the same.[21]

Apart from coalition government, the greatest structural source of support for unity among city politicians was and remains the dominance of professional administrators in city politics. The city's

20. For a more extended consideration of the effects of public criticism on politicians, see Chapter VI, below.
21. The same conclusion can be applied to suburban governments, where proportional representation and a tradition of administration either by committee or plural executives encourage a wide-ranging consensus on municipal affairs. For a comment, see Hancock, *op. cit.*, pp. 94–95.

career public service—large in number, well trained and well re-
warded—has traditionally enjoyed a very high degree of access to the
political elite. Indeed, the absence of restrictions against political
office-holding by administrators has enabled career administrators to
double as influential partisan figures in local affairs. The result has
been an elite extraordinarily receptive to administrative definitions
of issues and to professionally prescribed solutions to problems.[22]
Thus it was no accident that a nominally "socialist" party could argue
for massive governmental reorganization in 1950 without even men-
tioning "income inequality," social "injustice," or other ideological
symbols. For the "socialists" of 1950, irrationality and the need for
better coordination was a more powerful argument. For the governing bourgeois coalition of a few years later, waste and inefficiency,
rather than individual freedom, rationalized the same demand for
reorganization. Only an insider could see any real differences in these
different emphases. From the outside, which is where suburban officials of all political affiliations were, the city's view of the metropolitan world seemed dogmatic, more than slightly self-righteous, and
quite unaffected by partisan differences.

The possibility that a political party might serve as an informal
mechanism to overcome formal decentralization of public authority
in Greater Stockholm therefore seemed remote in mid-1950. Given
the social composition of the suburbs, only the Social Democratic
party could serve as a vehicle of integration, but its suburban leaders
were too independent and too entrenched, and its city leaders were
too nonpartisan in their view of appropriate public policies, to provide such a vehicle. Another mechanism would have to be found if
this system of decentralized authority and dispersed power were to
be altered.

BUILDING INSTITUTIONS

In September of 1950, the bourgeois parties regained control over
the city government. Though the general thrust of city policy hardly
changed at all, the political shift removed whatever slight hope there

22. Richard D. Cunningham has examined the occupational backgrounds of
city councillors and members of the various administrative boards during the
period 1966–1970. His data convincingly show that the city is governed by a
managerial elite: only 4 of 100 councilmen and 16 of 263 members of the boards
were classified as workers. See his "Stockholm Metropolitan Government: The
Administration and Politics of City Planning" (unpublished seminar paper, University of Pittsburgh, 1971), pp. 39, 55–56. Mimeographed.

may have been that party similarity could bring city and suburb together. Instead of facing a socialist-dominated city administration, suburban socialist bosses were now confronted with a bourgeois government led by Dr. Yngve Larsson, who had been instrumental in formulating the city's expansionist aims in the suburbs.[23] Larsson initiated several efforts to reopen negotiations with suburban governments. When these efforts failed, he proposed that the city change its stance: since there was no way to solve the organizational problem, the reasonable alternative was to forget it. This strategy of avoidance was not fully rationalized for several years,[24] but the city's actions after the 1950 elections made clear that, from its point of view, the action had moved to other fields.

The Regional Planning Association, for one thing, was still struggling to get off the ground. A national government order had created the association in 1949, but the battle for its control was still being waged between the city and its suburbs. Though the association was to be controlled nominally by an eighty-member elected council, it was understood that real power would be in the hands of a nine-member executive board, and each side was anxious to gain access to that power. Under the new city administration a compromise was reached in February of 1951 which gave five of the nine executive board seats to the suburbs, but which gave the board chairmanship to the city. Since the association was merely an advisory body with no legal authority to compel action, this compromise may have seemed enough to get work underway. Its effect, however, was little more than to shift the battle line somewhat. The next issue was the question of securing a full-time director for the association and here, too, the city and suburbs disagreed, with each side demanding appointment of someone from its side of the boundary.[25] Quite evidently, the suburbs were taking the regional planning agency seriously, regardless of its limited formal authority, and were determined to be neither pressured nor maneuvered into a position of organizational inferiority.

What really was bothering the suburbs became clear in May, at a meeting called by Dr. Yngve Larsson, who had moved from his posi-

23. For Larsson's background and accomplishments, see David Pass, *op. cit.*, pp. 192–201.

24. Commissioner Helge Berglund formulated the rationale in *Stadskollegiets Utlåtanden och Memorial, Utl. nr 172 år 1959*, pp. 1530–1534. Hereafter cited as *Utlåtande nr 172, 1959*.

25. Interview, Commissioner Joakim Garpe, June 10, 1971.

tion as City Planning Commissioner to the presidency of the Council's Executive Board with the recent change in government. In another attempt to improve city-suburban relations, Larsson offered a proposal to create a permanent committee to deal with problems of cooperation. All of the most important city officials were present, including the new socialist leader Hjalmar Mehr, as were the most weighty suburban socialist bosses—Nils Eliasson of Huddinge, P. A. Sköldin of Sundbyberg, Gustaf Berg of Täby.

Suburban spokesmen wasted no time in arguing that the most important cooperative problem for them was the lack of cooperation from the city in its purchases of land in their municipalities. The city, it turns out, was not only attempting to buy up land in the suburbs, but it was often doing so without informing suburban officials. Given the city's known intentions for development, such behavior could hardly encourage a high level of confidence or trust among suburban politicians. Suburban complaints had led to some improvement, suggested Eliasson, but what was really needed was full information disclosure on the city's part: suburban governments had to be informed, in writing, of any city effort to purchase land in their territory. With other suburban spokesmen supporting both the analysis and the recommendations put forward by Eliasson, Larsson quickly agreed that the city would henceforward keep the suburbs informed about city land purchases. Furthermore, Larsson added, since the incorporation of Hässelby and Spånga (in 1949), the city had no further desire to expand its area through incorporations of suburban territory. The implication was clear: though the city might continue to buy suburban land, it would no longer attempt to dictate the disposition of that land by itself.[26]

Larsson's statement, made in the presence of all major city leaders and recorded in the official minutes of the meeting, represented a basic shift in city policy: the city would no longer use whatever resources it had to push the suburbs around. Suburban officials remained skeptical, particularly since city spokesmen repeated their earlier well-publicized assertions that the city would run out of land for housing by 1960. If the city *was* sincere, on the other hand, a basis for cooperation was self-evident, for the suburbs, too, were feeling the pressure of increasing demand for housing. Over the next several months it became clear that a "deal" had been consummated,

26. This summary of events is taken from a typewritten "Protokoll" (Minutes), dated May 21, 1951.

though no one had ever spelled it out: the city gave up its drive for large-scale organizational reform in return for suburban cooperation in housing. By April of 1952, the Regional Planning Association had not only hired a director, it also had begun work on its first major assignment: a study of the preconditions necessary to meet the housing needs projected forward to 1960.

A year later the regional planning office issued its report on the housing problem, arguing the need for comprehensive measures to deal with it. This report provided an opportunity for a dramatic demonstration of what the city had achieved through its change in attitude toward the suburbs. Responding to the housing report, the suburban majority on the nine-man Executive Board argued that the housing situation was so manifestly serious that action had to be taken even before work was completed on the regional plan itself. In order to increase the production of new housing, these suburban officials thought, some form of "immediate municipal cooperation was necessary," particularly for Stockholm and its closest neighbors. Noting the inadequacy of existing cooperative organizations, the suburbanites stated their "intention to take the initiative in bringing about a more detailed consideration of forms for voluntary cooooperation in certain questions of implementation [of new housing] among the affected suburban municipalities." Finally, these officials proposed that the regional planning office be assigned the task of developing information that could provide a basis for a "suitable and achievable program for housing production in the Greater Stockholm area." [27]

References to "voluntary cooperation" obviously were intended to reaffirm suburban opposition to any kind of imposed reorganization, but even with this qualification in mind, the suburban response seemed unusually significant. For the first time, representatives of the suburbs had asserted a responsibility for a non-local problem. For the first time, too, the suburbs had asserted a responsibility for action to resolve the problem, rather than mere participation in "studies." Either way, the suburban response marked an obvious departure from earlier attitudes.

With both city and suburbs softening attitudes toward one another, largely through the vehicle of a regional planning agency and the opportunities it provided for reaching common understanding, the situation seemed ripe for further institutional development. Again, a city election provided an appropriate occasion. Although

27. *Utlåtande nr 172, 1959,* p. 1530.

the socialists failed to win the 1954 election, they did increase their strength somewhat, relative to the governing bourgeois coalition.[28] Since the margin of difference between the two groups was now even thinner, socialist complaints over their allocation of only three of the eight seats on the Board of Commissioners became even more pointed: with close to half the vote, less than 40 per cent representation in the center of power was intolerable. Many bourgeois politicians, steeped in the proportional representation tradition, were sensitive to this complaint, but saw no easy solution. There were only eight commissioners, after all, and increasing the number of socialist commissioners to four would result in virtually equal representation for minority and majority parties. Though increasingly annoyed at constant socialist criticism, bourgeois politicians were not prepared to go that far.

One of them, however, thought he saw a way to solve the representation problem, and, at the same time, improve the city's ability to deal with the surrounding ring of socialist-controlled suburbs. The idea, according to Yngve Larsson, was to expand the Board of Commissioners to nine members, and place the new commissioner in charge of the city's relations with its suburbs—a sort of "Foreign Minister" in city government. The new commissioner would of course be a socialist, thus satisfying the political demand for increased representation. With skill and luck, the new official also might promote closer relationships with socialist suburbs. Socialist city leader Hjalmar Mehr readily agreed to this plan—he and Larsson always had taken very much the same view of city problems—and by the end of the year the new position was officially approved.[29]

THE "COMMISSIONER FOR GREATER STOCKHOLM AFFAIRS"

The man Mehr and Larsson agreed should become the first "Commissioner for Greater Stockholm Affairs" was Joakim Garpe. Like Larsson and Mehr, Garpe had "grown up in City Hall," having held a succession of positions, beginning as secretary to a former Commissioner for Social Affairs in the early 1930s. As head of the Long-Range Investment Committee set up by the city in 1949, Garpe was well versed in the problems associated with planning the city's future. In fact Garpe had written the economic portion of the 1952 Stock-

28. The Social Democrat-Communist coalition gained only one seat—from 48 to 49—but the Liberal party lost four seats. For the figures, see Hadenius, Molin, and Wieslander, *op. cit.*, p. 296.
29. Interviews, Commissioner Yngve Larsson and Commissioner Joakim Garpe.

holm master plan. As party activist, Garpe had good relationships with many socialists throughout the city and suburban area, and a particularly close relationship with party leader Mehr.[30] Both the new institution and the man chosen to head its activities thus symbolized the city's determination to adopt a metropolitan, rather than city, approach to metropolitan-wide problems.

Garpe's mission seemed straightforward enough—on paper. Inside the city administration, he would attempt to coordinate the various relationships city agencies had with suburban governments. If he carried out this responsibility cleverly enough, he could expect to achieve an informal centralization of power that might be of great potential significance in dealing with the suburbs. Outside of the city, he would attempt to expand opportunities for city-suburban cooperation in matters of joint concern. By this time (early 1955), of course, the general policy framework within which these objectives would be pursued was relatively settled: the city was no longer interested in total governmental reorganization, but would instead pursue cooperative solutions to individual problems as they arose. By this time, too, a reasonably clear consensus had developed on the nature of the area's priority problems. The recent statements of suburban leaders made clear that they, no less than city officials, saw housing as the most vital problem they faced. Garpe, therefore, was stepping into a situation in which both general and specific policy priorities already had been developed in the political system. This simplified his problem considerably, but hardly came close to solving it. Deep-seated suburban hostility to Stockholm was still there, even if a common interest in housing had emerged, and that hostility meant that everything would depend on *how* Garpe chose to act.

INITIAL STEPS

His choice was to begin by attempting to establish both his and the city's credibility in a series of small but important areas. He negotiated an agreement that enabled the municipality of Huddinge, where Nils Eliasson was boss, to purchase thirty-five hectares (roughly fourteen acres) of city-owned land located within Huddinge's borders. He reached another agreement with Solna over the location of a major traffic artery that permitted Solna to begin a large housing development. Garpe negotiated an agreement with Lidingö for joint planning of a new bridge connecting that municipality with Stockholm—a connection necessary for further development in Lidingö.

30. Interview, Commissioner Joakim Garpe. See also Kubu, *op. cit.,* p. 60.

Discussions were begun with officials from Huddinge, Nacka, and Järfälla which led ultimately to connecting those municipalities to the Stockholm sewer system. An agreement was reached with Järfälla making city high school facilities available to students from that municipality, at cost. Joint city-county planning for a regional health-care system was begun, as was planning for a Stockholm-suburban water supply system.[31]

Taken individually, none of these agreements was very significant. Taken together, they represented a clear-cut pattern: the assertion of city willingness to utilize its resources to help solve problems of significance to several neighboring municipalities. It was precisely this demonstration that the city as an organization wanted to establish, and that Garpe as an individual *had* to establish. Except for Lidingö, all of the suburbs with which Garpe achieved agreements in this period were socialist-controlled, and these suburban socialists recalled vividly that their party colleague Garpe, as chairman of the city's Long-Range Investment Committee in 1949, had helped to initiate Stockholm's petition to the national government requesting a regional governmental reorganization. Garpe, no less than the city, was on trial.

A HOUSING PROGRAM

Garpe and his new city agency were not the only actors who were busy during this period. The staff of the Regional Planning Association was in the process of completing a draft regional plan, to be circulated in 1956, which included an inventory of municipal resources available for new housing construction. In 1955 the national government initiated another in its series of five-year planning studies and this, too, was known to be aimed in part at the problem of housing.[32] Against this background of broadening interest in the housing problem, Garpe moved to exploit the existing regional consensus. At his initiative, a meeting of city and suburban officials was held in December 1955. These officials agreed to authorize "an inventory of resources available for housing construction in the various area municipalities together with a survey of the predominant obstacles to increased housing production." [33] Since information on

31. These early negotiations are summarized in *Utlåtande nr 402 år 1956,* pp. 3117–3119.

32. *SOU 1956:53*, pp. 196–198, report the result of this interest. See below, Chapter III, for further discussion.

33. *Bihang nr 51 år 1957*, p. 7.

available resources had been gathered already by the regional planning office, the "bite" in this assignment was the survey of obstacles. This was clearly a political problem: it was not information about resources that was desired but information about what had to be done to get at those resources. The political significance of the group's action was further underlined by the delicate assignment of responsibility for the work to be done. Two individuals were asked to carry out the project. One, Garpe, represented the city, while the other, Axel Granath, County Housing Director, represented the suburbs as Garpe's coequal. Consensus or no consensus, it was important that no political agreement between city and suburb show the slightest sign of suburban subservience.[34]

That this was in fact a political agreement became evident several months later, in May 1956, when the same representatives, having reviewed a report prepared by the Garpe-Granath team, now authorized them to work out specific proposals for a joint housing program. Reaching agreement on specifics, Garpe later recalled, was far more difficult than gaining acceptance of a policy that was already in general favor.[35] Few of the suburbs had either the technical or financial resources necessary to launch a significant program of housing construction. For some, launching such a program would necessarily curtail other, equally desirable, municipal activities. But this time Garpe and his city had the powerful assistance of the national administration.

In responding to the regional plan sketch that began circulating in 1956 the national Housing Board argued that earlier estimates of housing for the Stockholm area were faulty and needed upward revision. If any serious dent was to be made in the area's housing shortage, the board concluded in the fall of 1956, the area would have to begin producing new units at the rate of some 14,000 per year. Interestingly, the same figure was reached by the national commission working on the five-year national planning projection. This provided even more support for some form of organization that would be able to coordinate the desired increase in housing production.[36] With both the national government and the city administration pushing, the suburbs had nowhere to move but straight ahead. Garpe, Gra-

34. Years later, Garpe recalled that he had been extraordinarily sensitive to his position of "superior inequality" and had gone out of his way to prevent others from concluding that the city was pushing the suburbs around. Interview.
35. Interview, Commissioner Joakim Garpe.
36. *SOU 1956:53.*

nath, and other city and suburban officials retreated to the charming medieval town of Sigtuna in November of 1956 to hash out the details. When they emerged they carried with them both a metropolitan housing program and a plan for the first operating metropolitan governmental authority in Stockholm's history.

The housing program—officially styled the "Program of Action for Housing Supply in Greater Stockholm, 1957–1961"—repeated the national government's target of 14,000 new units per year for Greater Stockholm by the end of 1961. While this represented a 40 per cent increase over existing production of 10,000 units per year, the change called for was in fact far more dramatic. Of the current 10,000 units per year, some 7,000 were being produced by the city, in the city, with only 3,000 being built in the suburbs. But, as city officials had been insisting since 1949, land available for new construction inside city boundaries would be used up by 1960 or so, which meant that the bulk of the construction necessary to reach the target of 14,000 new units per year would have to be built in the suburbs. By 1961, according to the "Action Program," city construction would be down to only 3,000 units. The suburbs, by that time, would have to be building 11,000 or more new units per year—almost a 300 per cent increase over 1956–57 production levels! [37]

That kind of a change obviously required some drastic measures of implementation. If there was to be any chance of meeting the goal in five years, large-scale, concentrated developments would have to be given priority. The Garpe-Granath inventory of municipal resources had pinpointed several areas suitable for the kind of quick and comprehensive exploitation recently accomplished in the "new town" of Vällingby, which served as a model of what was now necessary.[38] Large areas of virgin land were available in Solna, Sundbyberg, Täby, Nacka, Huddinge, and Botkyrka. Construction of housing for thousands of persons could be accomplished efficiently in each of these areas, and the Action Program proposed that they be given priority. Other areas could be exploited later, as need and opportunity dictated.

Special arrangements would have to be made with national authorities for the construction credits and labor permits necessary for such large-scale undertakings. It was even more important that an agency be created to plan and coordinate the totally new activities about to be undertaken by many suburban municipalities. To this

37. *Bihang nr 51 år 1957*, pp. 29–34.
38. Vällingby was specifically cited as a model for emulation. *Ibid.*, p. 30.

end, the report proposed that a new "Greater Stockholm Planning Board" be created. Composed of representatives of both city and suburbs, the new board would handle necessary negotiations with the national government on the one hand, and coordinate local housing plans on the other. Though the proposed board would be permanent and have formalized instructions, the Action Program authors were careful to point out that they did not envision an agency whose decisions would "bind" individual municipalities. Just how such a board could function without binding individual municipalities was a question the authors preferred to leave unanswered. Presumably, such details could be worked out by the cooperating municipalities later, if they could agree that such an agency was necessary.[39]

That Garpe was able to bring about agreement on a metropolitan housing program of such magnitude was a major political achievement—brought about, it is clear, partly by Garpe's patient efforts to establish the city's good faith, partly by the city's withdrawal from earlier efforts to press for large-scale governmental reform, and partly by open and obvious pressure from the national government to deal more effectively with the housing problem. How much of an achievement it was became clear in June of 1957, when the Stockholm City Council debated whether or not to give its approval to the plan outlined in the Action Program report.

While no council member disagreed with either the analysis or the recommendations presented in the report, Liberal party councilmen challenged the realism of plans to organize a major expansion of housing in the metropolitan area through voluntary agreements. The problem, they argued, was not simply to arrange cooperation during the development stage, but also to organize "what comes after in the form of administration and supervision of all the housing areas, traffic connections, schools, and other things that are necessary to meet Greater Stockholm's needs." What was required, and what would have to come eventually, argued the Liberals' P.-O. Hanson, in terms identical to those used by the socialists in 1949 and 1950, was "an official study leading to an administrative reorganization of the entire Greater Stockholm area into such communal work forms as are capable of handling the development that has taken place in the area." [40] To solve the difficulties produced by that development "with boundaries and arrangements that are hundreds of years old,

39. *Ibid.*, pp. 39–41, presents the rationale for the new board.
40. Stockholms Stadsfullmäktige, *Protokoll Jämte Yttranden, 1957*, Nr 6, p. 392. Hereafter cited as *Protokoll, 1957*, p. 392.

when the whole area has completely changed character, cannot be possible." [41]

For the socialists, now out of power, their former policy seemed to lead into a blind alley. In a revealing statement, socialist leader Hjalmar Mehr argued that

All of us know that every municipality outside Stockholm refuses to follow the path recommended by Mr. Hanson. There is not a single municipal government that is not suspicious of Stockholm. We can believe that to be justified or not, but what we think is irrelevant when all are afraid of being sucked up by the giant Stockholm. There is not a single municipal government, in a city or town, which will not defend itself against Stockholm at any price. . . . Mr. Hanson can hardly find a single municipal leader who will stand to speak for the point of view he takes because they all oppose it. That is the situation in which we find ourselves.

Even to discuss such a study, Mehr continued, particularly after so many assurances from the city that it would not attempt to absorb the suburbs, would create more suspicion. If such a proposal were made, suburban municipalities would simply refuse to participate and all the hard work of the Commissioner for Greater Stockholm Affairs would be sabotaged.[42] Garpe himself joined the debate to argue that the council had a choice: doing something about housing or proposing massive governmental reorganization, but not both. To him, proposing reorganization would simply kill any hope for a common housing program,[43] and neither he nor Mehr was willing to sacrifice a present achievement for the dubious opportunity of arriving at an even greater achievement in the future. "We must proceed step by step," concluded Mehr, "on the way to reform."

THE GREATER STOCKHOLM PLANNING BOARD

The willingness of the city socialists to trade in earlier demands for total reorganization in return for a meaningful housing program brought all the tumblers into alignment: national, city, and suburban authorities were all agreed that something should be done. Bourgeois criticism in the council thus represented not so much opposition as symbolic reaffirmation of what professional city administrators knew to be the rational, efficient, and therefore "right" thing to do. Though many politicians—even socialists—doubtless shared this conception of what was right, they also recognized that what was practical was quite different. The Action Program sailed through the council on June 3, 1957, and within a few months, negotiations between city

41. *Ibid.,* p. 402.   42. *Ibid.,* pp. 403–404.   43. *Ibid.,* p. 403.

and suburbs led to the establishment of the Greater Stockholm Planning Board, precisely as proposed in the Garpe-Granath report.

Yet, for all its importance as a joint city-suburban authority to *do* something of metropolitan scope, creation of the planning board rested on political foundations that were fragile to the point of delicacy. Hjalmar Mehr's perception of suburban hostility was reflected in every paragraph of the "instructions" for the new agency worked out by city and suburban representatives. The planning board was an agency for "voluntary cooperation" between two "equal" partners, whose decisions could only "influence," not bind, the various member communes. As if to underline this delicate relationship, two chairmen of the board were to be elected, one by the city members, the other by the suburban members, and leadership of meetings was to be shared on a rotating basis.[44] Clearly enough, this was no decisive breakthrough to a totally changed situation. It was, instead, a small and halting step, taken cautiously, by men whose old antagonisms toward one another had not been wiped away, in the hope that the existing situation might be improved. To have come this far was surely significant; whether any further distance could be traveled remained very much an open question.

STRUCTURAL CLEAVAGES AND THE PROCESS OF CONSENSUS

From one point of view, the interactions between Stockholm and its suburbs during the period 1947–1957 could only be regarded as inconsequential. After all, nothing concrete had actually been accomplished. Worse yet, the problems that seemed serious in 1947— housing, transportation, related services—were even more serious in 1957, after a decade of development. To be sure, city and suburban officials had at least begun talking to each other in a regularized way, thanks to the creation of formal agencies such as the Regional Planning Association. But talking and planning were a long way from action, particularly when the planning agency itself possessed no authority to implement its plans. Moreover, for all the talk, it seemed clear in 1957 that old hostilities between city and suburb had not withered away. They may have been covered over to some extent, but, as the debate over the Greater Stockholm Planning Board suggested, suburban officials remained suspicious of the city, and the city retained a somewhat haughty view of its neighbors.

44. *Utlåtande nr 330 år 1957.*

These actor perceptions were firmly rooted on both sides. The laymen-politicians of the suburbs, operating for the most part with little or no professional staff assistance, were defending a position— i.e., their existence as "independent" municipalities—that had no rational defense if "problems" were as serious as claimed by the city. Housing expansion could not be accomplished without large administrative organizations, and suburban governments had no such organizations. Dealing with the housing question, or any other question, thus necessarily implied assistance from the city, and once that assistance was given, it would be infinitely harder to prevent both *de facto* and *de jure* absorption of suburban governments by the city. The only defense available to the suburbs was the Swedish "tradition" of municipal independence, which was powerful enough to stall action while more "competent" suburban administrative structures were built up. Once such structures were available, of course, more "professional" arguments could be developed to rationalize suburban independence. At this point in time, however, the suburban position was organized around a politics of status, in which both individual and municipal status positions were implicated.

The city, on the other hand, was determined to pursue a politics of administrative service, in which identification of serious "problems" was followed by efforts to devise "rational" and "efficient" solutions. In this view, what was central to suburban officials— preservation of their independence—became merely a secondary roadblock obstructing the rational solution of common problems. Centered around the city's large and expert bureaucracy, following its "professional" ideologies, this view gradually lost credibility in the face of suburban opposition. It fell to the politicians to devise a more pragmatic approach, emphasizing a case-by-case search for progress. This adjustment made possible some movement toward agreement on housing and hospital care, but it needs to be emphasized that the city's core interest remained a more comprehensive solution to the metropolitan problem and that this interest was never abandoned. Suburban officials appreciated this fact, which accounts for their continued caution, and frequent hostility, in dealing with city counterparts.

NATIONAL INTERVENTION

These contrasting and largely contradictory views help to explain the absence of much concrete accomplishment during this decade. Indeed, left to their own devices, city and suburban officials might have totally refused even to begin talking to one another. On a number of important occasions, however, the national government refused to leave the two parties to their own devices: in 1949, when creation of a regional planning association was ordered; in 1950 and 1953, when the government sided with the suburbs in opposing a metropolitan governmental reorganization; in 1955–56, when it prodded area governments to set higher housing goals; and in 1957, when it agreed to commit its resources to meeting those housing goals. Clearly enough, the national government was closely and continuously involved in regional affairs, as a potential ally for either the city or its suburbs. Like the suburban politics of status and city politics of service, the national government's politics of intervention was a constant. But the direction in which that intervention might point was a variable that could lend weight to either side of the local conflict. Though it had not supported the city through the early and mid-1950s, there was always a possibility that it might do so, with decisive consequences.

A COMMON UNDERSTANDING

If one views the events of this decade from a process rather than structural point of view, however, it seems clear that, despite an absence of accomplishment, something very important was going on. Intellectually, a common understanding of the problems of the region, together with an appreciation of the steps required to solve them, was being spread among an ever widening set of officials. Work on the proposed regional plan involved numerous meetings between city and suburban representatives to set priorities for a variety of future development alernatives. Success in setting such priorities implied that city and suburban officials had agreed on an estimate of what had happened and what should happen. This, in turn, implied an even wider circle of acceptance of such estimates, as local politicians communicated their understandings to constituents.[45] Nationally, too, increasing attention to problems of the Stockholm region had led to general agreement on the priority of housing, if not on other planning matters. As time passed, then, local and national officials came increasingly close to consensus on regional problems. However much suburbanites may have suspected Stockholm, increasingly they came to use the same terms in describing both their

45. Regional Planning Director C.-F. Ahlberg has made a similar argument in his "The Regional Plan for the Stockholm Area," *Stockholm Regional and City Planning* (Stockholm: City Planning Commission, 1964), pp. 37–54.

predicament and the city's. Rationalized disagreement had begun to replace blind antagonism.

Socially, the meetings and discussions had created familiarity—in some cases friendship—between individuals who had formerly been known only as signatures on letters or names in a newspaper. Since most suburban and city officials enjoyed and looked forward to long tenure, growing familiarity effectively undermined the social bases for hostility: no one could afford (or would want) to be hostile to a colleague with whom one would have to work for some time into the future. Moreover, familiarity opened new, and broadened old, lines of communication. As officials came to realize that "he isn't such a bad guy after all," the telephone call or personal visit became more common as a way of dealing with problems. Better communications meant reduced antagonisms, if only because they made formal appeals to the mass media less necessary. But they also multiplied opportunities for agreement by reducing the time necessary to "test" the acceptability of any given proposal. Thus by the end of this ten-year period, familiarity and better city-suburban communications among a small and stable elite had transformed the environment of regional interaction. Development of social foundations for the growing political consensus seemed well under way.

Despite the fact that nothing very tangible had yet occurred then, a great deal of social learning had taken place in the Stockholm region by early 1958. City politicians had tested their preferred alternative and learned that it was unacceptable. Suburban politicians had learned, for their part, that the national government expected more from them than unrelieved hostility to Stockholm. These lessons had been learned with hesitation, cooperative agreements had been entered into with great caution, and no commitments had been made that could not be withdrawn. But if nothing was settled, the Greater Stockholm Planning Board suggested at least that both sides were willing to continue discussions. Little as this may seem, it represented a significant increment of trust among politicians whose predicaments forced them to be extraordinarily wary of one another.

CHAPTER III

HOUSING: THE POLITICS OF CAPACITY

TENUOUS though it may have seemed, the consensus on housing reached by Stockholm area politicians came at a time when national politicians, too, were becoming more concerned with housing policy. The so-called "Red-Green Coalition" between the Social Democrats and the Farmers Party had produced few new programs since 1951, when the coalition government came into existence. Meanwhile problems piled up. In Stockholm alone, the number of persons registered in the city's housing queue reached 100,000 in 1956, and complaints about "the queue society" became more insistent. Both of the governing parties suffered in the 1956 parliamentary elections, and the Social Democrats dropped to their second lowest level of support in twenty-five years.

These results further weakened the coalition, already strained because of a divergence of opinion on the question of a supplementary pension program. Early in 1957 the Social Democrats appointed Torsten Nilsson as Social Minister, with responsibility for bringing about a solution to the pension question. A rare public referendum on the question was held in October 1957, and the coalition was dissolved when this too revealed a divergence of views between the governing parties. For the time being, the Social Democrats would govern alone, determined to push forward with their pension plan and other programs that could revive voter support.[1]

The next three years proved to be among the most active and important in recent political history, as the pension question was fought

1. For a review of these events, see Hadenius, Molin and Wieslander, *op. cit.,* pp. 199–212. Sweden has held only three public referenda in the twentieth century: in 1922 (prohibition), 1955 (right-hand traffic), and 1957 (pension reform). The results of these referenda are reported on p. 293.

out to a resolution. Social Minister Nilsson led the fight for the Social Democrats, who succeeded in pushing their plan through a closely divided parliament after an unusual special election and a series of local elections—in September 1958—that became still another referendum on the issue.[2] As Social Minister, of course, Nilsson had other governmental responsibilities, including housing.

Equally significant was Nilsson's political position as chairman of Stockholm's "arbetarkommun," the party organization for the city. Nilsson maintained that position throughout his tenure as a cabinet minister, and was thus closely attuned to the city's problems.[3] Indeed, he could hardly be otherwise in view of his close personal relationship to Hjalmar Mehr, who became Commissioner of Finance after the September 1958 electoral victory. The political consensus that had created the Greater Stockholm Planning Board thus could be carried forward after 1958 by a socialist city government, socialist suburban governments, and a socialist national minister already working hard to implement new programs to win voter approval.

THE ORGANIZATION OF PERCEPTION

Within the framework of this structural and political consensus, it was well understood that Stockholm had the biggest headache. The city's planned decrease in housing production at a time when the waiting list for housing was climbing rapidly above 100,000 was only the most obvious sign of the headache.[4] Less obvious, but just as critical, were the consequences of decreasing production to the units engaged in it: the city's nonprofit housing companies. Responding to incentives offered by the national government, which was eager to provide tools to increase local housing production, Stockholm had created three such companies in 1947, to complement two already in existence. Though organized as private, joint-stock companies, the shares in these companies were held by the city—entirely or predominantly—giving it total control over company activities.

Because these companies were governmentally controlled, they

2. Björn Molin's *Tjänstepensionfrågan* (Göteborg: Akademiförlaget, 1965) will probably remain as the definitive study of this issue.

3. Nilsson later became Foreign Minister. Even then, he retained his Stockholm party chairmanship.

4. Figures on the growth of the housing queue from 1948 to 1970 are provided in Thomas J. Anton and Oliver P. Williams, "On Comparing Urban Political Systems: Residential Allocations in London and Stockholm." Paper prepared for delivery at the 1971 Annual Meeting of the American Political Science Association, Chicago, September 1971. Mimeographed.

were eligible for 100 per cent financing from the state, that is, the state would guarantee 100 per cent of the value of housing units constructed by the companies. And because such companies were organized as private stock companies, they could avoid troublesome legal restrictions upon public organizations: contracts for work were not required to be made public, nor were prevailing salary scales for public employees applicable to company officials. These were considerable advantages, enabling Stockholm and other municipalities to create and operate productive and effective housing companies.[5]

Of the five city companies, three were primarily administrative organizations, arranging contracts and managing newly built housing units, but not themselves engaging in construction work. The other two did their own construction work as well, and thus in time built up large numbers of employees. Of the two, Swedish Housing, Inc. had by far the largest organization. Moreover, it had incurred the greatest political obligation among city officials for its work in developing the new suburb of Vällingby, at a time when no private contractors were willing to undertake such a large and uncertain project. For all of the city companies, but especially for Swedish Housing, Inc., with its large complement of workers, machines, architects, and financial experts, any significant reduction in city housing production would be a disaster.

Unfortunately for the public companies, their futures were in considerable doubt in the mid to late 1950s, despite the agreed upon five-year Action Program for housing. For Swedish Housing, Inc., work on the Vällingby project was all but finished by 1955, and the only project large enough to offer any prospect for long-term utilization of its capacity was Farsta, a new suburb proposed for development on the southernmost border of the city. Since Farsta was the last large area of open land available inside city boundaries, Swedish Housing, Inc. competed vigorously for the project. In April of 1956, however, the bourgeois-controlled city government awarded the project to a consortium of bankers and private contractors, leaving the city's largest housing company with no substantial work beyond what was already in the pipeline, and leaving the city itself with no further large areas of developable land.[6] In this situation, Conserva-

5. Figures reported in *SOU 1965:40*, p. 38, show that between 1945 and 1965 an average of more than twenty such companies were created each year. For the Stockholm companies, see *Kommunalt Bostadsbyggande i Stockholm* (Stockholm: De Allmännyttiga Bostadsföretagen i Stockholm, 1966).

6. David Pass, *op. cit.*, pp. 263–273, discusses the decision to award Farsta to a private consortium.

tive party members of the City Council took the position that the city companies should gradually be phased out of construction work altogether, leaving them only administrative management duties. With no more city land, and plenty of private building companies interested in work, conservatives saw little point in maintaining the public companies.[7]

In preparing their five-year Action Program, on the other hand, Commissioner Garpe and Housing Director Granath took a different view. They concluded that only large projects of the Vällingby-Farsta type could make a significant impact on the housing problem, and aimed their investigations at discovering available land resources of sufficient size to accommodate such projects. They seriously doubted, however, that all of the suburban municipalities had the resources necessary for carrying through such projects. Nor did they believe it to be "rational or even possible" for every municipality to put together the financial and administrative apparatus necessary for large-scale community development.

COMBINING REGIONAL RESOURCES

Instead, they offered the possibility of combining regional resources in the areas where development would take place. Without daring to propose it directly, they suggested that the question of using city resources to aid suburban governments could hardly be avoided in the future. And the city resources they were talking about were the city building companies. Having identified the suburbs as the only available source of land, Garpe and Granath were now implying that the most efficient way to transform vacant land into housing units was to utilize the city companies to do what none of the suburbs was tooled up to do.[8] For Garpe and Granath, this strategy was the only alternative to the relatively rapid disappearance of the city companies.

The September 1958 election altered perspectives on the question of who should build where. Though the pension question dominated the campaign in Stockholm, as in other municipalities across Sweden, Stockholm socialist leader Hjalmar Mehr's campaign statements promised energetic movement on a number of fronts, particularly housing and city development. An expert on urban problems the world over, Mehr promised that "We shall not repeat America's mis-

7. For expression of these themes, in the context of the first five-year program, see Stockholms Stadsfullmäktige, *Protokoll, 1957*, pp. 377–411.

8. *Utlåtande nr 140 år 1957*, esp. pp. 934–935.

takes." [9] The socialist victory gave him a chance to redeem that promise as Finance Commissioner and thus head of the government. To
help him Mehr retained Joakim Garpe as Planning Commissioner,
with continuing responsibility for Greater Stockholm problems.

In addition, councilman Albert Aronson became chairman of the
city's Executive Board, and vice-chairman of the Real Estate Board,
which was responsible for the purchase, maintenance, and disposition
of all city-owned property. This combination of responsibilities was
particularly interesting, since Aronson was at the same time managing director of Swedish Housing, Inc., and had been in that position
since 1947—which is to say that it was Aronson who, perhaps more
than any other single individual, was responsible for the development of Vällingby. Both Garpe and Aronson were close to Mehr personally. Indeed, Aronson was married to Mehr's sister. In dealing
with the problem of housing, then, Mehr could count on two colleagues who were not only expert in their respective areas of public
responsibility, but who were also closely tied to him by personal and
political relationships.

Mehr, of course, had other resources as well. As party leader of the
majority group in the City Council, he was in total control of actions
taken by that body. As Finance Commissioner, he was in a position to
influence all activities of the city's administrative units if he so desired. In addition to all this, Mehr became chairman of the board of
another private stock company controlled by the city, AB STRADA.
The city had bought this company from its former owner to give
him a tax dodge, in return for which the city gained access to a large
building in the path of a proposed subway extension. Since the city
wanted the building, not the company, nothing was done with the
company except to allow it to lead a paper existence.

A LAND-PURCHASE COMPANY

In 1956, however, frustrated by difficulties in purchasing needed
land from sellers reluctant to chance the vagaries of city politics, the
city determined to convert AB STRADA into a land-purchase company. Again, use of the private company device would permit the
city to avoid troublesome problems: negotiations for purchase could
be done without publicity, except for an innocuous annual report
that would say very little. Price gouging could thereby be avoided, as
well as undesirable publicity in the event the city purchased land out-

9. Quoted in Kubu, *op. cit.,* p. 51.

side its own borders. From the sellers' point of view, meanwhile, presence of the city's Finance Commissioner on the board, along with the other major party leaders, could provide a guarantee of sorts that the city would in fact purchase land once agreement to do so had been reached. Mehr, who was determined to expand the city's land holdings, thus had a specialized agency to work with that included all major party leaders among its controllers. Unless they opposed him, this would surely be an important policy tool.[10]

OPPORTUNITY

Not long after these resources and men came together in a position of city leadership an opportunity arose to test their capabilities. By this time, the five-year housing program had been in existence for more than a year, and Commissioner Garpe, in seeking to implement it, was discovering that the predicted difficulties were at least as great as he and Granath had suggested. Though some of the suburbs were building more housing units, none had yet even considered the large-scale developments Garpe thought necessary to make a significant impact, largely because they simply lacked the administrative know-how to get such projects organized.

SUBURBAN PROBLEMS SURFACE: TYRESÖ

Instead, suburban governments were forming private companies of their own and moving into partnerships with the two housing co-operative organizations, HSB and Svenska Riksbyggen. The trouble with this, apart from the small number of apartments being con-structed, was that cooperative apartments required down-payments, often of considerable size. But most of the people waiting for hous-ing in Stockholm could not afford down payments of even modest size. They needed rental units at low cost, but this is not what the suburbs were building. In 1958 the complex of problems created by this situation surfaced all at once in the municipality of Tyresö, southeast of the city.[11]

Several years earlier Tyresö had purchased a large piece of prop-erty, intending to use it for some form of industrial employment.

10. Information about AB STRADA is taken from interviews with agency officials. See also Shirley S. Passow, "Land Reserves and Teamwork in Planning Stockholm," *Journal of the American Institute of Planners,* Vol. XXXVI, No. 3 (May, 1970).

11. This discussion draws heavily on Torsten Wergenius, "Lex Bollmora," *Svenska Stadsförbundets Tidskrift,* Vol. 5 (1965), pp. 216–222.

Efforts to find an industrial employer soon proved successful, and in 1957 the municipality signed a contract with HSB for the construction of some 2,000 cooperative apartments, presumably to accommodate the housing needs of the workers who would shortly be coming into the community. HSB set to work on preliminary planning for the project, but both sides soon became uneasy. It gradually dawned on municipal officials that few workers would be able to afford the cooperative units. This could only mean trouble for the new local industry.

Meanwhile, HSB gradually lost confidence in its ability to carry through the project. One of its new cooperative apartment buildings had just opened in the developing Farsta area, and customer resistance to that project did not encourage HSB to think it could do any better in Tyresö, which was further away and not serviced by a subway connection. By the middle of 1958 HSB had begun discussing ways of dealing with its problem with the city housing company that shared its office building, Family Housing, Inc. Would it not be a good idea, HSB wondered, for Family Housing, Inc. to take over part of the project in the Bollmora section of Tyresö?

Both Commissioner Garpe and his chief administrator Inge Hörlén—like Garpe an expert administrator, committed socialist, and close associate of Hjalmar Mehr—were fully aware of what was going on in Tyresö, partly because they had recently concluded negotiations leading to the sale of city water to the municipality. Moreover Garpe, as chairman of the Regional Planning Board, had received copies of projected plans for the Bollmora area. With the election victory as signal, therefore, a meeting of HSB, Family Housing, Inc., Tyresö, and Stockholm officials was arranged to discuss the idea. All present agreed it was a good one.

Unfortunately for these participants, it was also made clear that the city companies lacked legal authority to operate outside the municipal boundaries. Albert Aronson, however, thought he saw in this difficulty an opportunity to solve both the problem of land access and the problem of future work for the public housing companies. Aronson encouraged Family Housing, Inc. to request the Real Estate Board (of which he was vice-chairman) to look into the legal and technical problems that would require solution if the city companies were to extend their activities to the suburbs.

Not long afterward, this investigation concluded that a legal change would be necessary to permit the city to provide financial guarantees for projects built outside its borders. If this change could be made, there were no other major difficulties. Accordingly, a delegation of Stockholm and Tyresö officials visited Social Minister Torsten Nilsson in the spring of 1959 to request his support for such a change in national statutes. Nilsson, sensitive as always to the city's problems, agreed immediately, and set his staff to work drafting the proposed legislation. Meanwhile Albert Aronson had devined another problem in the coming sequence of events, and set the staff of the city's real estate department to work on a proposal to reserve access to most remaining public land *within city boundaries* to the public housing companies, reserving what was left for the housing cooperatives. If the city companies were to expand their work outside the city, their productive capacity would have to be maintained until such expansion was initiated. And that, reasoned Aronson, could be accomplished only by reserving remaining city land for city companies.[12]

In the Council debate over this proposal on June 15, 1959, Aronson pointed out that during the previous ten years—i.e., the period of bourgeois control—private builders had been granted 30 per cent of city-owned land, with 58 per cent going to the public companies and 12 per cent to the cooperatives. Because of the land shortage, however, housing production in the city would be cut in half in the next few years. Half of that reduced production would take place on privately owned land and would be constructed by private builders. The effect would be to reduce the proportion of total public company construction to only 30–33 per cent over the next few years, while increasing the proportion of private construction to 50 per cent. "A loss for the public companies and for cooperative organizations," Aronson concluded, "can be prevented only if all of the City's land is retained for these organizations."

Aronson's proposal, coupled with the use of city companies in the suburbs, gave some hope of dealing with what Liberal City Commissioner Frank called the "absolute necessity" of increasing housing production for the tens of thousands waiting in the housing queue. Conservative party spokesmen in the debate professed to see Aronson's plan as another effort "to move society in a more socialist direction" through a "monopolistic" policy that constituted an "unwarranted discrimination against private companies." But few listeners were sympathetic to this view. As Liberal party leader Gunnar Hjerne argued, the conservatives' principles might be correct, but they had

12. *Utlåtande nr 210 år 1959*, p. 1850.

little to do with reality. The reality for him and his party was the "tens of thousands of apartment seekers with no chance to get an apartment inside Stockholm, and in that situation, practical realities must overcome principles." [13] They did.

LEX BOLLMORA: THE CITY BUILDS OUTSIDE

These political themes were further developed in February 1960, when the City Council debated the proposal for a contract with Tyresö which would allow Family Housing, Inc., to build 500 apartments in the Bollmora section of Tyresö. Eighty-five per cent of the new units would be made available to registrants in the Stockholm housing queue. By December 1959 the Riksdag, acting with unusual dispatch, had enacted legislation—since known as *Lex Bollmora*—permitting the city to build outside its borders, adding only the proviso that the city had to be invited in by the other municipality. Within two months the city had a contract ready for approval.

Once again the Conservative party representatives charged a "socialistic" maneuver that could turn out to be financially irresponsible if the city was ever called upon to make good the fiscal guarantees it was now planning to give. Instead of allowing the public companies to expand into the suburbs, the conservatives demanded that they gradually withdraw from housing construction altogether. Few took this proposal seriously. Communists, Liberals, and Social Democrats all agreed that it was pointless to restrict the public companies when so many people were seeking apartments. As Aronson put it, "From the point of view of those standing in the housing queue, it makes little difference *who* it is that is building housing; what is essential for them is *that* housing be built."

But if the Social Democrats professed to find little significance in who the builders of new housing might be, they now found reason to be concerned about *what form* the housing should take. Introducing the bill, Commissioner Garpe noted that more and more of the housing units being produced in the suburbs usually required high down-payments, typically because they were segments of cooperative apartment buildings. In 1959, in fact, fully 55 per cent of all finished suburban units were down-payment units. The great majority in the housing queue, on the other hand, wanted to *rent* apartments, because they could not afford the 20,000 or 25,000 crown required to

13. Stockholms Stadsfullmäktige, *Protokoll, 1959,* pp. 699–713.

purchase cooperative units. If the waiting list was to be reduced, therefore, large numbers of rental units would have to be built—and rental units were precisely what the public companies were authorized to build.

Although Liberal party spokesmen were less certain about this argument than was Garpe, they were just as determined to provide more housing. The proposed contract between the municipalities of Stockholm and Tyresö sailed through by a vote of 58 to 18. *Lex Bollmora*, the legislation of December 1959, had achieved its first result.[14] Fittingly enough, it was Aronson's own company, Swedish Housing, Inc., which ultimately contracted to build 2,000 of the 2,500 apartments built by the city in the Bollmora section of Tyresö municipality.

Lex Bollmora was a major turning point in city and regional housing and development policy. Over the next few years it led to ten agreements between Stockholm and eight suburban municipalities for the provision of 31,000 new housing units. Of those new units fully 70 per cent, or 22,000 apartments, were placed at the disposal of the City Housing Exchange. In the process, the physical shape of Stockholm for the next century was effectively determined. Indeed, the *Lex Bollmora* agreements were so important that it is imperative to take a closer look at the manner in which they were achieved. Though it would generally be accurate to view these agreements as merely the working out in detail of an over all political agreement stated in the 1957 Action Program, it is striking that the earliest agreements affected areas that were given very little attention by the authors of the 1957 program.

Both Tyresö and Järfälla municipalities presented problems for the large-scale building projects envisioned in the 1957 program. Lack of adequate transportation, in particular, relegated them to second, or even third, priority, compared to other locations. Nevertheless, the earliest agreements focused the bulk of city building activity on these two areas. This suggests a flexibility with regard to the 1957 agreement which is worth some attention. Similarly, most of the later (1963–66) agreements affected Salem, Botkyrka, and Huddinge—municipalities which lie southwest of the city, in the path of then-contemplated extensions of city subway lines. More interestingly, they were all municipalities in which the city either

14. The debate, including the quotations cited above, is found in Stockholms Stadsfullmäktige, *Protokoll, 1960*, pp. 88–125.

TABLE 1

Lex Bollmora Agreements

Municipality	Date	Number of apartments	Percentage to Stockholm
Tyresö	1960	500	85
Tyresö	1962	500	70
Tyresö	1963	1,500	70
Järfälla	1961	2,500	70
Nacka	1960	750	50
Salem	1963	3,400	85
Österhaninge	1964	1,000	67
Botkyrka	1965	15,000	67–75
Boo	1966	1,000	70
Huddinge	1966	5,000	70

Total apartments: 31,150
Average % available to Stockholm: 70

Source: *Utlåtande nr 442, 1968,* pp. 3972–3974.

owned, or was purchasing, large quantities of land. This, too, deserves further attention.

PARTY POLITICS AND SUBURBAN HOUSING

How can we account for the city's failure to follow the 1957 priorities in the initial thrusts of its public housing companies? All three of the first municipalities to accept city companies—Tyresö, Nacka, and Järfälla—were traditionally Social Democratic suburbs. But since most of the other municipalities involved in the 1957 agreement were also Social Democratic, factors other than party strength obviously were involved in determining which communities were first.

Still, the debate over Tyresö exposed a political dimension of the problem that would continue to be significant, namely, the partisan implications of building rental vs. cooperative housing. The downpayments required in the cooperatives being built in the suburbs in the late 1950s provided an income screen that effectively prevented most working-class families from obtaining suburban apartments. Because social class and income are closely related to partisan voting, continued emphasis on cooperative apartments in the suburbs could only lead to loss of socialist control of suburban municipal governments. Plainly, suburban socialist politicians could attempt to maintain their power by building rental instead of cooperative apartments

—a consideration that neither they nor the city building companies was likely to ignore. Behind the apparently innocuous issue of rental vs. cooperative housing, therefore, was the vital political question of whether suburban socialism, in encouraging development, was not also digging its own grave.

Increasingly, then, suburban socialist politicians began to see the advantages of accepting city housing companies within their borders, whether or not "plans" existed for such developments. Facing their own "survival" problems, the city companies similarly were interested above all in getting their future work organized, again regardless of "plans." How these pressures came together in a specific case was previously well illustrated in the Tyresö case—a case that can usefully be compared to the other large commitment of the early period, Järfälla.[15]

MULTIPLE PRESSURES: THE CASE OF JÄRFÄLLA

A small, working-class, and solidly socialist suburb west of the city, Järfälla had been coveted by Stockholm in the early postwar period. As the city's complicated annexation of Hässelby and Spånga, adjacent to Järfälla, drew to a close in 1949, city agents quietly inquired about the possibilities of purchasing large tracts of vacant land in Järfälla. Following so swiftly on the heels of the annexation of neighboring land, these inquiries magnified the potential threat to Järfälla's independence and spurred a variety of responses from local officials.

Already committed to growth, Järfälla socialists now moved rapidly to implement that commitment. Within three years two public building companies had been created. Within another year a property development corporation, also publicly controlled, was in existence to develop an industrial park capable of attracting jobs to the municipality. These organizations soon produced results that were good enough to guarantee Järfälla's continued independence. Ten thousand people lived in the suburb in 1954, up from 4,400 in 1945, and an expansive master plan was in preparation. Järfälla was well on the way to its eventual status as the Stockholm area's most rapidly growing municipality.

Not surprisingly, rapid growth placed more and more pressure on municipal agencies. Since Järfälla was responsible for guaranteeing

15. Unless otherwise noted, the following discussion of Järfälla is based wholly on my "Politics and Planning . . . ," *loc. cit.*

76   HOUSING: THE POLITICS OF CAPACITY

the fiscal soundness of each housing project within its borders, a general expansion of communal fiscal and administrative organs was mandatory. Moreover, the community was required to have a representative on the governing board of each housing cooperative formed within its borders, forcing Järfälla to recruit a large number of persons to represent the municipality in the ever increasing cooperatives. And as the suburb grew, the problems of providing public services and facilities (streets, lights, water, etc.) grew more and more pressing.

Indeed, these problems grew faster than Järfälla's ability to handle them. As a consequence, local officials found it expedient to draw upon the expertise of neighboring Stockholm, particularly after 1954, when their socialist colleague Garpe became Commissioner for Greater Stockholm Affairs. A Järfälla-Stockholm agreement of 1955 permitted high school students from the suburb to attend city schools; Järfälla supported the 1957 housing program and placed its Socialist party leader on the Executive Committee of the Greater Stockholm Planning Board; and in 1959 an agreement was reached to connect the Järfälla sewer system to Stockholm's sewerage treatment facilities. It was against this background of prior contact and agreement that Stockholm and Järfälla decided, in 1961, to make use of the new *Lex Bollmora*.

At the time, the suburb had begun constructing its new central business and shopping center, modelled after the Vällingby center. Much of the area was being built by the local property development company but, because of limited resources and technical competence, a large portion had to be left in the hands of private developers. Hoping to avoid excessive commitment of their own capital, the private developers requested that they be allowed to develop their property in the form of cooperative housing units. Doing so, of course, would have entitled them to 95 per cent financing from the government rather than the 85 per cent allowed for private construction. This request posed a difficult dilemma for Järfälla's leaders: though they badly wanted and needed the units planned by the developers to complete the center, acceptance of such a proposal would require additional local employees to review project financing for government loans and to represent the municipality on cooperative boards. Apart from the difficulties involved in finding such persons, there was also the issue so recently prominent in the Stockholm debate: building more cooperatives would provide very limited help for either the city housing queue or the Social Democrats in Järfälla. At a party dinner, therefore, Järfälla socialist leader John Ljungkvist suggested to Commissioner Garpe that this might be an opportune moment to apply the new national legislation (*Lex Bollmora*).

A CITY-JÄRFÄLLA AGREEMENT

The discussions that followed led ultimately to a proposal that was beautifully designed to satisfy all parties. Järfälla agreed to allow Homes of Stockholm, Inc., another of the city's public housing companies, to purchase the properties in question from the private developers and to arrange for the construction and management of rental housing units on those properties. In return, the municipality agreed to reserve 70 per cent of the 2,500 new apartments for the city and its housing queue registrants. Finally, the city agreed to use the private developers whose property had been acquired to do the construction work on the new housing units. Everyone gained something, and Järfälla obtained a substantial contribution to both its housing supply and its new center, without any of the financial and administrative headaches normally associated with projects of such size. Not inappropriately, the Järfälla Social Democrats also gained residential areas that later provided the municipality's heaviest socialist voter turnout.

In Järfälla, as in Tyresö, growth-related difficulties created situations that made city assistance a realistic consideration. In both communities these situations were perceived as opportunities for cooperation because of past cooperative agreements. In both communities these perceptions were transformed into action through existing structures of communication, both administrative and partisan. In both communities solutions to specific problems were developed that neither arose from, nor were defined by, a preexisting plan. Finally, speedy action was taken in both communities, once the problem at issue was defined in terms of the fundamental interests of the involved parties. This pattern of action also characterized other *Lex Bollmora* agreements, as suburban and city politicians responded quickly and flexibly to unexpected problems that they defined as opportunities. We shall consider this pattern of *opportunistic problem-solving* in some detail at a later point. For now it is enough to note its significance in many of the *Lex Bollmora* agreements.

THE POLITICS OF LAND

A second and quantitatively more important pattern for these agreements emerged from Finance Commissioner Mehr's determination to expand the city's land holdings.[16] Assuming office in 1958, Mehr recognized that Stockholm had exhausted its land available for development. Apart from Farsta, whose future use already had been decided, the only other land areas within city boundaries suitable for large-scale development were Sätra, southwest of the city, and Järva, to the northwest. Järva was owned by the Swedish Defense Department and used as a military training area, effectively precluding city acquisition unless the military authorities could be brought to agreement.

Sätra was owned by three charitable foundations, all of whom had rejected a city offer of 11 million crowns for their property. Knowing that the city badly wanted their land, which was in the path of both a natural extension of city housing and of the planned city subway system, the foundations employed architects to draw up another development plan. According to that plan, the area could be exploited at a level that made a price of 57 million crowns more reasonable than the city offer. Unable to bridge a gap of this magnitude, the city brought the matter to court, seeking expropriation.[17] The Sätra question was being litigated when Mehr came into power, giving him little alternative but to seek land in suburban jurisdictions, using the city's land-buying company, AB STRADA. By the fall of 1960, with the matter still in the lower courts, another three to four years of waiting seemed likely before Sweden's highest court made a decision.

A FAR-REACHING ACTION: PURCHASE OF SÄTRA

The situation provided an opportunity for far-reaching action, this time by Sten Källenius, director of the Associated General Contractors and House Builders of Sweden. Källenius was a member of both the Riksdag and the Stockholm City Planning Board, whose chairman was Commissioner Garpe. Acting for the builders, Källenius approached Garpe and pointed out that the city's 1959 decision to deny private builders access to remaining city-owned land had caused them a good deal of hardship. The builders, he said, had always cooperated with the city and preferred to continue that relationship, if they could. For example, the builders thought they saw a way to settle the dispute over Sätra between the city and the three founda-

16. See Passow, *loc. cit.*, for figures on city land-purchase activities. Kubu, *op. cit.*, pp. 77–78, cites suburban land purchases as one of Mehr's three most significant accomplishments as Finance Commissioner.

17. These details are reported in *Utlåtande nr 115 år 1961.*

tions. They wondered whether the city would be interested in their mediation. Because of their central position in the Swedish economy, Källenius continued, the builders had powerful financial friends, and were prepared to exert as much influence as they could, particularly if the city was prepared to take a more sympathetic view of the builders' problems.[18] Garpe was interested enough to discuss the matter immediately with Mehr, who shortly thereafter authorized AB STRADA to begin negotiations. After several months of hard negotiations a deal was concluded in February 1961, and approved by the City Council in May.

In another "something-for-everyone" arrangement, the city agreed to pay 30 million crowns for the property. This was 19 million more than it wanted to pay, but on the other hand the land became available immediately. Three of Sweden's largest building firms (John Mattson, Skånska Cement and SIAB) agreed to compensate the foundations for court costs incurred, and to help the city arrange bank loans to finance the 30-million crown purchase. In return, the city agreed to allocate 45 per cent of the buildable land acquired in Sätra to the private builders. Another 45 per cent of the Sätra land was allocated to the public companies, and 10 per cent to the largest cooperative organizations, HSB and Svenska Riksbyggen.[19] Having been frozen out of the city only a few months before, the private builders were now back in, with a large and guaranteed piece of the building cake. Before the City Council, Mehr expressed his satisfaction with an agreement that saved the city three to four years in developing new housing units for about 30,000 people. In a change of emphasis from the 1959 debate, he added that "The Social Democrats have always worked together with the private building sector." [20]

NEXT STEP: ANNEXATION OF VÅRBY

Though important enough in itself, the Sätra acquisition assumed a greater significance because of its location, as city-owned property was now extended to the city's southwest legal boundary. Beyond that

18. This version of events, obtained in an interview with Källenius, differs slightly from other versions. Källenius himself is a good example of (a) overlapping: a private-sector manager who holds several public positions directly related to his private interests, and (b) coordination: a local official who is also a member of parliament. It is useful to note that Källenius opposed *Lex Bollmora* in the Riksdag.
19. *Utlåtande nr 115 år 1961.*
20. Stockholms Stadsfullmäktige, *Protokoll, 1961,* p. 450.

boundary lay 1,100 hectares (445 acres) of land the city had bought
for a pittance in 1931. That land now looked extraordinarily attractive to Mehr and Garpe. If developed on the same scale and in the
same time frame as Sätra, the Vårby property could provide room for
still another 30,000 people. Indeed, economies of scale, possible
through coordination of housing construction and subway extension
through the next "natural" site for exploitation, made any other development scheme virtually irrational.

The easiest way to facilitate such development, of course, was to
annex the Vårby property into the city, but two obstacles stood in
the way. One was the city's 1951 promise that no further suburban
annexations would be requested.[21] The other, and far more significant, obstacle was Nils Eliasson, the suburban socialist boss in Huddinge, where the Vårby property was located. Eliasson's dominating
position in county politics was built largely around his opposition to
Stockholm expansion.

Nevertheless, for Mehr and Garpe the Vårby opportunity was too
good to pass up. In great secrecy, Garpe arranged to travel out to
Huddinge for a meeting with Eliasson in March of 1961, at which
time the Vårby property was presented to Eliasson as a matter of
great urgency for the party. An election was coming in 1962, Garpe
reminded Eliasson, and the bourgeois opposition already had begun
to attack the city socialists for not having done enough in the housing
area, even focusing on Garpe himself. The 1957 housing program
would come close to its target but that, Garpe argued, was almost insignificant, in view of the much larger numbers in the housing
queue. The city socialists badly needed some tangible housing accomplishment to present in the coming campaign. Vårby, Garpe argued,
could provide just that. Taking it into the city was thus politically
"necessary."

Garpe's direct, partisan approach worked. Garpe said later that
Eliasson was "too good a politician" not to appreciate the problem
confronting his party colleagues in the city, and too clever a negotiator not to see a chance to gain something for Huddinge. Accordingly, Garpe and Eliasson agreed to the annexation in principle, thus
commiting themselves to a more detailed exploration of the matter.
Eliasson emphasized that, to be productive, the coming negotiations
would have to be conducted in absolute secrecy until the very end.
Even a rumor that he, Stockholm's most determined and most vigor-

---

21. See Chapter II, above.

ous opponent, was considering a "deal" with the city would be enough to bring his local opposition, as well as the city newspapers, down on his head in sufficient strength to make the annexation impossible.[22]

What followed was in the best tradition of European spy thrillers. Apart from Mehr and Garpe, only two other men in the city administration, both administrators in boards headed by Garpe, were informed of the matter. Similarly, Eliasson informed only his chief administrator in Huddinge of what was going on. None of these people was permitted to work on the problem at his office or to keep any relevant papers there, and no related activity was permitted during regular working hours. After several weeks of secret weekend meetings, late evening negotiations, and tramping through the snow-covered fields of Huddinge with measuring tapes, an agreement was ready.

On Monday evening, June 5, 1961, the city councils of both Stockholm and Huddinge met at 7:00 P.M. Only the Social Democratic leadership group in Stockholm had been informed beforehand, and no one had been informed in Huddinge. Shortly after 7:00 P.M., Garpe passed a note describing the deal to his colleague, Liberal party Real Estate Commissioner Waldo Frank, and to the press. In Huddinge, Eliasson convened the meeting of his Council which, in short order, approved the deal he had made. The fact that Commissioner Frank had not been informed about a matter directly affecting his responsibilities was a direct violation of the rules of the game in City Hall, and led to a major political crisis. Liberal party commissioners, strongly supported—"egged on" would perhaps be a more accurate description—by the liberal morning and evening newspapers, threatened to resign, thus destroying the tradition of coalition governments, and leading possibly to a system of majority rule in city politics. That crisis was resolved, however, and the coalition system survived. More important from the Social Democrat point of view, Vårby would be incorporated.[23]

Interestingly enough, the term "annexation" was not used.[24] In-

22. Interview, Commissioner Joakim Garpe.
23. This account is drawn from Kubu, *op. cit.*, pp. 140–164. Kubu tells the story with great skill and humor.
24. To avoid confusion the term "annexation" has been used wherever the meaning is the addition of new territory to an existing city. The more literal translation of the Swedish term would be "incorporation," but in usage in the United States, "incorporation" means creation of a new and independent municipality.

stead, a "boundary regulation" would transfer 385 hectares (156 acres) of land, already owned by Stockholm, from Huddinge to the city. In return, the city agreed to sell 775 hectares (314 acres) of its land to Huddinge for the extremely low price of ½ crown (10 cents) per square meter. The land transferred to the city would be used to extend the intensive exploitation planned for Sätra (the "new town" of Skärholmen opened in 1968 on portions of this Vårby acquisition), while Huddinge agreed to reserve the land it bought from the city as an open-space recreation area. In keeping with the new language of 1961, the city also promised that it would not, in the future, pursue any further "boundary regulations."

The Vårby annexation thus was a major political accomplishment. Space was acquired for an additional 30,000 people, making possible a more efficient and rational extension of both the subway and the housing developments. At the same time, significant new open-space reservations for outdoorsmen and environmentalists were provided. For the Social Democrats, then, there could be "no doubt that the agreement reached here is the best solution from Stockholm's point of view. . . . With over 100,000 registrants in Stockholm's housing queue and with unreasonably long waiting times in this queue, increasing housing production and providing access to as many apartments as possible becomes one of the city's most urgent responsibilities." Against bourgeois criticisms that the city need not have sold any land to Huddinge, and certainly not at a "giveaway" price, the socialists pointed out that the sale was a condition for Huddinge's cooperation. Moreover, continued the socialist leadership in a passage that deserves quotation, this was

a matter of transfer to a neighboring municipality of land set aside as open space and which is guaranteed to remain in that state for the common use of both Huddinge and Stockholm. Those Stockholmers who settle in the Vårby area, like Huddinge residents, will be able to use these beautiful nature reserves for recreation the year round. In Huddinge's ownership, the Vårby area will fill the same function in southwest Stockholm that the Nacka reserve fills in southeast Stockholm.[25]

EXPANDING HORIZONS

It was therefore no surprise that Commissioner Garpe, initiating Council debate on the Vårby acquisition and a new five-year housing program on October 16, 1961, sounded more like a political cam-

25. The quoted passage is found in *Utlåtande nr 270 år 1961,* pp. 2301–2302. The previous quotations are on p. 2320.

paigner than a Planning Commissioner. Treating a bird in the bush as though it were in hand, Garpe saw the potential acquisition of Järva as still another feather in the city's cap:

If the City leadership in Stockholm can now reach agreement with the Crown for housing in the Järva area, as it has achieved agreements with private land-owners in Sätra and with Huddinge municipality in Vårby, that will mean that altogether, we will have put together land on which we can build housing for around 100,000 people—housing for 100,000 people inside the City's boundaries.

Mr. Chairman—new housing for 100,000 Stockholmers! I repeat my motion that the Executive Board's proposals in both areas be approved.[26]

For reasons noted earlier, the political significance of these ambitious housing plans is difficult to estimate, though the Social Democrats did indeed win again in 1962. From a housing point of view, on the other hand, it is impossible to overestimate the significance of the Sätra and Vårby acquisitions, not only because they made possible a relatively rapid construction of new apartments for 60,000 people, but also because, in the same way that Sätra had made Vårby accessible, Vårby opened access to Botkyrka, beyond Vårby, and Salem, beyond Botkyrka. In both these latter municipalities, city purchase of large parcels of land provided a lever to induce agreement on the production of new housing. Whereas the city merely took advantage of opportunities as they arose in the first series of *Lex Bollmora* agreements, its aggressive land policy enabled it to manufacture new opportunities in reaching the later agreements—as in the Vårby case.

Ironically, neither side kept the Vårby agreement. Annexation of 375 hectares took place as scheduled on January 1, 1963, but the city, claiming "technical difficulties," delayed the sale of its 775 hectares to Huddinge. Meanwhile, believing it had a valid contract with the city, Huddinge began selling land which it did not yet own to commercial interests. In 1963 Esso, the supermarket chain Metro, and the furniture chain IKEA purchased land in the Vårby area from Huddinge, paying 20 to 25 crowns ($4–$5) per square meter for land the municipality thought it had purchased for ½ crown (10¢) per square meter.

Despite the absence of a legally required town plan, and despite the city's known intention of developing a large shopping center in the Skärholmen portion of the Vårby land, IKEA proceeded immediately to begin what was to become the largest furniture store in

26. Stockholms Stadsfullmäktige, *Protokoll, 1961*, p. 840.

Europe. By the time the city learned of these developments it was too late to stop them, though the city now had grounds for insisting on a new agreement with Huddinge. Among the effects of that new agreement was the construction of large housing estates on those "beautiful nature reserves for recreation" about which Stockholm's socialist leaders had written so lyrically in 1961.[27]

THE INGREDIENTS OF AGREEMENT

The *Lex Bollmora* agreements, then, resulted from the city's determination to expand its housing supply and its ability to seize or manufacture opportunities that could be used to implement that determination. The other crucial ingredient, of course, was the willingness of suburban politicians to accept agreements with the city, producing the results shown in Table 2. That willingness was a compound of many factors: a desire to do something about the serious housing shortage, an interest in growth and the additional tax resources growth would bring, a hope for partisan advantage through tangible accomplishment. At bottom, however, it was the knowledge that failure to cooperate would most probably lead to loss of municipal independence. Both the bourgeois press and bourgeois politicians

TABLE 2

Apartments Completed in the Greater Stockholm Area
1957–1968

Year	City	Suburbs	Total
1957	6,466	4,549	11,015
1958	7,117	4,642	11,759
1959	5,538	5,629	11,167
1960	5,525	7,853	13,388
1961	4,166	9,365	13,531
1962	3,789	9,837	13,626
1963	4,187	8,443	12,630
1964	3,884	9,046	12,930
1965	5,907	9,164	15,071
1966	4,523	10,032	14,555
1967	5,719	10,653	16,372
1968	8,565	12,532	21,097

Source: Storlandstingskommittén, *Regionalt Bostasbygge* (Stockholm, 1968), p. 19, and *Statistisk Årsbok för Stockholms Stad 1969*, p. 386.

27. A late but effective storm of newspaper publicity forced the city to reveal and respond to these events. See *Protokoll, 1965*, pp. 901–906.

in Stockholm had been campaigning for a "total reorganization" of the region's governments since at least 1957, and the Social Democrats, while they had not yet advanced such a proposal, knew that it would command wide-spread support if it were offered. By cooperating with the city, suburban politicians—particularly socialist politicians—could hope to ward off such a proposal and, at the same time, retain far more control over their future development than would otherwise be the case.

In short, suburban politicians were left only two alternatives. They could either steadfastly refuse to cooperate with the city in housing and related matters, and thus bring on a relatively rapid loss of independence, or they could "choose" to cooperate, and thus hope to exercise some leverage on a future in which they could at least expect to survive. A few predominantly upper- and middle-class "villa suburbs" chose the former alternative, but there were enough predominantly socialist suburbs which chose the latter, and thus made possible the large-scale production of apartments in the Stockholm region. As Botkyrka's socialist leader said recently, "I cannot imagine that we would have been permitted to remain as an independent municipality if we had said no." [28]

TOWARD INTEGRATION

The housing policy of the Stockholm socialists was thus institutionally conservative, however progressive it otherwise may have been. The city pushed the suburbs into building because only the suburbs had the necessary land. By building, the suburbs justified their continued existence. Continued existence, of course, meant that the resources the suburbs were now gaining—large numbers of new apartments—would be distributed by many housing agencies, rather than a single, region-wide administration. This, in turn, implied the application of a variety of different criteria in deciding who should live where.

A SENSITIVE ISSUE: WHO SHOULD LIVE WHERE?

Politically, this was a far more sensitive issue than the questions of whether to build and how much. For in deciding who should live where, there was virtually no way to align the interests of the city and the suburbs. It was quite unlikely that all the suburbs would emphasize the same values as the city in making housing assignments.

28. Quoted in Jonason, *op. cit.,* p. 260.

But even if all the units had precisely identical values, they had very different housing queues. In Stockholm, the number of registrants was well over 100,000 and rising, whereas a queue of more than a few thousand was an exception in suburbia. Nevertheless, each of the suburbs had a queue of its own, and the more a suburb made available to the city, the less it had left to meet the demands of its own residents. By "choosing" to cooperate with the city in housing production, a suburb could expect to maximize its leverage; but short of an oversupply of housing, there was no way to eliminate the interest conflict: what the city gained, the suburbs lost.

What there was to lose became clear in the struggle over the *Lex Bollmora* contracts. Because municipal budgets were supported primarily by personal income taxes, suburban politicians recognized that the more people residing in their communities, the better the tax base—*providing they were the right kind of people*. People with low incomes, people with insecure places in Swedish society (welfare recipients, alcoholics, etc.), or people who might demand more in services than they paid in taxes clearly were *not* the right kind of people. Seen from the suburbs, the danger was that the city, given access to housing units outside its boundaries, would dump its poor in the suburbs.

SUBURBAN CONTROLS

Suburban politicians had no difficulty appreciating this problem and, from the first contract signed with Tyresö to the last, insisted on a special clause providing that (a) in offering suburban apartments to people registered in the city housing queue, the city would "apply the same principles normally applied in Stockholm," and that (b) all offers of apartments would result from "joint consultations" between representatives of the city and suburban housing exchanges.[29] The first provision might be thought of as the suburban "anti-poor" law—technically, it was anti-rich as well—since it prohibited the city from sending out anything but a normally-distributed group of apartment seekers. The second provision amounted to a suburban veto over who would be allowed in. For all the aggressiveness of city policy, suburban bosses had managed to retain full control over what was, after all, most important to them.

The struggles over the *Lex Bollmora* contracts were not the only

29. See, for examples, *Utlåtande nr 41 år 1960* (Tyresö) or *Utlåtande nr 185 år 1963* (Salem).

TABLE 3

Families Placed by Common Housing Exchange,
1954–1958

	1954	1955	1956	1957	1958
Number of households provided housing	24	126	115	193	243

Source: *Stadskollegiets Utlåtenden och Memorial, Bihang nr 99, 1959*, p. 64.

suburban efforts to frustrate the city's desire to arrange housing for its thousands of registrants. As early as January 1950, the city had initiated efforts to reach a joint city-suburban housing exchange. More than four years dragged out before a housing exchange of sorts began on April 1, 1954. This agreement encompassed a limited exchange, designed to help people move closer to their jobs, through the *voluntary* participation of the various municipal housing bureaus. Only ten municipalities even bothered to join, and only four of these managed to register more than twenty families per year in the period 1954–58. Stockholm was by far the most important municipality, registering almost 3,300 persons in that period, out of a total of 4,400. But, as is evident from Table 3, an average of only 140 households per year ever benefited from this exchange—at a time when the city queue was growing from 80,000 to 105,000! The trouble, later investigators discovered, was that journey-to-work time was far less important to Stockholmers than getting a bigger and better apartment, particularly in the center of the city. Getting a "better" apartment was the major motivation for registration in no less than 91.3 per cent of all cases and, as these investigators remarked, "Hardly any of the registrants have indicated an interest in moving from the inner city to an apartment of similar size and quality in the suburbs." [30]

CONTINUED CONTROVERSY: A COMMON HOUSING EXCHANGE

The advent of the 1957 Action Program for housing, and the Greater Stockholm Planning Board to oversee that program, provided a new opportunity for initiatives by the city. Among the first of these was the creation of a small research group to study the operations of the Common Housing Exchange with a view toward revising its program. The result was a recommendation to replace the existing

30. *Bihang nr 99*, 1959, pp. 60–64.

exchange with one composed of more area municipalities, committed
to the development and application of uniform rules throughout the
region, and commanding a quota of apartments of its own to dispose
of, without regard to municipal boundaries.

This plan went into effect on December 1, 1960, and its fundamental weakness soon became obvious. Like its predecessor, the new exchange was entirely dependent on the voluntary participation of the
suburbs. Although 18 municipalities agreed to participate, their
"participation" provided a total of only 186 apartments for the common register in its first two years of operation. By the end of 1963
only 497 apartments had been made available, and more than half of
these were contributed by just two municipalities: Huddinge and
Järfälla.

Stung by this obvious failure, the Planning Board sent around a
proposal that each municipality agree to allot 10 per cent of its annual production of new apartments to the common register. Nine of
the inner suburbs officially accepted the proposal, but seven of the
ten outlying suburbs rejected it, placing 16 of the 28 suburbs in official opposition. Actual opposition proved even stronger: of 12,930
housing units produced in greater Stockholm in 1964, only 159 were
allocated to the Common Exchange.[31]

Why was there such determined opposition to a common housing
exchange, even as agreements were being made for the production of
housing? The answer emerges from the following figures summariz-
ing the work of the city and suburban housing exchanges in 1964 and
1965. Of all apartments handled by suburban exchanges in 1964, for
example, more than 73 per cent were allocated by municipalities to
their own residents. Quite understandably, suburban politicians
were taking care of their own problems first. As long as their problems remained—that is, as long as each suburb had more registrants
than it had available housing units—there would be no reason to
expect them to turn their backs on their neighbors and coworkers in
favor of persons currently living in other municipalities.

Moreover, there is no doubt that suburban politicians felt their
problems to be quite different from those of the central city. Just
how different can be seen in the distribution of priority housing allocations by Stockholm and its suburbs in 1965. In that year, the city

31. These facts were gathered by the Greater Stockholm Planning Board and
reported to a Royal Commission in March 1965. They are printed in SOU
1965:51, pp. 31–36.

TABLE 4

Apartments Allocated by Suburban Exchanges, 1964, by Municipality of Registration

Apartments allocated to persons registered in:	Number	Percentage
Allocating municipality	5,084	73.1
Stockholm	521	7.5
Other Stockholm suburb	327	4.7
Other, Sweden	584	8.4
Unknown	440	6.3
Total	6,956	100.0

Source: Adapted from *SOU 1965:51, Gemensamma Bostadsförmedlingar,* Stockholm, Inrikesdepartementet, 1965, p. 33.

allocated 8,345 housing units, of which only 162 were allocated "out of turn." During the same year 6,860 apartments were assigned by suburban exchanges, of which 2,642—or 39 per cent—were assigned on such a "priority," nonqueue basis. Without doubt, suburban officials were treating housing as an important municipal resource which, in a time of severe housing shortage, could be used to support values or activities regarded as essential, and they appear to have been doing so to a far greater extent than were city authorities.

What values or activities did they regard as essential? At least a tentative answer is provided by Table 5. Stockholm, the capital city, devoted almost all of its priority allocations to community employees, or persons in "socially useful employment." Medical personnel, teachers, policemen, and even an occasional foreign minister fell into this category.[32] Though the suburbs also used a substantial portion (30 per cent) of their priority allocations to attract and keep useful community employees, they allocated an even higher percentage to industrial workers, indicating the zeal of their efforts to attract industrial plants and thus avoid the "dormitory suburb" curse.

For suburban governments, then, housing was deeply involved in economic and financial policy, as well as social policy. For them, a "common register," applying uniform rules to all metropolitan municipalities, would be something close to a disaster. In the absence of uniform rules, a registrant could lose his turn in any one of thirty

32. Kubu, *op. cit.,* pp. 129–136, writes entertainingly about the city's manner of allocation housing priorities.

TABLE 5

City and Suburban Priority Housing Allocations
1965

	Total	Industrial employment	Construction employment	Community employment	Other employment	Social need	Other
				Based upon:			
Stockholm	162	0	29 (18%)	133 (82%)	0	0	0
Suburbs	2,642	847 (32%)	68 (3%)	799 (30%)	236 (9%)	352 (13%)	340 (3%)

Source: Adapted from *SOU 1967:1 Kommunal Bostadsförmedling*, Stockholm, Inrikesdepartementet, 1967, p. 151. The figures here are based on reports from 22 of the 29 area municipalities.

different ways, despite years in a queue. As a result, the use of "connections" to arrange housing gradually became both more understandable and more widespread.

ACTION UNDER DURESS: NATIONAL INTERVENTION

The sense of injustice thus generated brought about national intervention in 1962, when a Royal Commission was appointed to investigate the entire housing exchange question. By 1963 Interior Minister Rune Johansson had decided to broaden the Commission's charge to include the possibility of *imposing* a common housing exchange in areas where this seemed necessary. When the first of the Commission's two reports was circulated for comment in late 1965, the Greater Stockholm Planning Board seized the opportunity to propose a framework for a new common exchange. The report made it clear that the national government would impose a common housing exchange on the Stockholm region if area municipalities failed to act. To avoid this loss of freedom, the Greater Stockholm Planning Board proposed action to ensure local control over the form the new exchange would take.[33]

Even with this pressure the suburbs balked. Seventeen gave positive responses but many responses contained reservations that betrayed a continuing reluctance for joint action. Five rejected the idea totally, while five others expressed a desire for "further considerations and additional investigations." [34] This reluctance became irrelevant the following year, when the Riksdag enacted legislation prohibiting the authorization of state housing loans in any municipality which—if part of a regional housing supply area—had not instituted an obligatory housing exchange. Since more than 90 per cent of all Swedish housing is constructed with state loans, the new legislation provided virtually total coverage. Another Planning Board circular issued in June 1967 pointed out that unless its earlier (now somewhat modified) plan was accepted in time to take effect on January 1, 1968, the region's municipalities would be forced to accept whatever form of common exchange the national government decided to propose.[35]

33. In interpreting the phrase "local control," it should be remembered that the city was the overwhelming force behind the Greater Stockholm Planning Board. The Board's "staff" personnel were in fact employees of the city's Division of Greater Stockholm Affairs.
34. Suburban responses are summarized in *Utlåtande nr 256 år 1967.*
35. *Ibid.,* pp. 3–12, discusses this circular.

"With the knife at our throats," as one official said later, the municipalities of Greater Stockholm once again "volunteered" to cooperate, not only with the city, but with each other. Though local exchanges still exist, since January 1, 1968 they have been merely branch offices of a single metropolitan housing exchange. The exchange agency has jurisdiction over all new apartments produced with state housing loans, and uses access rules that apply uniformly to all area municipalities. A large, centralized, and computerized bureaucracy now makes the choices formerly made by thirty different communities. For those seeking housing, Gargantua has replaced confusion.

CONCLUSION: THE POLITICS OF CAPACITY

In retrospect, it is clear that neither metropolitan-wide agreement on housing as *the* priority issue nor creation of the Greater Stockholm Planning Board to implement that agreement provided any guarantees that appropriate action would follow. Stockholm's planners had well-developed ideas about future city expansion along mass transportation routes, and the Garpe-Granath report was quite specific in pinpointing areas in which housing construction should take place, but neither of these two sets of "plans" was able to guide the development that actually took place. Instead, action was possible only when suburban "growing pains" became severe enough to legitimize requests for city assistance, or when the city, through its aggressive land policy, was able to structure situations that created new opportunities for housing construction. Having agreed that housing was all-important, it remained to bring together what the city had—technical, organizational, and financial capabilities—with what the suburbs had —large areas of vacant land. This could only be done by politicians, and only in the context of responding to specific problems with concrete proposals for action.

STOCKHOLM'S ORGANIZATIONAL RESOURCES

It would be difficult to overestimate the importance of Stockholm's organizational resources in generating both problems and solutions. By their very existence, the public housing companies structured support for one set of housing values. Moreover, when city land became scarce, these organizations pressed for policy innovations that could ensure their survival. This very practical and immediate organizational problem supplied the necessary link between general agreement on the need for more housing and the actual production of housing units in specific locations. As agreements were reached in one area after another, new organizational forms were created to keep pace with the expanding capacity of area governments.

Thus the movement from the relatively small contracts of the early *Lex Bollmora* period to the larger contracts of the later period was accompanied by the generation of new organizational forms capable of developing whole communities. In Botkyrka, for example, a joint city-suburb company was formed to develop a community for 45,000 people, with all responsibility for technical matters and financial commitments agreed to in advance of construction. Similar organizational forms are now being followed in Salem and in the new Järva area, north of the city.[36] In these latter cases, as in the earliest agreements, however, the city companies have provided the initiatives and plans, as well as the administrative competence necessary to ensure success. As much as anything else, then, the politics of housing in Stockholm has been a politics of organizational pressure and growth.

None of this should be taken to mean that *only* public companies prospered. On the contrary, the dimensions of the housing problem made ideological positions less and less relevant to actual housing decisions, thus eliminating any operative bias against private contractors. To be sure, the public positions taken by various local party leaders remained strongly ideological. Conservatives and liberals denied the legitimacy (or efficiency) of public participation in the provision of housing, while socialists decried the exploitation produced by private capitalism.

PRACTICAL REALITIES: THE NUMBERS IN THE QUEUE

Toward the end of the 1950s, however, the waiting lists had grown so long that party competition over housing in fact came to focus on what the liberals referred to as the "practical realities." By this they meant the numbers in the queue. Thus in 1961, following the socialist successes in acquiring land in Sätra and Vårby, the issue was no longer *who* should build, but *how much should be built?* Socialists supported the Action Program recommendation of 75,000 new apartments in the 1961–65 period, but the bourgeois parties, clearly seeking to steal an election issue, demanded a program for 80,000 apartments instead. Since the conservatives somehow managed to retain

36. A joint stock company, with Stockholm and Salem as shareholders, has been formed to develop that area. Järva is being developed by a consortium that includes Stockholm and four other municipalities.

their insistence on doing away with the public companies while demanding more units, some ideological purity remained, although in a quite silly fashion. Nevertheless, the conservative demand for 80,-000 units emphasized the absence of real disagreement on the bourgeois side on the urgency of housing production.

IDEOLOGY BE DAMNED

Meanwhile, on the socialist side, Finance Commissioner Mehr had no difficulty accepting the Sätra agreement, which guaranteed private companies almost half of new production, while arguing simultaneously that "Our central ambition in all contexts has been to keep up the municipal housing companies." [37] In fact, Mehr had no difficulty applying the Sätra agreement to virtually all large housing developments initiated during his tenure. As a result (see Table 6), private builders increased their share of construction on city land from 30.0 per cent to 39.3 per cent under Mehr's tenure, and did so largely at the expense of the public companies. These figures represent only land inside city borders, but the figures for the entire Greater Stockholm region are similar: during Mehr's tenure the *metropolitan distribution* between public, cooperative and private builders was, respectively, 38.9 per cent, 26.5 per cent, and 34.6 per cent.[38] Despite all the contrary rhetoric, Stockholm socialists have been even better friends of private capitalism than have their bourgeois colleagues. Implicitly, if not rhetorically, the city's controlling assumption has

TABLE 6

Housing Supply by Type of Builder Under
"Bourgeois" and "Socialist" Governments

Period	Public companies	Cooperatives	Private companies
1950–1959 Bourgeois	58%	12%	30%
1960–1969 Socialist	47.3%	13.4%	39.3%

Source: *Stadskollegiets Utlåtanden och Memorial: Utlåtande Nr 210, 1959*, p. 701 and *Kommunstyrelsens Utlåtanden och Memorial: Utlåtande Nr 183, 1971*, p. 1406.

37. Stockholms Stadsfullmäktige, *Protokoll, 1961*, p. 450.
38. Note that the time periods designated as "bourgeois" or "socialist" do not correspond exactly to electoral periods (bourgeois parties were in control from 1950 to 1958, and socialists from 1958 to 1966). The time lag between initiation and completion of projects, however, suggests that it is not unreasonable to divide the years in this way.

been this: use all means available to deal with the housing problem, and ideology be damned.

FLEXIBILITY AND INNOVATION

The development of organizational capacity, within a framework of nonideological agreement on priorities, helps provide an explanation for the high level of housing production achieved by Stockholm area municipalities. But to repeat: none of the actions necessary to this level of success was guaranteed. Each step along the way took time, patient effort, frequently a high level of ingenuity and, just as often, a well-developed capacity for flexibility and innovation. A pattern of "opportunistic problem-solving," together with a related pattern of "opportunity creation," make clear that area politicians generally, and city politicians in particular, were strong supporters of interventionist policies. Repeatedly, these politicians demonstrated their ability to respond to new challenges and to "make things happen." While today's Stockholm region is not the "planned city" it is often said to be, neither did it "just grow." Instead, it was developed, consciously and through flexible design, by activist political leaders.

NATIONAL INTERVENTION: ANOTHER DIMENSION OF CAPACITY

These same leaders, however, could not agree on the issue of housing distribution. Given the differences in the size of housing queues in city and suburb, there was no way to harmonize city and suburban interests in apartment distribution. Anything done to reduce waiting time for city residents, such as adopting a common metropolitan exchange, would automatically increase waiting time for most suburban registrants. That prospect, coupled with suburban anxiety over the characteristics of persons registered in the city's queue, was enough to prevent agreement, even though production agreements were proliferating. Repeated failures to resolve the issue locally brought national intervention, leading to an integrated metropolitan government structure to deal with housing distribution. Many local officials undoubtedly saw national intervention in this matter as a "failure." From an analytical point of view, however, it surely makes sense to view that intervention as an additional dimension of system capacity.

CHAPTER IV

TRANSPORTATION:
THE POLITICS OF INTEGRATION

NATIONAL INTERVENTION to resolve the issue of metropolitan housing distribution may have been a demonstration of system capacity, but it was also revealed how little the system had changed since 1945. By grafting a metropolitan agency to the existing set of public structures the government made it possible to deal more effectively with a limited—though exceedingly important—problem. Yet municipal independence, in fact as well as law, remained the foundation of the regional political system, fragmenting it into twenty-nine separate and jealously equal parts.

To be sure, municipal power had been coordinated in a number of policy areas through piecemeal contracts, signed one at a time. But national intervention in the housing problem could only emphasize the continuing strength of city-suburban hostility—notwithstanding all the piecemeal successes. Indeed, it was possible to argue, by the beginning of the 1960s, that city-suburban hostility had increased in at least one respect. The reason, of course, was that municipal bureaucracies had expanded so much in the suburbs that professional jealousies, as well as political competition, became important. None of this was, or could be, affected very much by the government's decision to centralize administration of the housing queue. The system was adjusted, perhaps, but its basic character remained very much the same.

PROBLEMS OF SUCCESS

Even as this adjustment was being made, however, pressure was building for more far-reaching change. The system's expanded capacity to produce housing generated much of this pressure. By locating new housing in large suburban concentrations, the politicians guaranteed the creation of large and difficult problems. To begin with, most of the new suburban residents continued to work in the city. Of those who worked outside the city, more often than not their jobs and residences were not located in the same municipality. Concentrating large numbers of new suburbanites in a few places necessarily aggravated the transportation problem, creating large crowds of rush-hour commuters where there had been none before.

COMMUTERS AND CONGESTION

Commuters were no special problem in areas such as Farsta or Bredäng or, later, Skärholmen, where the city owned the land and thus could coordinate housing and subway construction. But outside the city proper, thousands of new apartments had been negotiated for areas such as Tyresö, Huddinge, or Järfälla, which had neither subways nor any reasonable likelihood of obtaining them. Residents of those areas would thus be forced to rely on bus service, commuter trains, or, increasingly, automobiles. As frustration increased with poor train and bus service between the suburbs and the city, more and more commuters took to the private automobile, clogging highways that had not been designed for such heavy use and further aggravating the problem of mass transportation by bus.[1]

The result was constant decline in the quality of mass transit services, and constant growth in pressure to do something. Meanwhile, city politicians continued to press for more housing and more suburban land acquisition, in full knowledge that their activities could only worsen transportation difficulties and thus add to political pressures. Seeking to maintain their control of the city governmental machinery, the Social Democrats announced the Defense Department's agreement to leave its large training area, "Järvafältet," which was thereby freed for housing. Commissioner Garpe's earlier expectation thus came true and was used as a major election issue during the 1962 campaign.[2]

1. Yngve Larsson provides a valuable account of the impact of the automobile on Stockholm planning in his "Building a City and a Metropolis," *Journal of the American Institute of Planners,* Vol. 28 (1962).

2. Kubu, *op. cit.,* pp. 179–181, reports the significance of Järva in the 1962 campaign.

MANY TRANSIT AGENCIES

Political pressures focused initially on the practical difficulties of getting to and from work conveniently. But public debate quickly revealed some deeper causes of these difficulties. Perhaps the major cause was the sheer number of different organizations, public and private, that were engaged in providing transportation services for Stockholm area residents. Within the city the municipal company, Stockholm Street Railways, operated comprehensive mass transit services, including subways, trolleys, and buses. In the suburbs, on the other hand, a dozen private and public companies provided various kinds of service. The biggest of these was the national government's State Railways (SJ) which, in addition to three commuter train lines, operated a number of bus routes throughout the region. The municipality of Lidingö operated three different bus companies to carry its residents to and from the city. Sweden's most influential banking family, the Wallenbergs, operated both a suburban train and a bus company, and a variety of other private companies operated bus and boat traffic companies.[3]

Except for minor agreements between the Lidingö companies and the city, and between SJ and the city, there was virtually no coordination between these transit organizations, each of which had its own route, its own fares, and its own schedules. In most cases commuters could not even transfer from one company's line to another's—a circumstance that forced large numbers of suburbanites to pay two full fares to get from residence to place of work. It was in this matter that municipal boundary lines did their worst damage for, licensed in one or two municipalities, but not all, the buses of one company were forced to stop at a municipal border and discharge their passengers to the buses of another company instead of taking those passengers directly through to their destinations. Municipal and organizational fragmentation thus created a transit "system" to serve the suburbs that was inefficient, expensive, and for most commuters, downright ridiculous.[4]

"RATIONAL SOLUTIONS"

The situation was sufficiently absurd to make the system itself a political issue. Beginning in 1961, writers for the metropolitan press

3. *Utlåtande nr 69, 1965*, p. 401, provides details regarding traffic companies in Stockholm.
4. Kubu, *op. cit.*, pp. 166–172, evokes the battery of discomforts experienced by the average commuter.

began what became a steady stream of editorials and articles critical of the "sandlot politics" that allowed suburban bosses to obstruct "rational solutions" to the area's transportation difficulties.[5] By 1962 Finance Commissioner Hjalmar Mehr was willing to be quoted publicly in favor of a "package solution" to the problem, which would treat the whole area as a single unity.

Mehr's trial balloon was quickly punctured, however, by Nils Eliasson of Huddinge who, at a public meeting to which Mehr had been invited, declared unambiguously that "never in his life" would he tolerate a single solution to the metropolitan traffic problem. Eliasson's fellow bosses, Gustaf Berg of Täby and Arthur Sköldin from Sundbyberg were known to be of like mind, giving Eliasson strong support to augment his own power as head of the County Council's Administration Committee.

With both individual suburban bosses and the county government in opposition, the city had no alternative but again to deal individually with each municipality in turn. Accordingly, the city persuaded the municipalities of Solna and Sundbyberg to join with it in building a subway extension to portions of the Järva area, to be acquired from the national government. A second agreement to extend the northeastern subway line was also made by the city with Lidingö.[6] Both of these important agreements were reached in 1963. Despite such progress it was quite clear that a great deal more time would be required to conclude enough individual Stockholm-suburban agreements to cope with a rapidly worsening transportation problem.

"FIRST WE AGREE UPON OUR GOALS . . ."

Before 1963 was out, however, all political calculations had to be revised. Nils Eliasson, who had pledged a lifetime effort against a comprehensive solution to the traffic problem, died on October 4, removing the city's most powerful and most vocal antagonist from the scene. A week later the County Council passed a resolution, supported by all parties, instructing the Administration Committee to appoint representatives to participate in the various negotiations then under way to find some solution to the traffic problem.

Meanwhile, Mehr and Garpe persuaded the last of the remaining suburban socialist bosses, Arthur Sköldin, to change his position on the traffic problem: Sköldin now saw the virtue of dealing with trans-

5. *Ibid.*, p. 165, reports the significance of massive press intervention.
6. *Utlåtande nr 69, 1965*, p. 402.

portation on a metropolitan-wide basis. He also shared the understanding that Mehr and Garpe had reached, namely that city and
suburban interests were once again in direct conflict. The most rational and efficient "solution" to the traffic problem on a metropolitan-wide basis would be to extend the city's subways into the surrounding suburban municipalities. But who would pay for such extensions, how much, and when? The city was quite willing to extend
its subway system, provided that the suburbs assumed a fair share of
the financial burden for doing so. Suburban politicians were eager to
expand the subway system but, never having operated mass transit
systems in the past, were wary of assuming a burden that might be
both large and unpredictable. Both sides badly wanted a metropolitan subway system, but they were equally determined to avoid the
signing of any blank checks.

A THIRD PARTY

Hjalmar Mehr saw an obvious way to seek a solution, employing
a third party whose interests were directly involved: the national
government itself. Having changed Sköldin's mind, Mehr now persuaded him to attend a meeting with the Minister of Communications to consider the possibility of national assistance. The national
government not only operated trains and buses into the area but,
perhaps more significantly, its financial support for highway and road
construction directly affected the level of support available for other
mass transit facilities.[7] Clearly, if there was to be a metropolitan
solution the State would have to be involved. With Mehr and Sköldin pressing, the national government agreed in October 1963 to appoint an official "negotiator" to work out the details of a regional
transportation program involving the city, the county (representing
the suburban jurisdictions), and the national government itself. The
Communications Ministry's chief political officer, Under Secretary
Nils Hörjel, was assigned the task of bringing this three-sided structure into existence. Since part of his job would be to look after national financial interests, his appointment made it clear that the
national government was prepared to participate—financially and
otherwise—in solving Stockholm's transportation problem.

THE GOVERNMENTAL SYSTEM

Achieving national participation was a major victory, but Mehr
had even bigger things in mind. He understood perfectly well that

7. *Ibid.*, p. 419.

the governmental system itself was now a major metropolitan political issue. The largest Stockholm newspaper had moved from criticisms of specific problems to a full-fledged campaign urging creation of a single municipal government for the entire region, the so-called "enhetskommun." [8] But the deaths of two of the city's three most powerful suburban opponents—Eliasson and Gustaf Berg of Täby—and the conversion of the third to a more friendly view, gave the system a decidedly different character in 1963, for none of the remaining suburban leaders had comparable status, or seemed likely to achieve it soon. Having secured a national government commitment to help resolve the city-suburban dispute on transportation finance, Mehr decided that the time had come to deal more directly with the governmental system itself.

On December 5, 1963, Mehr was scheduled to give his annual "State of the City" address before the City Council. Mehr briefed national officials in advance, and carefully timed his speech to maximize its exposure in the morning newspapers. He also informed his counterpart in the county government, Erik A. Lindh, successor to Eliasson, who would necessarily be a key figure in implementing the proposals Mehr was about to make.

"A NEW STOCKHOLM CONCEPT"

The cornerstone of Mehr's recommendations was the rapid development of the Stockholm area into an economic and political unit, involving both city and suburban jurisdictions in all major decisions. Virtually no problem, he thought, could any longer be discussed "without a debate flaring up over the appropriate administrative forms for greater Stockholm cooperation." The result was that

A new Stockholm concept and a new Greater Stockholm atmosphere continues to develop. Let me point to two factors. The first is our fundamental community of interests. Business, industry, the labor market, cultural life, amusements and vacation activities in reality function as a single unit and it therefore follows that the fundamental questions of housing, jobs, highways, mass transportation, health care, education and social institutions in general also become common problems. It is logical and natural that "Greater Stockholm" should replace "Stockholm" as the subject of development. The second factor speeding the process is that, because of a shortage of housing and land in Stockholm, people continue to move out. The new residents in our neighboring municipalities are for

8. *Expressen,* a Liberal party newspaper, had the largest circulation among city newspapers and was a strong supporter of a single metropolitan municipality to replace existing units. Kubu, *op. cit.,* p. 169.

the most part children of the middleaged generation of Stockholmers. Many move out after they marry in order to obtain an apartment but they continue to work in Stockholm. They feel themselves to be Stockholmers, they regard our trolleys and subways as theirs, our social and cultural institutions as theirs, and they have, naturally enough, significantly less sensitivity for administrative boundaries than older county residents.[9]

Mehr thought that these developments offered a basis for new administrative forms, but he also acknowledged the difficulty of designing the new forms. He pointed out that significant administrative reform was certain to redistribute the area tax burden. Local politicians in the area would therefore take a cold-blooded view of any proposal for change. But beyond that, the problems were extraordinarily complex. Cities in other nations—Mehr mentioned Toronto, London, and Copenhagen—were seen as struggling toward their own solutions, with mixed success. Failures in those cities, as well as their modest successes, should be kept in mind, he suggested, in devising changes in Stockholm institutions.

Mehr considered the consolidated single-government solution—advocated by many editorial writers—to be inappropriate. Combining the thirty area governments into a single municipality was a simple and appealing answer, he thought. Moreover, that kind of answer seemed to follow the worldwide trend toward rationalization and greater centralization. Yet such a drastic step would threaten a fundamental Swedish institution:

Has local self-government no worth of its own? For my own part I say that it does. In depth, breadth and significance, municipal self-government in our nation is unique, with its total sovereignty over essential community responsibilities. It trains women and men in responsibility; it anchors social consciousness and individual governing capacity in the citizenry; it is one of the cornerstones of Swedish democracy.

To Mehr, efforts to overturn an institution of such significance, because of unsolved problems of coordination, were dangerous and wrong-headed. A good deal of coordination already had occurred in important policy areas such as housing, water supply, and education. Indeed, it was precisely because of success in these areas that the discussion now could be carried further. These accomplishments, Mehr maintained, had produced a "wholly new spirit of understanding, respect and trust":

9. This and following excerpts are taken from Hjalmar Mehr, *Framsteg och Regional Samverkan* (Stockholm: Stadskollegiets Reklamkommitté, 1963). See Appendix for the text of the speech.

Stockholm views its neighbors as equally responsible and legitimate partners. Our neighbors view Stockholm as a municipality whose leaders seek intelligent and correct solutions that serve the best interests of citizens throughout the region, regardless of municipal boundaries. They know in particular that we do not seek any dominance or hold any quasi-imperialistic views. This is a sentiment of real political significance. If we now raise the question of developing cooperation even further through legislation, everyone knows that this is a reasonable and positive suggestion, not an effort to undermine or overwhelm smaller units. In the same spirit I begin, in the discussion to come, from the following position: that a regional solution to vital problems of coordination can be won with preservation of independent and active municipalities.

USING THE COUNTY COUNCIL

Mehr's assertions about the "new spirit of understanding" were exaggerated. Nevertheless, they provided a politically astute preface to specific proposals that placed great emphasis on continued municipal independence. Local independence, he argued, could be maintained only if a way were found to carry on urban functions effectively. That objective implied a transfer of some functions to a higher, regional, level of government. For such purposes, Mehr said, "wise fathers and lawmakers" had given us the County Council. Although it was then limited primarily to health care matters, Mehr saw the county as the institution most capable of taking over a number of regional policy responsibilities. The alternative was to transfer those responsibilities to the regional offices of the national government or, to put it differently, to choose "bureaucratic administration" rather than "citizen control" over municipal affairs.

Mehr strongly preferred the County Council, with locally elected and thus locally controlled representatives. Accordingly, he proposed that the city join with the county in forming a new "Greater Stockholm Council" to deal with the following regional responsibilities:

1. Regional planning
2. Coordination and support of municipal housing production
3. Common water supply and sewer systems
4. Mass transportation, in conjunction with the national government
5. Health care
6. Secondary education

Mehr admitted that this was a tentative list, subject to future modification. Indeed, given the complexity likely to be encountered in rearranging municipal and county functions, modification would almost certainly occur. But, for the moment, he regarded these functions as having the most "regional" significance, and thus as most suited to supramunicipal control.

For the county, adopting Mehr's proposals would mean a substantial expansion of responsibilities to include several major activities in addition to continued operation of hospitals. Mehr's plan would also require a total overhaul of the county legislative body, the *landsting*, to accommodate city and county representatives on a basis different from the past.

For area municipalities, Mehr's proposals implied a considerable loss of authority, but the municipalities would be retained and would continue to operate independently in those functional areas left to municipal control. Mehr proposed that, while the details of all this were being worked out, the Greater Stockholm Planning Board be given the task of bringing regional housing production up to an annual figure of 20,000 units. He also proposed that city, county, and national governments pursue solutions to the traffic problem, as well as the equally pressing problem of capital supply for future development. The latter proposals implicitly recognized the resistance likely to be found on both sides. Nevertheless, as Mehr said in conclusion,

An initiative to adjust administrative forms to demands of the time and needs of the situation, coming from supporters of municipal self-government, is an expression of municipal vitality and capacity. I invite everyone to cooperate.

In the debate that followed Mehr's speech, Liberal party spokesmen renewed their demands for a single metropolitan municipality. Some even suggested that the local monopoly over planning—long regarded as a municipal sacred cow in Swedish politics—be taken away from area municipalities. This policy stance permitted Mehr and his Social Democratic colleagues to appear as sole occupants of a more moderate, middle-of-the-road position. That position was presented as a defense of municipal independence, and the Social Democrats were thus able to picture their proposed reforms as a direct outgrowth of Swedish tradition.[10] These debating positions were interesting only because they provided another indication of weakness in bourgeois party tactics. As a practical matter, socialist control of the City Council meant that any socialist proposal would carry regardless of bourgeois arguments. Far more interesting and significant was

10. Kubu, *op. cit.*, pp. 169–170, reviews the debate.

the absence of any serious or sustained suburban criticism in the following months. Mehr had successfully coopted his counterpart in the County Council, Erik Lindh, as well as Arthur Sköldin. No other socialist leaders appeared to feel competent enough to challenge the plan put forward by their party colleague in the city.

THE CASE AGAINST

Among the few bourgeois leaders in the suburbs there was opposition, but little of it was expressed in public. Igor Holmstedt, the Conservative party leader in the municipality of Lidingö, regarded Mehr's plan as "a coup against the suburban governments" and published an article attacking the need for a new regional governmental unit. He analyzed each of the six functions Mehr had proposed for regional attention and concluded that only one—mass transportation —was likely to benefit from creation of a regional unit. Moreover, he pointed out, that benefit would accrue primarily because, for political reasons, both the State Railways and Stockholm Street Railways were operated at a deficit. Not even the suburban governments most interested in helping finance subway extension wished to assume the burden of a city-created deficit. Thus a solution to the traffic mess might best be sought through some regional unit. On the other hand, there was no real reason to suppose that a regional unit ought to handle anything beyond transportation. Apart from transportation, Holmstedt found nothing in Mehr's proposals that could not be done better—indeed, that was not *already* being done better—by existing structures of intermunicipal cooperation.[11]

THE GREATER COUNTY COUNCIL COMMITTEE

Holmstedt's case was powerfully argued, but his was a lone public voice among suddenly complacent suburbanites. Mehr had timed his move perfectly: the forces of suburban opposition were suddenly leaderless and unable to withstand the double thrust of public outcry combined with city pressure. Mehr now increased the pressure by arranging a meeting of ten leading politicians in March 1964. Five were appointed by the City Council and five by the County Council.[12] An advance memorandum prepared by Mehr repeated the

11. Igor Holmstedt, "Storlandstinget och stockholms-regionen," *Svensk Tidskrift,* Årgång LI (1964), pp. 346–354.
12. For the membership and minutes of the March meeting, see *Bihang nr 81, 1966,* pp, 138–141.

arguments he had made three months earlier. It proposed that these ten representatives of the city and county governments constitute themselves the Greater County Council Committee (*Storlandstings-kommité*) for the purpose of conducting non-preconceived studies leading to "regional, legally-regulated cooperation." The group agreed, and a staff composed of officials from the city's Department of Greater Stockholm Affairs was appointed. Each "regional" function proposed by Mehr was assigned to an agency for study, except for transportation, which was already being dealt with by a state negotiator.[13]

The Greater County Council Committee was thus totally dominated by the city: its work plan was *precisely* the plan laid out by the Stockholm Finance Commissioner, and its staff personnel were in fact city employees. Overshadowing that, moreover, the very name given the new committee in effect changed the terms of future debate. A set of proposals advanced tentatively a few weeks before now became a goal agreed upon, at least for these representatives of the city and county governments. Despite much talk about organizing studies without preconceptions, the new committee clearly had a strong preconception built into its very title. There were many alternatives to a Greater County Council, but it would now be difficult to have serious discussions about them.

Mehr had succeeded in defining a new goal. Henceforward the question was no longer, "What to do about the Stockholm regional problem," but rather, "How to implement the Greater County Council plan for solving the Stockholm regional problem." Having coopted his principal opponents, the city's Finance Commissioner had now succeeded in setting an entirely new agenda for regional politics and regional politicians. If there was a *coup* against suburban political entities, this was surely it.

". . . THEN WE DECIDE HOW TO REACH THEM."

Most of the organizations and actors who might have been expected to offer alternatives to the Greater County Council plan had been put to work by the Greater County Council Committee. The Regional Planning Commission, the Greater Stockholm Planning Board and its various subcommittees, and the Regional Health Care

---

13. *Ibid.* In view of developments that occurred later, it may be worth noting that Mehr's preliminary memo urged all participants to bear in mind that "the housing problem was and will continue to be the largest problem in the entire complex of problems affecting the Greater County Council issue."

Committee all had accepted commissions to perform studies for the Greater County Council Committee.[14] Interim reports from any of these organizations—virtually all of whose staff resources were being provided by the city—or public comment about their ongoing work thus became directly linked to the Greater County Council concept. The more this process went on, unhampered by any references to metropolitan governmental alternatives, the more the Greater County Council came to seem the natural and logical future.

In September 1964 the Committee hired a full-time Staff Director and two secretaries to coordinate the work of the various study groups. Lennart Nyström, the new Staff Director, was a twelve-year veteran of the city personnel office, with wide experience in city affairs, while the other two employees were in fact put on the city's payroll. But apart from coordinating the several investigations under way, the Committee did very little during the remainder of the year. Instead, it watched the negotiations over the traffic problem being conducted by Nils Hörjel and waited for the outcome.

THE GREATER STOCKHOLM TRAFFIC ASSOCIATION

The remarkable result came in December of 1964, after months of hard bargaining that often included acrimonious exchanges between Mehr and Hörjel over the question of who should pay for what. According to the "agreement in principle" reached in the early morning hours of December 17, the city and county governments agreed to form a municipal association to plan, develop, and operate a comprehensive metropolitan transportation system. The new organization, called the Greater Stockholm Traffic Association (*Storstockholms local-trafikförbund,* or SL), was to be governed by a legislative body with equal city and county representation, although the city was assigned all the important committee chairmanships for the first four years.

A new private corporation, called Greater Stockholm Local Traffic, Inc., was to be created by restructuring Stockholm Street Railways, operator of the city's surface and subway transit facilities. The new corporation would be the Municipal Association's operating arm, with responsibility for administrative and economic aspects of those operations. The parent association would be responsible for planning a mass transit system for the entire region, for building new subway lines into the area surrounding the city, for developing stand-

14. *Ibid.*

ards of service and fares, and for financing a comprehensive system of surface and underground transportation. The agreement specifically committed the two parties to seek, for residents of outlying portions of Stockholm County, transit services as good as those available to residents of Greater Stockholm itself.[15]

An ideology of equalitarianism and rationalism underlies the agreement. In terms of transit to and from the central city, the goal was service of a uniform standard, available to all regional residents, regardless of location. This clearly would not be possible for residents of distant county areas, but stating the goal was politically important from the point of view of the county, whose taxpayers would be committing themselves to an entirely new financial obligation.

ALL REGIONAL TRANSIT

In terms of rationality, moreover, it was both sensible and important to design a system suited to the reality of a region that constituted a cultural and economic unity. Accordingly the new association and its operating company assumed responsibility for *all* regional transit activities: the several private organizations operating in the suburbs were to be purchased and their routes incorporated into the association system; negotiations with the State Railways were to be held for the purpose of coordinating and/or purchasing their services; and, of course, the subways to be extended to the new residential areas in Järva and Botkyrka were to be constructed, so far as was possible, before the residents arrived. This was part of an agreement for a totally new third subway line, running north-southwest, to complement the two subway diagonals (south-west and southeast-northeast) then in existence. All this would take care of the region's mass transit needs for the foreseeable future, giving Stockholm a transit system second to none in any city in the world.[16]

These were large and comprehensive goals, and large sums of money were involved. The cost of the new subway extensions alone was reckoned at more than 1.5 billion crowns ($300 million). Almost another 500 million crowns ($100 million) was pledged by the State Railways in improvements to its facilities, bringing total anticipated capital expenditures to more than 2 billion crowns ($400 million).

15. For the text of the agreement, see *Utlåtande nr 69, 1965*, pp. 445–451.
16. *Ibid.* In keeping with the Swedish tradition of moderation in public pronouncements, none of the participants offered the sweeping judgment made above. The Board of Commissioners was prepared to suggest, however, that the contemplated system would be "high class." See p. 442.

Beyond that, substantial annual operating deficits were projected, adding further to financial burdens about to be assumed by the city and county.

THE NATIONAL CONTRIBUTION

That such fiscal obligations were accepted at all was due entirely to the third party in these discussions: the national government. Reversing a long-standing policy, the government agreed to include funds for the support of subway construction in its budget for road and highway development. Specifically, the national government pledged 95 per cent of the costs of underground and related construction work (tunnels, bridges, viaducts) for the new subway extensions.[17] Since these costs represented almost 60 per cent of the estimated total of 1.5 billion for the new subways, the government's commitment represented more than half the cost of the new lines. For the city and county, this financial commitment was a condition for their agreement to form an Association to deal with mass transit. For the national government, the commitment represented the cheapest solution to a difficult problem. In presenting his annual authorization bill to the Riksdag in March of 1965, the Minister of Communication argued that

A major calculation behind the proposal that state contributions for subway construction should be drawn from the budget for road and highway construction—and thus be counted against automobile tax funds—is that a rationally developed subway system within a metropolitan region can lead to a reduction of public investments for a road network of similar size and capacity.[18]

The national contribution thus represented a dual policy breakthrough: (1) to national support for subways and (2) to the use of automobile tax revenue to provide the necessary funds. Over all, the national government wound up pledging roughly 1.3 billion of the 2 billion crowns of new capital expenditures required by the new plan.

THE REMAINING COSTS

The remaining costs were to be shared by the city and county, according to a formula that was even more remarkable, politically, than the breakthrough to a national subway subsidy. As noted above,

17. The national government's "pledge" later turned out to be ambiguous, but both the city and the county considered it binding. *Ibid.*, pp. 406–420.
18. *Kungl. Maj:ts proposition 1965:107*, p. 7.

a new transit company, Greater Stockholm Local Traffic, Inc., was to be created through sale of Stockholm Street Railways to the new municipal Association. The Association, it was now agreed, would purchase all of the city's shares in its transit company for the sum of 17.6 million crowns ($3.5 million). Up to then the city had invested a total of more than a billion crowns—for subway tunnels, stations, stock, etc.—of which half already had been amortized.[19] Thus the city agreed to sell assets of 500,000 million crowns for only 17.6 million crowns. In effect, the city gave away its subway system, which had been bought and half paid for by city taxpayers!

Moreover, the city's agreement to distribute costs on the basis of tax base meant that city taxpayers would continue to bear the bulk of the financial burden for developing and operating the expanded transit system. This was because the city's population was larger and wealthier, on the average, than the county population. Finally, although the Greater Stockholm Traffic Association was to be formed in 1966 and begin activities in 1967, the county was not required to assume its full share of the costs until 1972. It is easy enough to imagine that discussions between Mehr and Hörjel over these points were indeed heated. Nor should there be any difficulty in appreciating the vastly understated conclusion offered by the City Finance Office:

through the agreement reached here the City is assuming far-reaching financial and economic responsibilities for the continued development of the subway system, among other things, which will substantially benefit inhabitants of the City's neighboring municipalities. These responsibilities have been motivated by, and are aimed at, those advantages that a coordinated transit system offers, not only from the point of view of transportation and fares, but even more from the point of view of good city planning in general in the capital city region.[20]

THE CITY'S MOTIVATIONS

A more detailed discussion of the structural conditions that enabled city politicians to subsidize residents of other municipalities must await a later chapter. At this point we should simply try to understand why city leaders were moved to accept these agreements. Quite obviously, Mehr and his city colleagues were strongly motivated to create a metropolitan transit system that could move people to and from the city more efficiently and in larger numbers than the

19. *Utlåtande nr 69, 1965,* p. 412.
20. *Ibid.,* p. 440.

existing system. Much of the new housing being built in the suburbs, after all, was constructed by city companies, to accommodate people registered in the city's housing queue. Moreover, since all the subway diagonals crossed in the city center, extending them out and building them well was a way of guaranteeing the future health of the core city, whatever the short-run costs.

Beyond that, the national government made the provisions very difficult to reject, not only through pressure to reach agreement, but also through the very substantial financial contribution it offered. Had the offer been turned down, another might have been difficult, if not impossible, to arrange. But, at bottom, city political leaders saw their problems primarily in regional, rather than local, terms. As professionally trained administrators, they accepted ideologies that stressed efficiency and rationality in the organization of public services. Failure to follow those ideologies would have represented a denial of background, training, and tradition. In short, when they talked about good city planning, they meant it.

THE STRATEGY AND TACTICS OF MANIPULATION

The "agreement in principle" negotiated by Under Secretary Hörjel can with some justice be regarded as historic. Not only had the national government consented to support urban mass transit from automobile tax revenues, but the city and county also had agreed to a binding form of cooperation for purposes that one government knew nothing about and that the other government would largely finance. Nevertheless, it was clear that Hjalmar Mehr had other, equally historic, prospects in mind. His Greater County Council Committee was functioning during 1964 and, after the traffic agreement had been reached, the issue became whether, and how, the traffic negotiations could be worked into the larger question of the Greater County Council. Mehr put the staff of the Greater County Council Committee to work on the question. By January 29, 1965, their answer was ready.

In a memo of that date circulated to members of the Greater County Council Committee, the staff (all current or former city employees) noted that negotiation of the traffic agreement naturally suggested the possibility that other problems of common interest could be handled similarly. Before the Greater County Council actually came into existence, the staff suggested, it would be quite useful to have an organization to prepare the way. The Municipal Association could well play such a role in addition to its traffic responsibilities. Accordingly, when plans for the new association were being drawn up, the staff proposed that simultaneous consideration be given to making the association flexible enough to permit the assignment of additional functions.[21] Such assignments would facilitate a rational and orderly transition to the new Greater County Council.

THE IMPRESSION OF CONSENSUS

Apart from the committee's ten members, of course, no one had yet accepted the inevitability of the Greater County Council. Indeed, the press and bourgeois party spokesmen were continuing a vigorous campaign for a much more comprehensive solution. Neither was there any logical or factual reason why the Greater County Council idea should be tied to the traffic agreement. But Mehr's tactic was to refuse to acknowledge the existence of other points of view, thus adding to the impression of political unanimity among the government "experts." The Greater County Council Committee meeting of February 5 circulated the proposal to other regional bodies for comment, rather than endorsing it outright, but the press release prepared for the meeting implied that the idea was fully endorsed and that only details of implementation remained. Using the Traffic Association to deal with other matters was the "simplest way," according to the release, to move toward the Greater County Council. The association could assume some of the work of existing regional bodies and, if it took on some additional regional responsibilities, it would constitute a governing body capable of representing all portions of the county.[22] Only a Swede, perhaps, can appreciate the political power that arises from the feeling of consensus, although in this case the feeling was largely the product of one man's assertiveness.

The impression of consensus was strengthened by the expected positive responses from the regional bodies that had been asked to comment on the Traffic Association's proposed expansion. Two of them, in fact, had already been co-opted by the city, or were in large measure creatures of the city: the Regional Planning Board and the Greater Stockholm Planning Board. The third regional organization,

21. Storlandstingskommittén, "Protokoll," 5 februari 1965, p. 304. Mimeographed.
22. The press release was identified as a product of the Greater County Council Committee's staff, and was dated February 2, three days *before* the Committee meeting was held. The Committee itself *tabled* the proposal for expanding the responsibilities of the traffic association, pending further review.

the Stockholm Suburbs Cooperative Association, existed primarily to focus suburban opposition to the big city.[23] Only a few of the members of this organization had been given positions in other regional bodies controlled by the city. Most remained unco-opted and un-co-optable. They had not been informed in advance of Mehr's December 1963 speech, and had never had an official chance to respond to his plans for the future of the Stockholm area. Now they had that opportunity.

SUBURBAN REJECTION

Meeting to discuss the matter on March 19, 1965, the suburban officials quickly concluded that the traffic agreement was a good thing, and that further city-suburban cooperation was a good idea, at least in principle. Whether it would be a good idea in operation depended on what responsibilities were to be assigned, and to whom. These questions were not specifically addressed in the Greater County Council Committee proposal. The suburbanites therefore could find no basis for a definite response. Although not stated in so many words, their reply was a flat rejection of the Greater County Council idea, based as it was on a reallocation of urban functions. It followed, then, that the suburbs could not accept the notion of using the traffic agreement as a first step toward a new governmental system:

The Board, however, finds reason to question whether creation of a municipal association for mass transportation justifies broadening that association to include activities that affect primary municipal responsibilities. The memorandum circulated does not establish the need for such a broadening. In the memorandum it has hardly been demonstrated that a broadened municipal association would bring about conditions for a more rational and satisfactory resolution of Greater Stockholm questions. It may in this connection be suggested that Greater Stockholm problems are not, in the first instance, questions of new administrative forms for local government. The most essential problems are related to factors apart from any form of local administration or organization. The intended studies and discussions therefore ought to be directed at, among other things, the elimination of barriers to more satisfactory community development that are beyond local competence.[24]

The message from the suburbs was clear: any efforts to change the existing system of boundaries and funtions—"primary municipal responsibilities"—would provoke a fight. If there was a "real" prob-

23. See Lind, *loc. cit.,* for the history of this organization.
24. Storlandstingskommittén, "Protokoll," 13 maj 1965. Mimeographed.

lem, it was economic. Just give the suburban governments enough money and technical resources, and they would do a fine job of organizing development.

A NEW TACTIC

Even without strong suburban leadership, this position represented a powerful challenge to Mehr's plan, largely because so many of the suburban governments were controlled by his own party colleagues. In a written response, Mehr had his staff point out, gently, that accepting the suburban argument would leave unchanged the very organizational mess that had produced the current difficulties. Sooner or later, he urged, the problems would have to be dealt with by bringing the various organizations together.[25] Meanwhile, Mehr decided to see what might be done about bringing the politicians, if not their programs, together.

Provisions of the traffic agreement had yet to be worked out in detail, and it had been assumed that the staff of the Greater County Council Committee would work out the details. But the committee itself had only ten members, and Mehr began to see the advantages of creating a larger group. A larger committee would offer more places for suburban political leaders and provide opportunities to coopt them into agreement. If enough suburban leaders could be brought into line, any remaining dissenters would appear to stand outside a prevailing consensus of public "experts," and could thus be ignored. Accordingly, Mehr arranged for a new group—the "Planning Committee"—to work on the traffic agreement.

The new committee was composed of twenty-six people, thirteen each from the city and the county. Temporarily, they were to assume the Greater County Council Committee's role. To help ensure that the new group understood the nature of the consensus soon to be reached, Mehr and his county counterpart, Erik Lindh, publicly announced their support for a broadened Traffic Association, even before the Planning Committee held its first meeting.[26]

Mehr and Lindh were selected as vice-chairmen of the Planning Committee at its May 26 organizational meeting. In a memo circulated two days before the Planning Committee's first meeting, Mehr laid out the group's working procedures and agenda. According to Mehr, the most pressing immediate problem was the question of passenger transfer privileges between the various transit companies

25. *Ibid.*   26. *Ibid.*

in the area, particularly the state and city companies. The second problem on Mehr's agenda was the detailed projection of subway extensions from the city. The third item was future investment by the State Railways.

THE CONSTITUTIONAL QUESTION

There also remained the problem of arranging a constitution for the Municipal Association, but a draft already had been prepared by the Greater County Council Committee and Mehr was content to leave that aside temporarily. If the issue of single or multiple responsibilities could be resolved, the constitutional question would simply be a matter of careful legal drafting. For each of the two immediate problems outlined, Mehr proposed a separate and smaller working subcommittee, each of which was an extension of an existing city committee, and each of which would be staffed by city experts. By accepting everything that Mehr proposed, the 26-member Planning Committee showed that Mehr's latest tactic would be even more successful than expected. Failure to oppose at this juncture signaled suburban willingness to be co-opted.[27]

At a second meeting about a month later, Planning Committee actions verified earlier indications. A detailed plan for future subway extension was presented by Anders Nordberg, a long-time associate of Mehr and head of the city's General Planning Group. His presentation was accepted as the basis for the Planning Committee's recommendations. Mehr presented another proposal for transfers between all transit systems operating in the area—drafted by the city's Special Committee on Transit Fares. After some discussion it was approved.

Acceptance meant that, for the first time, there would be a uniform set of fares and transfer rights throughout the region, regardless of company or mode of transportation. Weekly and monthly rebated tickets would be issued, cutting travel costs for commuters to less than one-third of previous rates. The estimated first-year deficit of seven to eight million crowns would be apportioned between the partners in the new municipal association according to the 1964 agreement, i.e., Stockholm would bear 65 per cent of the cost. As of January 1, 1966, then, commuters would begin to see some tangible results of the political negotiations. The city, it should be noted,

27. Stockholms stads och Stockholms läns landstings gemensamma planeringskommitté för den kollektiva trafiken, "Protokoll," 26 maj 1965. Mimeographed. County representatives by this time had been assured that national use of auto taxes for subways would not harm allocations for county highways.

would bear most but not *all* of the cost of the projected deficit—as would have been the case without the traffic agreement. The third agenda topic—future investments by the State Railways—was not yet ripe for discussion, leaving only the constitutional question as a major matter for consideration.[28]

On that issue Mehr distributed the draft constitution prepared by the Greater County Council Committee staff. The draft contained the almost ritualized assertion of what was not yet agreed to: namely, that "The proposed municipal association for mass transportation is a significant step along the way toward a Greater County Council as the form of administration for regional questions." [29] The association would necessarily be temporary, but precisely because of its temporary nature, it should be assigned broad, rather than limited, responsibilities. Apart from traffic, the only other immediate candidate for inclusion in association responsibilities seemed to be regional planning. But others were certain to be agreed upon and when they were, the association's form should be flexible enough to include them without further complicated political and legal negotiations. As part of that flexibility, the draft authors proposed a name for the new association that would express its future potential: "The Municipal Association for City and County of Stockholm Regional Problems"—*Kommunalförbundet för Stockholms stads och läns regionala frågor*—or KSL for short.[30]

"SEEMINGLY LIMITED STEP . . ."

On the surface the proposal offered by Mehr's lieutenants seemed quite innocuous. It asked only that the Municipal Association be so organized as to permit it to deal with other matters than traffic problems, without specifying what those problems were, and also without committing the organization to dealing with them. Yet everyone understood that accepting this seemingly limited step would make it extraordinarily difficult to turn back later, particularly if nontraffic responsibilities were assigned to the new association.

Behind a limited-purpose facade then, Mehr was in fact asking the Planning Committee to approve *his* plan for future regional administration, and he was doing so in a context that could be expected to brand any disagreement as unreasonable. Everyone was anxious

28. Planerings Kommittén, "Protokoll," 30 juni 1965. Mimeographed.
29. The draft, essentially as proposed, is available in *Utlåtande nr 311, 1965*, pp. 2382–2384.
30. *Ibid.*

to resolve transportation difficulties, and grateful for the expertise offered by the city that permitted most details to be ironed out by the end of the summer. Opposition to this proposal in the face of wide agreement on transit matters would thus appear—or could be made to appear—extremist and unreasonable. Those sponsoring such opposition would clearly face grave political risks. Suburban socialists already had indicated their unwillingness to take those risks. Would the bourgeois party leaders do the same?

A reform as limited as the Greater County Council presented a difficult problem for bourgeois party strategists. Rejecting Mehr's plan because it was not sufficiently comprehensive might not only brand them as obstructionists, but might also emphasize the fact that the bourgeois parties, too, were split on the issue. Although leaders of the conservative and liberal parties *in the City* were persuaded that Mehr's plan did not go nearly far enough, many *suburban* conservatives and liberals felt that the proposal was comprehensive enough to pose a real threat to municipal sovereignty. With no obvious way out of this dilemma, bourgeois party representatives moved to table the issue until the post-vacation meeting of the Planning Committee, scheduled for the end of August. Even then the bourgeois parties had not decided what position to take, although most of the details of the transit problem had been worked out by that time, adding further pressure to decide.

Finally, at a special meeting held on September 13, 1965, the bourgeois groups announced their position. They would accept the proposed constitution, including the provision allowing the new association to deal with problems other than mass transit. But they specifically refused to support Mehr's Greater County Council idea. In a separate statement, all bourgeois members of the Planning Committee pointed out that several studies of regional problems were not yet completed. Until the studies were completed, they argued, it would be improper to "take a position on which administrative form would be best suited to the common problems of Stockholm city and county." [31]

This statement, which was the Planning Committee's nearest approximation to a recorded vote, allowed the bourgeois groups the option of proposing more drastic reforms at some later date. At the same time, it also enabled Mehr to report unanimous committee sup-

---

31. Planeringskommittén, "Protokoll," 13 september 1965, p. 2. Mimeographed.

port for a new, metropolitan-wide municipal association whose principal responsibility would be mass transportation, but which could add other regional responsibilities whenever agreement could be reached.

TOWARD A GREATER COUNTY COUNCIL

Moreover, since virtually all city officials were constantly referring to the traffic agreement as a "step toward" a Greater County Council, the proposed solution was gradually assuming the character of an inevitable outcome. A final meeting of the Planning Committee was held in November to ratify the agreements and otherwise tie up loose ends, especially with respect to investments to be made by the State Railways.[32] Promptly on schedule, December 15, 1965, the new Municipal Association for City and County of Stockholm Regional Problems came into existence, ready to do business on January 1, 1966. A regional structure to handle regional transportation was now in existence, with potential authority to handle other problems as well. The remaining question was whether this temporary structure could find a more permanent form of organization.

OUTCOMES

With the work of the Planning Committee finished, it remained for the Greater County Council Committee to find a way to move from a single- to a multiple-purpose Municipal Association, and from there to the new regional government that was Mehr's ultimate goal.

RECOMMENDED: AGREEMENT IN PRINCIPLE

In mid-February 1966, Mehr and his co-chairman Erik Lindh proposed to the Greater County Council Committee that they recommend another "agreement in principle" to city and county governments. Since developing detailed plans for transferring functions between governments was so complicated, Mehr and Lindh suggested that the task could be simplified by fixing a definite date for such a transfer. They proposed that the Committee urge the city and county governments to agree "in principle" before the end of June 1966

32. Although the details are too complicated to discuss here, another subcommittee headed by former Commissioner Helge Berglund and aided by a staff of experts from the city transit company worked through the summer to clarify the obligations of the State Railways. These were important matters, which demonstrated again that the city bureaucracy was clearly superior to the state bureaucracy: negotiating memos prepared by the city experts repeatedly revealed the inadequacy of national calculations in harsh, but precise, language.

that a Greater County Council should come into existence, and to set January 1, 1971 as the target date.[33]

The Committee could derive a rationale for such action from the studies, commissioned earlier, that were now being finished, and could indicate the areas possibly subject to functional transfer, as well as the necessary organizational changes. With this proposal there was, at last, no place to hide. After all the preliminary maneuvers and partial steps, some hard choices were now being suggested concerning future allocations of power among area governmental units, within a specified period of time.

BOURGEOIS PARTY REACTION

Bourgeois party reaction, as expected, struck out at the administrative timidity of Mehr's Greater County Council plan. "The natural and rational administrative jurisdiction of the region," argued the party leaders in an official response to the Mehr-Lindh proposal, "ought to be based upon economic and geographic criteria—not on outmoded county and municipal boundaries." Where people shopped, worked and lived had little or nothing to do with political boundaries; therefore the boundaries should be discarded in considering ways to deal with future administrative needs. Instead, a study of people's utilization of the region for basic social and economic activities ought to guide the design of a regional government. Such a study, the bourgeois leaders felt, would justify the need for a regional-level municipality to handle "all municipal questions," not merely the short list Mehr had in mind. Planning questions in particular had to be dealt with in a less prejudicial way, in order to satisfy increasingly critical regional housing needs. To cope with the housing problem, a regional municipality should be assigned responsibilities superceding the traditional "planning monopoly" of local governments. If such a "super municipality" were created, bourgeois leaders suggested, it would be equally necessary to somehow preserve and enlarge citizen influence in a far more centralized governmental system. All of this could be achieved only if more comprehensive studies were done. While they were willing to contemplate creation of some form of super municipality on January 1, 1971, bourgeois leaders insisted that it be comprehensive, centralized, and capable of overriding existing municipal units in all matters of administrative significance.[34]

33. *Bihang nr 81, 1966,* p. 149.
34. *Ibid.,* pp. 150–151.

Given the obvious contradictions in the bourgeois position, it is not easy to judge how serious they were. Demanding more centralization and greater citizen participation in the same statement was curious enough by itself. Combining that with an open challenge to a "sacred cow" of Swedish politics—the local planning "monopoly"— seemed almost calculated to place Mehr squarely in the middle of the reform road, precisely where any Swedish politician would like to be.

THE SUBURBAN MESSAGE: LEAVE HOUSING ALONE

Meanwhile, the suburban socialists on Mehr's other flank observed the bourgeois response with some trepidation. Although it was not likely that Mehr would back off from his earlier support for continued municipal independence, the bourgeois position made clear that local "autonomy" would very much depend on what functions were left to municipalities after all the reforming was over. From the suburban point of view, loss of the planning monopoly would be disastrous, for it would not only remove local authority to control development, but it would also undermine local ability to influence population mix through housing construction. The suburban socialists' message to Mehr was simple and direct: if you want our support for your Greater County Council, leave housing alone.

Mehr might have ignored this message, but chose instead to take it very seriously during the negotiations then under way. This became clear on May 16, 1966, when the Greater County Council Committee officially adopted a three-part proposal:

1. that the Committee propose to the Stockholm City Council and the Stockholm County Council that they each decide to unite the City and the county in a new "secondary municipality" with the working title of "Greater County Council";
2. that the responsibilities of the new secondary municipality would include mass transportation, health care, regional planning, and long-range planning for water and sewer systems; and
3. that January 1, 1971 be the target date for creation of the new Greater County Council.

Of the other responsibilities proposed earlier for inclusion in the regional government, some, such as secondary education and mental health, were left out for technical or legal reasons not related to the political positions of the principally involved actors.

But the major omissions here—housing and local planning—were left out because they simply could not be included without risking a serious fight. The proffered back-up position was that "more research was required before a position could be taken" on the housing question, and that such research was under way. But everyone understood that the housing issue was still much too sensitive for local politicians to expect them to relinquish their control of it. Put differently, this was the best deal Mehr could get. He took it rather than risk the loss of a Stockholm metro in any form. One month later both the city and county councils officially approved the proposal. Stockholm's regional government, the Greater County Council, was born.[35]

EPILOGUE: THE METROPOLITAN GOVERNMENT

The period between June 1966 and January 1971 was marked by many technical and legal complexities. Indeed, the complications of rearranging and reassigning urban service functions were so great that the national government was again asked to help, this time lending a two-man team of "experts" to solve the legal questions involved in the new metropolitan government.[36] Nevertheless, what emerged on January 1, 1971 was essentially the governmental plan prepared by the Greater County Council Committee. In 1968, after necessary legal changes, both regional planning and water-sewer planning were temporarily assigned to the Municipal Association for City and County of Stockholm Regional Problems (KSL), which was already operating the mass transit system.

Later, in January 1971, these functions became part of the metropolitan government, along with the health care functions formerly administered by the city. More than one-third of the city's employees —17,000 of 48,000—became employees of the new Greater County Council, thus shifting more than 1.1 billion crowns in annual operating costs to the new metropolitan government. Most of these were persons employed in hospitals and other health-care facilities, which now became part of an integrated metropolitan system of public health facilities. Thus, while the new Stockholm metro was not, as of January 1971, doing all that Commissioner Mehr had proposed years before, in December of 1963, it was in fact a substantial organization, with large operating programs (mass transportation and health), important intelligence functions (regional and water planning), a large payroll, and its own tax base. This was a messy solution compared to the more comprehensive reforms that might have been,

35. *Utlåtande nr 217, 1966.*
36. For a sense of the complications involved, see *Utlåtande nr 414, 1968,* passim.

but the Greater Stockholm Council represented a considerable step away from what was.

THE EXTENT OF THE CHANGE

The extent of the change can be appreciated by comparing the Greater County Council to the other "metropolitan government" created in the same period: the housing queue administration (see Chapter III). Apart from the fact that the housing solution was forced upon the region by the national government, there are two crucial differences. First, the constituent units in the queue administration are municipalities. These are represented on the governing board, and their costs are apportioned as *municipalities*. In contrast, the constituent units of the Greater County Council are individual citizens residing in the Stockholm city and county region, with representation from districts related to, but not determined by, municipal boundaries and with costs apportioned to individual citizens.

Second, the Greater County Council enjoys its own taxing authority and is not dependent on taxes levied by member municipalities, as is the queue administration. Whereas the queue administration is nothing more than a contract between municipalities to perform a single service, the Greater County Council is a government acting directly upon citizens in a variety of functional areas. It also has the potential for adding other functions of regional significance. In short, the Greater County Council is a true metropolitan government, whose significance is virtually certain to increase over time.

MEHR'S MAJOR CONTRIBUTIONS

If one asks "Why this kind of change, at this time, in this way?" the answer, clearly, must begin with Hjalmar Mehr. Mehr's quick mind and wide reading had established him as a leading Marxist intellectual among his Social Democratic colleagues, and he considered himself an expert on metropolitan problems the world over. But in these events his primary talent was not intellectual. Nor was it, by any stretch of the imagination, politically innovative: plans similar to his had been debated for years and officially proposed as early as 1928.

Instead, Mehr's major contributions were political. He identified the moment of suburban political weakness as the moment to act. He saw the possibility of tying a major governmental change to transportation policy change, and he proposed a way to achieve that linkage. Above all, he possessed the manipulative skills necessary to negotiate change, and he persevered in applying those skills for the best

CHART 1

STOCKHOLM GREATER COUNTY COUNCIL ORGANIZATION

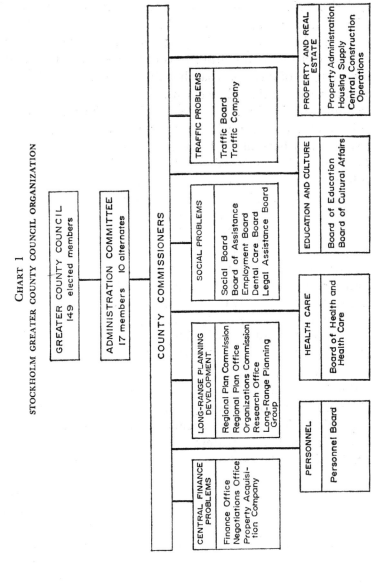

Adapted from *Information on the New County Council* (Stockholm: Greater County Council Committee, 1970). Note that this organization has probably been modified since January 1, 1971.

part of a decade. During this time Mehr maneuvered between sub-
urban-government representatives opposing any change at all, and
press or party forces demanding more sweeping reforms than he considered either tolerable or viable. What emerged was not what Mehr
originally desired. Neither did it represent anything that was desired
by any other politicians, most of whom had no clear-cut preferences
regarding system change when Mehr presented his. But the result *was*
something that metropolitan politicians could agree upon. Given the
continuing strength of city-suburban hostility, agreement itself must
be regarded as a substantial achievement.

Mehr would probably be the first to admit that he was only one
man working on a problem in which many others were involved. But
the alert reader will have noticed that few people except Mehr, his
party colleagues, leaders of the other political parties, and representatives of other governments, appear in the above recitation of events.
The reader may also wonder whether some other important actors
have been left out, and if so, why. Or he may have asked himself,
along the way, how it was possible for the leader of a city government
to literally give away assets paid for by his constituents, as part of a
deal which committed those same constituents to subsidizing residents of other municipalities. He may even wonder why the city was
interested in a Greater County Council, since the city lost its subways
and hospitals, with very little obvious return. Questions of this kind
cannot be answered simply by observing individuals in action, because action occurs in a structured setting which itself needs observation. Accordingly, attention now turns to a more careful consideration
of that setting in an effort to discover its contributions to the activities
described here. If he is not yet persuaded, the reader can assume that
Mehr, his political friends, and his enemies were all clever men. What
we need to understand is the pattern of constraints, and responses to
constraint, that shaped their actions.

Map 1 • STOCKHOLM COUNTY BEFORE 1971

STOCKHOLM COUNTY
(prior to reforms of 1971)

——·· — County boundary
— — — — Greater Stockholm boundary
——————— City of Stockholm boundary
——·—·— Commune boundary

1. SUNDBYBERG
2. SOLNA
3. DJURSHOLM
4. STOCKSUND
5. DANDERYD
6. SOLLENTUNA
7. SALTSJÖBADEN
8. NORRTÄLJE

125

MAP 2 · STOCKHOLM COUNTY AFTER 1971

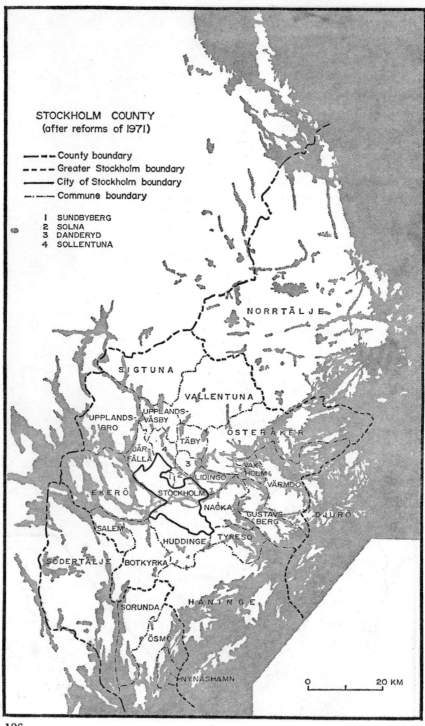

STOCKHOLM COUNTY
(after reforms of 1971)

━ ━ ━ County boundary
━ ━ ━ Greater Stockholm boundary
━━━ City of Stockholm boundary
━·━·━ Commune boundary

1 SUNDBYBERG
2 SOLNA
3 DANDERYD
4 SOLLENTUNA

NORRTÄLJE

SIGTUNA

VALLENTUNA

UPPLANDS-
BRO

UPPLANDS-
VÄSBY

ÖSTERÅKER

TÄBY

JÄR-
FÄLLA   4

3   VAX-
                HOLM
2 LIDINGÖ
EKERÖ   1   VÄRMDÖ
        STOCKHOLM
                      NACKA
SALEM   GUSTAVS-   DJURÖ
                            BERG
        HUDDINGE   TYRESÖ

SÖDERTÄLJE BOTKYRKA

                HANINGE
SORUNDA

ÖSMO

NYNÄSHAMN   0   20 KM

MAP 3 • LAND OWNED BY THE CITY OF STOCKHOLM

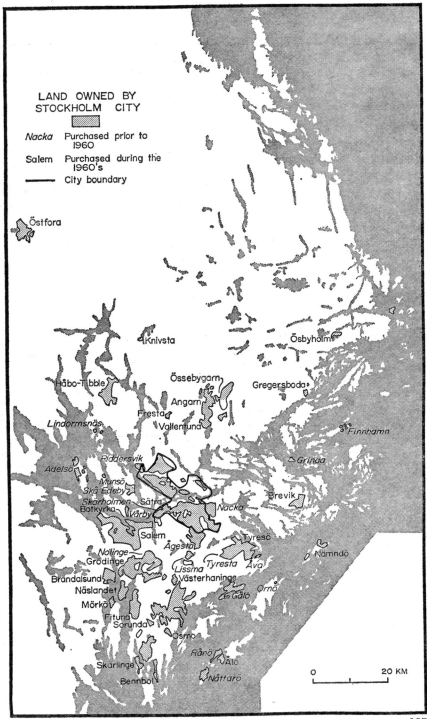

LAND OWNED BY
STOCKHOLM CITY

Nacka   Purchased prior to
1960
Salem   Purchased during the
1960's
———   City boundary

Östfora

Knivsta

Osbyholm

Håbo-Tibble

Össebygarn

Gregersboda

Angarn

Fresta

Finnhamn

Lindormsnäs

Vallentuna

Riddersvik

Grinda

Adelsö

Munsö

Skå Edeby

Brevik

Skärholmen

Sätra

Botkyrka

Nacka

Vårby

Salem

Tyresö

Ågesta

Nämndö

Nolinge

Grödinge

Lissma

Tyresta

Åva

Brandalsund

Västerhaninge

Näslandet

Ornö

Mörkö

Gålö

Fituna

Sorunda

Osmo

Rånö

Skärlinge

Ålö

Bennbol

Nåttarö

0   20 KM

MAP 4 • THE CITY OF STOCKHOLM AND ITS SUBURBS: MAIN ROADS, EXISTING
AND PROPOSED

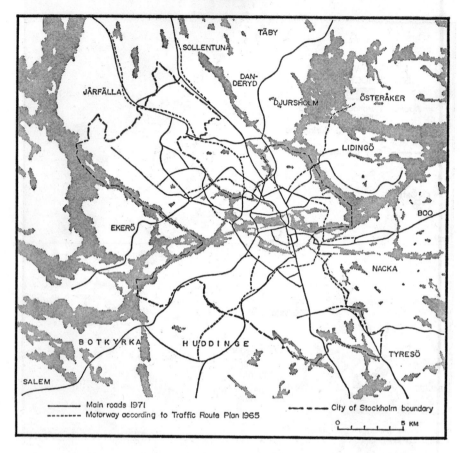

Main roads 1971
Motorway according to Traffic Route Plan 1965

City of Stockholm boundary

0   5 KM

MAP 5 • THE CITY OF STOCKHOLM AND ITS SUBURBS: RAIL TRANSIT, EXISTING
AND PROPOSED

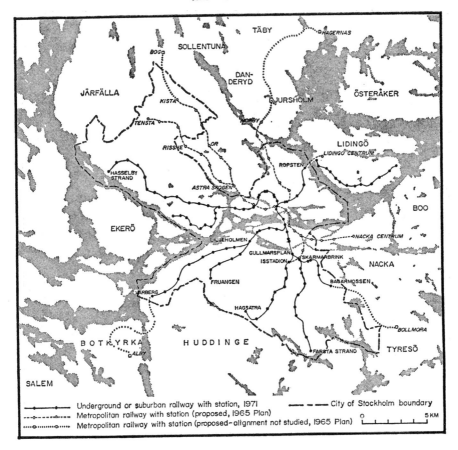

Underground or suburban railway with station, 1971
Metropolitan railway with station (proposed, 1965 Plan)
Metropolitan railway with station (proposed-alignment not studied, 1965 Plan)
City of Stockholm boundary

0   5 KM

Part Three

PATTERNS OF PARTICIPATION

CHAPTER V

THE STRUCTURAL BASES
OF SYSTEM PERFORMANCE

THE PERFORMANCE of urban Stockholm's political system since 1945 provides abundant justification for the widespread view that Stockholm is among the best-governed and best-organized urban environments in the world. In slightly more than two decades an additional 450,000 people have been accommodated in a series of new communities within and outside of the core city. Moreover, the city itself has been extensively renewed, and urban services ranging from water supply to one of the world's most impressive subway systems have been provided for a population that has grown constantly in sophistication, as well as number. Clearly enough, this political system has done more than simply survive: it has significantly altered its environment and has transformed itself in the process.

COMMON "EXPLANATIONS"

Observing these developments over nearly three decades allows us to reject some of the more common but inaccurate explanations for the success of Stockholm's politicians. One explanation, rooted in an indvidualistic model of causation, suggests that the Swedes are simply better planners than other people, implying that they have either better ideas or better technology, or both. Proponents of this view typically base it on the *physical characteristics* of portions of the Stockholm area, where the provision of housing has been coordinated with transportation and social services, where buildings serving various purposes have been placed in a rational relationship to one another,

133

and where the natural landscape has been used, rather than destroyed.[1] Many such areas can be found in and around Stockholm, but knowledgeable observers will look in vain for anything distinctively "Swedish" in the underlying ideas or technology. Stockholm politicians and administrators agree that all of their major planning concepts were borrowed from other countries, primarily Britain and the United States.[2] Similarly, nothing in the technology of Swedish urban development is particularly innovative. Swedish urban architecture is severely limited by a highly concentrated construction industry, using techniques that are common to all advanced nations.[3] Even if there were something new or different about these ideas and techniques, it would remain necessary to account for their implementation—a problem that necessarily calls for an examination of social structure.

On this point, one set of assertions has been widely accepted, although seldom examined. The population of both Sweden and Stockholm is so homogeneous, it is said, that deep political divisions are avoided and occasional conflicts easily resolved. In this view, high-quality performance results from the absence of conflict. Low conflict levels, in turn, are attributed to the relative absence of social cleavages.[4] At one level, of course, this set of assertions is true enough and is appealing as an "explanation." During most of the period after World War II Stockholm had no large concentrations of non-Swedes, and political difficulties arising from ethnic diversity never developed. Yet readers of the preceding chapters will probably agree that this explanation is entirely inadequate, largely because the links in

1. See David R. Godschalk, "Creating New Communities: A Symposium on Process and Product," and "Comparative New Community Design," *Journal of the American Institute of Planners*, Vol. XXXIII (1967), pp. 370–387.

2. Both former Commissioner Yngve Larsson and Göran Sidenbladh, Director of City Planning, have pointed this out in their contributions to *Stockholm Regional and City Planning* (Stockholm: City Planning Commission, 1964), pp. 8, 56.

3. The Swedish building industry is becoming increasingly concentrated into fewer and fewer large firms, each tied into one of the few large Swedish banks. Mert Kubu has recently pulled together information on these trends in his *Bostadspamparna* (Stockholm: Bonniers, 1971), pp. 21–36.

4. This is a view often put forth by Swedes themselves, no less than foreign observers. Used by Swedes, the argument invariably carries overtones of "success" and "progress," since it suggests that Sweden has achieved a greater degree of equalitarianism than other countries. Used by foreigners, the argument can often be bitterly critical. For a marvelously obtuse example of the former, see Kaj Björk, "Individualism and Collectivism," in M. Donald Hancock and Gideon Sjoberg, eds., *Politics in the Post-Welfare State* (New York: Columbia University Press, 1972), pp. 246–256. For an example of the latter, see Roland Huntford, *The New Totalitarians* (New York: Stein and Day, 1972).

its presumed causal chain have little or nothing to do with the real world.

To begin with, no one familiar with postwar Stockholm could associate effective performance with the absence of conflict. The preceding narrative demonstrated that conflict was endemic, difficult to manage, and occasionally beyond resolution (consider control over municipal housing policy). Indeed, fragmentation of public authority into twenty-nine constitutionally independent governmental units was a structural guarantee of recurring conflict. When fragmentation was accompanied by social class segregation in a fashion that united municipal boundaries with class boundaries, deeply rooted conflict was unavoidable. If ethnicity were the only basis for social cleavage, and if there were no other structural causes of political disagreement, the "homogeneity" argument might make sense. But the facts are otherwise, and they reduce that argument to one that explains nonexistent conditions by nonexistent causes. That the argument continues to be offered is, as I have suggested elsewhere, primarily due to the kinds of statements Stockholm officials are prepared to give to people who inquire only superficially into these matters.[5]

How, then, do we account for the remarkable performance of Stockholm's political system since the war? The detailed descriptions of policy-making behavior provided earlier offer an answer by revealing *patterns of action*, ranging from the comparatively obvious to the obscure. One obvious behavior pattern is limited participation, i.e., only a very few people were involved in these policy-making activities. Moreover the same people participated actively for long periods of time. Hjalmar Mehr, for example, began his political career in city hall in the 1930s. He became a City Commissioner in the late 1940s, and was still a Commissioner in 1971, when Stockholm's new metropolitan government came into existence.

Another pattern is what has been referred to as "opportunistic problem-solving." This pattern includes both a high level of flexibility toward past commitments and a willingness to experiment with public programs. A less obvious pattern is the reliance of Stockholm politicians on organizational, rather than public, settings as arenas for negotiation and conflict resolution. A more obscure, but im-

5. Unless an investigator knows the language, he or she will be unable to penetrate the largely self-congratulatory and formalistic views typically offered by Swedes for foreign consumption. Since few foreign observers take the time to learn the language, their understanding is bound to be limited by the "cover" statements I have touched on in my "Policy-Making and Political Culture in Sweden," *loc. cit.*

portant, pattern is the preference for unanimity as a foundation for policy or, to put it differently, the reluctance to impose policy where there is significant disagreement.

BEHAVIOR PATTERNS

These are termed *patterns* of behavior because they recur frequently. Because they occur repeatedly, we are justified in assuming thought patterns that cause different individuals to respond to similar events in similar ways. In short, we are justified in viewing these actions as products of *organized human interactions*—or, to repeat an earlier phrase, games. This view encourages us to explore the social bases of repetitive action. Instead of considering policy to be merely the responses of single individuals to situational stimuli, let us imagine that those individuals are players, connected in some determinate way to on-going games of various kinds. Let us assume that responses to policy-making situations are limited (1) by *constraints* imposed by other actors, and (2) by *satisfactions* they pursue in various kinds of social structures. Finally, let us assume that, given knowledge of these constraints and satisfactions, we might be able to predict both the styles of interaction and the resulting policies. These assumptions are not entirely valid, but they need not be wholly true to be useful. Let us see how far they take us toward a more satisfying explanation of urban Stockholm's political performance.[6]

PLAYERS IN THE GAME

GOVERNMENT OFFICIALS DOMINATE

Almost without exception, the actors involved in developing major urban policies for postwar Stockholm have been government officials. To be sure, there is plentiful evidence that the city's economic elite —particularly the banks—have been deeply involved in land purchase and speculation in ways that were more or less legitimate.[7] But it must be recalled that the city itself is the largest speculator in the region, owning virtually all of the undeveloped land inside city boundaries and nearly as much in the inner suburbs as the inner-

---

6. See below, Chapter VII, for a review and extension of these ideas.

7. Naturally, information of this kind is extraordinarily difficult to locate, although "everyone knows" that such activities are common. For a rare, published report of a transaction in which land assessed at 1.6 million crowns was sold to a consortium of Sweden's largest builders and banks for 27.5 million crowns, see "Viksjöaffären," *Järfälla-Bygden*, Årgång 32 (1963), pp. 3ff.

suburban governments themselves. Further, Stockholm owns nine times as much land in the outer suburban area as the outer suburban municipal governments.

MINOR ROLE: DEVELOPERS AND BANKERS

Compared to the city, the private developers are minor actors, with correspondingly limited capacity to influence future development through control of land. Nor can it be forgotten that primary responsibility for housing rests with city and suburban governments, not with the private developers and their banking allies. Although private power remains active and significant, the wielders of public power can beat the private interests at their own game.

A TAME PRESS

In addition to developers and bankers, the metropolitan press has occasionally taken an active part in generating issues (e.g., the Vårby crisis reported earlier). But the Stockholm press is crisis-oriented, vague, sporadic, and, like the press in other western cities, tame in its reporting of metropolitan politics. The lack of newspaper aggressiveness was emphasized not long ago by an enterprising reporter doing research for a book on Stockholm politics. Noting that Swedish law requires that all documents handled by public officials be available for public inspection, he pointed out that this requirement even extends to correspondence:

The letter files of city commissioners are common public documents. Anyone at all can ask to look at them in city hall or, in some cases, in the Stockholm city archives. *However, until now, no outsider is thought to have made such a request. . . .*[8]

The sources of newspaper timidity are varied, ranging from the natural tendency of a capital city press to concentrate on national affairs, to the affiliation of the metropolitan press with party organizations—a linkage that discourages incisive criticism of public actions involving party colleagues.[9] Moreover, newspaper reporters, like other citizens, traditionally have accorded city officials all the respect and deference that Swedish society gives "government experts." This

8. Kubu, *Det politiska spelet i stadshuset* (Stockholm: Almqvist & Wiksell, 1968), p. 8. My italics.

9. Recall, too, that the press is closely linked to the formal governing institutions. Cunningham, *op. cit.*, reports that there were eight journalists on the 1966–70 Council, and nine journalists on various city Boards.

TABLE 7

Ownership of Undeveloped Land, Stockholm Region (1967 Data)
(Hectares)

Location	Area	Total Land—Owner					
		City	Other municipalities	Church and university	National government	Public housing companies	Private developers
City	18,600	2,400	14,800		200		100
Inner suburbs	127,300	11,700	1,700	3,300	9,600	600	4,000
Outer suburbs	133,500	14,700	1,600	3,400	13,300	800	2,300
County towns	291,300	9,700	5,900	7,000	20,400	900	3,400
Totals	570,700	38,500	22,300	13,700	43,500	2,300	9,800

Source: Storlandstingskommittén, *Regionalt Bostadsbygge* (Stockholm, 1968), p. 67.

discourages reporters from probing, and enables officials to use the newspapers for their own purposes.[10]

CITIZEN PASSIVITY

Regardless of the sources of newspaper timidity the consequences have been clear, beginning with the extraordinary passivity of the Stockholm population. Because newspaper coverage has been both intermittent and vague, citizens have had few "handles" to grasp in dealing with urban development issues. Lacking such leverage, citizen groups common in other areas—leagues of women voters, *ad hoc* groups organized around issues, neighborhood councils, etc.—simply have not emerged. Only after 1968, when Stockholm's leading newspaper, *Dagens Nyheter*, began a campaign against city planning policies by denouncing Skärholmen, the newest of the "new suburbs," did citizen organizations begin to form.[11] Hjalmar Mehr, although hardly a neutral observer in such matters, noticed the difference:

the planning questions for these neighborhoods (Sätra, Vårby, Bredäng and Skärholmen) were reviewed plan after plan, the site plan, area plan, general plan, neighborhood plan, successively during the whole period, in the city council, with public exhibitions for them all. Swedish Housing, Inc. [the prime developer] made two films and invited the press: not even a cat came. We sent out press material that was not published by the press and invited people to discussions: not a single person was interested in any of this during these past years. Afterwards the opening [of Skärholmen] was a huge success with 100,000 people, and a couple of days after that, the press campaign began.[12]

For virtually the entire postwar period, then, public officials dominated urban development policy-making, beating the economic elite at its own game, without significant hindrance from either a timid press or a compliant citizenry. Understanding Stockholm's urban policies thus requires an understanding of the forces shaping the behavior of this official elite.

10. Although I know of no systematic study, my impression (based on two years of careful reading) is that the vast majority of local stories consist primarily of quotations from official handouts.

11. For a review of these organizations and their origins, see Sören Häggroth, "Byalag m.m. i Stockholm 1968–1969" (unpublished seminar paper, Stockholm University, 1971).

12. Quoted in Nordal Åkerman, *Apparaten Sverige* (Stockholm: Wahlström & Widstrand, 1970), pp. 120–121.

THREE CHARACTERISTICS

Three structural characteristics noted earlier are worth repeating here. First is the fragmentation of public authority into twenty-nine separate municipal units in the Stockholm region (inner and outer suburbs included). Second is the constitutional independence of each of these units. Third is the influence of national political parties and national issues on local electoral campaigns. Fragmentation gave potential access to as many as twenty-nine different sets of local participants, and municipal independence was a guarantee that regional issues could only be settled by negotiation. But the core policy-making group was much smaller than these characteristics suggest, largely because of the national-local linkage.

THE NATIONAL-LOCAL LINKAGE

In the suburbs, the national-local linkage helped to insure long tenure for local party leaders, providing a remarkable degree of political continuity. Because candidates for local office ran on national party tickets, local election results reflected national programs and issues far more than local problems. Repeated Social Democratic party victories at the national level thus helped to solidify socialist control of most suburban communities—at least until 1966. Continuity, in turn, had two further consequences. On one hand, single party individuals were permitted to establish tight control over local party organizations, thereby reducing the potential pool of participants in metropolitan political negotiations. On the other hand, these suburban leaders were able to ignore demands from local constituents if they so desired. Instead of ensuring responsiveness, the nationalized electoral mechanism created and maintained suburban political organizations whose leaders were relatively free from localized political constraints.

The City of Stockholm also developed hierarchical control without significant local electoral constraint, but did so through different mechanisms. A more heterogeneous city population supported more party competition for control of the 100-member City Council. If we divide the five parties into two groups—those of the left (Social Democrats and Communists) and the parties of the right, or "bourgeois" block (Liberals, Conservatives, Center)—we see in Table 8 that each major bloc has won half of the elections since 1950. It thus appears that in evenly balanced Stockholm, unlike the one-party suburbs, slight shifts in support for the dominant socialist party are enough

TABLE 8

Distribution of the 100 Seats in the Stockholm City Council
By Party, 1950–1970

	1950	1954	1958	1962	1966	1970
Social Democratic	43	41	45	49	38	46
Liberal	35	31	20	23	24	22
Conservative	17	20	29	23	24	16
Center	—	—	—	—	4	10
Communist	5	8	6	5	10	7

Source: Stig Hadenius, Björn Molin, och Hans Wieslander, *Sverige efter 1900* (Stockholm: Bokförlaget Aldus/Bonniers, 1972), p. 296.

to bring about changes in party control of the local governmental machinery.

It does not follow, however, that the politicians in control of the city apparatus have been any more responsive to the local electorate than their suburban colleagues. City politicians themselves recognize that national rather than local issues determine their constituents' votes. In 1958 and 1962 the deciding issue was the national supplementary pension program. In 1966 it was probably a combination of price increases and housing policy. The 1968 invasion of Czechoslovakia created another form of national issue dominance in the 1970 election. These issues, rather than anything done by Stockholm politicians in planning or transportation policy, have determined winners and losers in local elections.[13]

Nor does it follow from the fact of political change that the city party organizations are any less hierarchically ordered than their suburban counterparts. Council seats are allocated in terms of total votes cast *for each party,* not for each individual. The electoral system thus gives party leaders a powerful mechanism of control, for it is the leaders who determine the names that will appear on the respective party lists. Each party typically nominates a somewhat larger number of candidates than the proportion of the total vote it expects to win. Because the expected vote for a party is reasonably predictable at any given time, positioning a candidate higher or lower on the party list is equivalent to electing or not electing him. It is easy enough to see what this system means for the individual councilman. In order to be elected, he must be granted a position on a list made

13. Several city politicians offered these judgments in conversations with the author.

up by the local party leader. In order to stay in office, he must persuade the same party leader to keep his name on succeeding electoral lists. The incentive for going along with the party leader is thus a powerful one, and is reflected in the rigid party discipline enforced in Council voting.[14]

In both city and suburb, then, the national electoral linkage has limited the ability of local electorates to enforce their preferences on local office-holders. As long as most suburbs were one-class communities, that link also solidified the tenure of one-party, hierarchically organized suburban governments. One-party control could not be maintained in the city, but hierarchy was nevertheless maintained through an electoral mechanism that gave a few party leaders control over the political fate of their subordinates. Domination of urban policy-making by a tiny governmental elite, therefore, has been a function of both the absence of competing centers of influence, and the absence of local electoral constraints. How little constrained these officials have been can be best appreciated by considering some of the more obvious forms and customs of policy-making in the city.

THE POLICY PROCESS IN STOCKHOLM

Control of the Stockholm City Council is the prize for which political parties compete, because it gives them the authority to control what the city does. Nevertheless, council activities are rarely more than perfunctory. Relatively few issues cause party divisions, and those that do are settled off the Council floor, in party caucuses or by party leaders. Voting on such issues is totally predetermined by party strength on the Council. The sometimes lengthy debates that often precede such votes would be surprising were it not for the presence of a few newspaper reporters in the otherwise vacant Council chamber, the interest of party leaders in "making a record," or the interest of the ambitious in showing how well they can play the highly stylized game of Swedish "debate." [15]

Similarly, the activities of the city's Executive Board (*Stadskollegiet*), a 12-member body appointed by the Council from among its

14. In the elm-tree dispute, discussed below (Chapter VII), all Social Democratic Council members were required to support the leadership, despite very strong sympathies against the leadership position among a substantial party minority.

15. Debating conventions in Sweden discourage direct confrontations between opponents by requiring those wishing to speak on an issue to register in advance with the chairman of the Council. Most contributions are thus prepared speeches, with only rare opportunities for question-and-answer exchanges.

members, are also usually perfunctory.[16] Though the board is responsible for supervising the implementation of all Council decisions, in fact it does little more than act as a conduit between another 9-member body, the Board of Commissioners, and the Council itself. Since commissioners develop all proposals to be acted upon by Council, this is not an insignificant function. But the commissioners, not the Executive Board members, sit at the center of power in Stockholm.

THE POWER OF THE COMMISSIONERS

The power of Stockholm city commissioners arises from the combination of resources at their disposal. First of all, they enjoy an unusually high level of prestige, grounded in the Stockholm "tradition" of high-quality public service. That prestige helps to justify salaries (135,000 crowns) that easily rank among the highest public salaries in Sweden. It is also reflected in impressive suites of offices, numerous staff assistants, and expense accounts to defray the costs of their various "official" duties. All these trappings of prestige give tangible evidence that commissioners truly are important men.

Commissioners also have direct access to the considerable resources of the city bureaucracy. The day-to-day work of city government— cleaning the streets, providing water, running the schools, etc.—is accomplished by operating agencies responsible to one of thirty-six different Administrative Boards. Each board sets policy in its area of responsibility and hires a professional civil servant—a *Direktör*—to administer that policy. Within established policy guidelines a Stockholm *Direktör* enjoys great freedom to utilize his agency subordinates as he sees fit. In setting policy, on the other hand, the Board has ultimate authority—and each Administrative Board is chaired by one of the nine city commissioners.

Placing a commissioner in charge of all administrative boards is partly a coordinating device: the thirty-six separate boards are grouped into nine Divisions (*rotlar* in Swedish), each headed by a commissioner. The commissioner thus provides a direct link to several agencies operating in the same functional area. At one point, for example, the Commissioner for Greater Stockholm Affairs (that is, head of the Greater Stockholm Division) was chairman of the Building Board, the Housing Commission, the General Planning Committee and the Greater Stockholm Planning Board.

If a commissioner does his job well, the activities of his several

16. For a brief discussion, see Calmfors, *et al., op. cit.,* pp. 35–36.

CHART 2

CITY OF STOCKHOLM ORGANIZATION

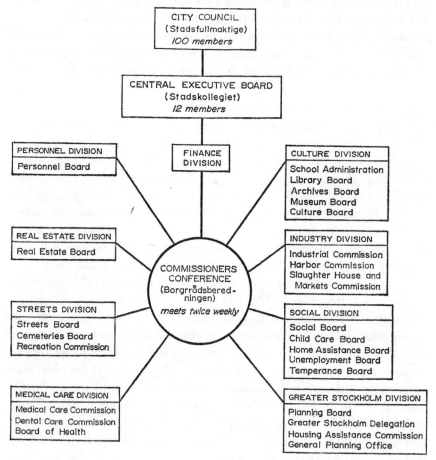

Adapted from Mert Kubu, *Det politiska spelet i Stadshuset* (Stockholm: Almqvist & Wiksell, 1968), p. 17, and Sjalvstyrelsentredningen, "Rapport" (Stockholm, 1970), Mimeographed.

agencies ought to be carried on with greater efficiency, and less conflict. But note that the strongest link here is between the commissioner and the *Direktör,* both of whom are full-time officials. Moreover, each of these officials "needs" the other in order to function well. A close relationship between commissioners and their several chief administrators is thus built into the structure of Stockholm city government, giving each commissioner direct and continuing access to the intellectual and other skills of a large bureaucracy.

Finally, commissioners command significant political resources. Partly because of the built-in financial and administrative resources, it is customary for the leaders of local party organizations to become commissioners, particularly in the more "weighty" divisions. The Finance Division, with its control over the budgets of all other divisions and boards, is by far the most weighty of the divisions; hence, the leader of the party securing the most votes in the City Council election becomes Finance Commissioner. Leaders of the other major party groups, in turn, compete for the other major divisions: real estate, streets and traffic, culture (which includes the school board), and, increasingly, the Greater Stockholm Division. The remaining commissionerships are distributed to other leading party figures, in proportion to party vote totals. All commissioners are thus politically potent, but the party leader commissoners, with their control over blocks of votes in the Council, as well as access to administrative expertise, are very powerful figures indeed.

LONG TENURE

This method of selecting commissioners means that electoral shifts normally produce little if any change in top-level personnel. Party leadership is a long-term assignment in Stockholm politics. When party vote totals change, the party leader does not *lose* his official job —he merely *changes* it to one that more accurately reflects the most recent vote totals. Consider again the example of Hjalmar Mehr who, with socialist control of the Council, became Commissioner for Personnel Affairs (the least important of the divisions) in 1948. When the bourgeois parties won the 1950 election, Mehr became Social Affairs Commissioner, and stayed in that position when the bourgeois groups won again in 1954. The socialist victory of 1958 promoted Mehr to Finance Commissioner, and the 1962 win kept him in that post. After the 1966 loss he exchanged jobs with Liberal Real Estate Commissioner P.-O. Hanson, and changed back again in 1970, when the socialists won again.

To be sure, Mehr had a comparatively long tenure as commissioner, but others have served for even longer periods. Indeed, the average tenure for *all* persons who have been commissioners since the position was created exceeds ten years.[17] During his tenure, a commissioner deals with a variety of major responsibilities in a system that *circulates* the city's political elite but seldom changes it. Perhaps the most significant consequence produced by this game of political chairs is that, in addition to their other resources, commissioners normally possess the indispensable one: experience.[18]

ROLE IN HANDLING ISSUES

Assigned direct responsibilities for important municipal services, and commanding blocks of votes in the Council, commissioners can exert great influence over the processes of generating and resolving issues. With few exceptions, issues arise through the normal deliberations of the administration board, in the course of considering recommendations submitted by their civil servants.[19] Board membership, like the commissioner selection process, is based on proportional representation of all parties, according to their electoral strength. Controversial issues or those the parties wish to make controversial, are thrashed out as this level, where party positions are developed and asserted. Depending on the kind of relationship he has with his administrative chief, a commissioner can exert considerable control over the number and kinds of issues that arise, and also determine whether such issues become topics of partisan controversy. At the very least, a commissioner knows what questions are likely to be raised in his bailiwick and can keep his party colleagues and fellow commissioners informed.

On matters requiring Council action, positions taken by the various boards are formalized in written proposals, complete with argumentation, for submission to the Council. The argument always includes statements of any minority opinions, as well as positions taken by the various party groups. Instead of going directly to Council, these proposals are submitted to the "Board of Commissioners," at

17. Names and tenure of all former Commissioners are available in *Stockholms Kommunalkalender* (Stockholm: Stockholms Stadskansli, 1970), p. 29.

18. From 1920, when the position was created, to 1970, only 39 people served as commissioner. *Ibid.*, pp. 28–29.

19. This is a conclusion offered to the author in interviews with present and former commissioners, and confirmed by observation of recent politics. See also Kubu, *Det politiska spelet i Stadshuset* (Stockholm: Almqvist & Wiksell, 1968), p. 53.

a brief, twice-weekly meeting of all nine commissioners. As a group, the commissioners then decide whether and how to submit a proposal to council. Their formal decision and accompanying report, complete with statements from minority party representatives if necessary, is then submitted to the Executive Board for transmission to Council.[20] Although this process seems weighty and complex, reality is more simple. Thus, once party positions are determined during board deliberations, a final policy decision has, in fact, been made. Subsequent activities, particularly those in Council, are sheer formalities.

Several characteristics of these issue-generating and issue-resolving procedures deserve special emphasis. First, there is direct and immediate involvement of high-level administrators in the process of *defining* issues, no less than proposing solutions. Most board proposals are initiated by the chief administrators, but even when a party group initiates an idea, it is expected that the administrative staff will research the proposal and give the board a plan of action signed by the *Direktör*.[21] Moreover, since the city's administrators form a highly qualified and very well-paid elite, with necessarily close relationships to the political elite, opportunities for administrator influence are enormous (a point to which we will return shortly).

Second, the commissioners, *as a group,* are insulated from the worst heat of political controversies. Because issues are normally first raised in the administrative boards, commissioners can argue very strongly for a point of view without antagonizing their fellow commissioners.[22] By the time a Board proposal is ready for submission to the Board of Commissioners, all arguments have been stated and dealt with, and party positions clarified. Commissioners, therefore, can more easily "agree to disagree," if they have to, without the emotional involvement often generated by heated political argument. Similarly, they can more readily discover bases for agreement, if they exist. This is not to suggest that Stockholm commissioners cannot stand the heat of the political kitchen; only that they work in a two-story kitchen, with the stoves one floor below.

Finally, it is important to note an unwritten rule of the City Coun-

20. A more formal view of these procedures is available in Calmfors, *et al., op. cit.,* pp. 38–54.

21. On the influence of administrators, see *ibid.* For the broad statements of administrative authority available to these officials, see annual copies of *Stockholms Kommunalkalendar.*

22. Unless, of course, a fellow commissioner is also a member of the Board.

cil that affects both the policy process and the role of commissioners: no Council member may question or criticize any proposal put forward by a board of which he or she is a member.[23] Board members are entitled to argue as long and as hard as they wish during board deliberations. But once a proposal has been accepted, all members are assumed to support it, unless they specifically withhold support, in writing. Normally support is withheld only in cases of partisan opposition, by minority party members.

When opposition does not exist—which is most of the time—the rule reduces the boundaries of open debate in the Council, limits the amount of issue-related information made available to the public, and above all, strengthens the commissioners, who need anticipate no further public difficulty once an acceptable board decision has been made. Combined with party discipline and the quite intimidating character of board proposals—on major matters they may number hundreds of pages, filled with charts, statistics, and other esoterica guaranteed to frighten an unknowing councilman—this rule of custom permits the clever commissioner to create a little monarchy for himself.

THE "LITTLE MONARCHIES"

From the point of view of efficient administration, the "little monarchies" that govern the city have several advantages. Direct involvement of politicians and administrators in each other's work contributes to more informed political debate and to a more responsive bureaucracy. Moreover, at its best the system embodies the sensitivity of a decentralized organizational weapon. Commissioners have their own individual responsibilities, which they are expected to carry out without interference from colleagues. But proposals for action by the Council are in fact a product of the Board of Commissioners. Proposals from individual commissioners that move forward thus take on the weight, and carry the impact, of recommendations by a unified group of city leaders. The political and administrative advantages of a system that promotes top-level unity surely help to account for the city's success in dealing with other governments.

There are also other, more subtle aspects of the system, beginning with the formal (and often real) involvement of each commissioner in the work of his colleagues. As noted, proposals from individual commissioners must be approved by all, before going on to Council.

23. Kubu, *Det politiska spelet i Stadshuset* (Stockholm: Almqvist & Wiksell, 1968), pp. 45–46.

Thus the other commissioners know a good deal about what their colleagues are doing. Over time, that knowledge helps build a community feeling that each commissioner has a stake in the good performance of his colleagues. If we recall that most matters handled by the Board of Commissioners are not controversial, and that the system is designed to shield commissioners from the most heated partisan controversies, we can begin to appreciate how the commissioners' involvement in each other's work creates incentives for cooperative behavior. These are men working together to solve difficult administrative problems, who often need and get each other's advice, and who have not been required to exchange the ultimate political insult. Instead, at this level, partisan conflict is ritualized: it is reflected in the Board reports, but it does not affect the Board's work. Here, as in other Swedish organizations, the participants would rather agree than fight.

The little monarchs of Stockholm are thus remarkably free from localized constraints. The scope of government services is large enough to permit the energetic city commissioners easily to overshadow private interests in the competition for power. Commissioners win or lose elections for reasons that have little to do with local issues. They remain in office for long periods of time, regardless of local electoral outcomes. And they operate in a system that gives them enormous resources of status, money and expertise, while simultaneously shielding them from the lowest forms of political in-fighting.

CITY-NATIONAL INTEGRATION

A system that allocates vast political resources to a tiny group of men, while simultaneously removing most local constraints on their behavior, appears to constitute an open invitation to corruption or other forms of official misbehavior. Yet evidence of such misbehavior is virtually nonexistent. Why? The answer is complicated, but it begins with the total integration of city and national politics.

As the capital city, Stockholm and its government are political issues themselves, and are treated as such. For example, when the military finally released its training ground, *Järvafältet,* to local officials for the construction of more housing, the Prime Minister made the public announcement, rather than a local politician. Later, when public tastes appeared to have changed, national party leaders led a campaign against city planning policies, debating the issue more often and with more fury in the national parliament than in the City Council. During all of his years as Foreign Minister, Torsten Nilsson retained the chairmanship of the Stockholm Social Democratic party organization, and often gave an annual address to that organization— on foreign policy! His successor, Krister Wickman, was at one time seriously considered as a replacement for a city commissioner who had allowed newspaper criticism of city planning policies to get out of hand. A former leader of the national-level Conservative party began his career as Secretary to City Commissioner Gösta Agrenius. During his quarter century as commissioner, Agrenius periodically made pronouncements on foreign policy. Hjalmar Mehr himself was selected as local party leader by the Prime Minister—but only after promising loyalty should the Prime Minister have decided to send over a Member of Parliament to assume control of the city organization.[24]

The integration of city and nation is not, therefore, simply a matter of easy and frequent interaction by administrators. National and local politicians also interact continuously because Stockholm represents the nation's largest block of voters. Accordingly, the way Stockholm is governed is a matter of some importance in determining national electoral outcomes. These interactions form an important constraint on the actions of local politicians, providing a major criterion against which to test any proposed policy change, i.e., the effect of policy on national party support. Since the task of predicting the effects of policy proposals on national electoral support borders on the impossible, local politicians need other, less ambiguous guidelines. It is convenient to think of such guidelines as "role orientations" and to ask: what orientations appear to guide the actions of a tiny and powerful elite, relatively free from localized constraints, but tightly integrated into the national governmental system?

ON BEING A COMMISSIONER: THE NORMATIVE GLUE OF A NATIONALIZED ELITE

At the outset it is important to bear in mind what the commissioners actually do. Each of them has significant administrative and policy-making responsibilities, through chairmanship of from two to eight administrative boards. Commissioners who are also leaders of the local party groups have those additional political responsibilities. This summary vastly understates the workload of a commissioner, however, for it omits a variety of other local organizations in whose activities he must participate—including the more than 100 private

24. All the events in the above paragraph are reported in Kubu, *ibid., passim.*

TABLE 9

Commissioner Membership in Public Organizations, 1950, 1960, and 1969

	1950	1960	1969
Number of commissioners	8	9	9
Number of memberships: Range	11–24	9–24	12–30
Average number of memberships per commissioner	17	18	22

Source: *Stockholms Kommunalkalender 1951, 1961, 1970.*

companies owned by the City of Stockholm. A simple tabulation of the number of formal appointments to public bodies (Table 9) can suggest the dimensions of the problem. Typically, a commissioner is a member of some fifteen to twenty decision-making bodies, and the number can go as high as thirty.

One commissioner recently revealed another dimension of the problem when he pointed out that each day he receives some four- to five-hundred pages of official paper: memos, reports, proposals, etc.[25]

A MULTITUDE OF MATTERS

Gösta Agrenius, recently retired after twenty-one years as a commissioner, aptly described his work in a letter of recommendation for his secretary, S-G. Åstrand:

What characterizes the job of commissioner above all is the multitude and changing nature of the questions and matters he must deal with. These involve problems of administrative, economic and technical nature in the Division's basic areas of responsibility: electric works, gas and water supply, harbor matters, together with slaughterhouses and market places [Agrenius was Commissioner of Industrial Affairs]. During the greater portion of Mr. Åstrand's period of employment legal and police matters were also included in the Division. Through my position as chairman of the City Council Conservative Party group, and during part of my time as chairman of the Stockholm area Conservative Party a considerable amount of purely political work was added. This involves covering virtually everything that comes under municipal responsibility, reviewing and taking initiatives in the whole field of municipal activities.

The rhythm of work is also particularly varied. A very few more quiet periods are followed by hectic periods, when rapid statements of position are demanded and the burden of work very high.[26]

25. Lars-Erik Klason, "Communikation i kommunala frågor" (unpublished dissertation, Stockholm University, 1970), p. 160.
26. Kubu, *op. cit.*, p. 59, provides this long quote from Agrenius's letter.

Agrenius's comments suggest the variety of different concerns that city commissioners must deal with, often in a very short period of time. Among other things, this means that a commissioner spends most of his time attending meetings, chairing meetings of his administrative boards, or discussing problems with his colleagues, usually by telephone. Without highly developed verbal skills, a commissioner could not function at all. He could not function *effectively* unless he combined those skills with a quick mind and the ability to be persuasive in small and large groups alike. A commissioner spends less time (roughly 15 per cent) than might be imagined in political ceremonies, such as school openings or bridge dedications, and rarely has time to meet ordinary citizens on an individual basis. His interactions are almost entirely confined to that small circle of politicians and administrators who participate in policy-making. His special business is seeing to it that decisions are made by the appropriate bodies, at the appropriate times.

COMMISSIONERS AND ADMINISTRATORS

Clearly enough, with fifteen to twenty-five different bodies to attend to, some of which will require active leadership in situations of potential conflict, no commissioner is able to achieve mastery of administrative or political detail. To keep track of appointments, arrange meetings, draft speeches, and take care of other necessary political leg-work, a commissioner is heavily dependent on his administrative assistant—typically a bright young man recently out of the Stockholm School of Social Work and Public Administration.[27] From a policy point of view, he is even more dependent on the chief administrators of the various boards he chairs. This, of course, is the single most important source of administrator influence. The administrative heads command all the information a commissioner needs to make policy decisions, but which, with his multitude of obligations, he cannot hope to get. Moreover, a commissioner cannot choose to deal or to not deal with a particular *Direktör:* administrative heads are civil servants, possessing permanent tenure and legally specified obligations to participate in the preparation of policy proposals. At this level, as well as at the national level, the structural independence of administrators breeds a psychological independence. In a real sense

27. Historically, this school, part of the University of Stockholm, has had close relationships with a variety of city agencies, creating something of an "old boy" network for securing administrative positions.

a commissioner needs his administrative chief more then the chief needs the commissioner—and both parties know it.[28]

These conditions structure the "special" relationship between commissioners and their administrative heads, although that relationship is masked in fairly conventional terms. Commissioners are all strong party men, but they begin with the presumption that they are responsible to the "city as a whole," and are most concerned with solving problems in a way that will benefit the entire city.[29] This is an easy enough assumption to make in the Stockholm context, as few questions generate party conflict among members of the multiparty boards. Having assumed the existence of a "city-wide" interest, commissioners typically go on to assert their special obligation to define it in particular cases: they develop policies and arrange to have them accepted by other city organs. That is a political responsibility, but it is not partisan. Neither is it administrative or technical—those more mundane tasks are willingly allocated by the commissioners to their chief administrators. The commissioners deal with policy; implementation is left to administrative heads. Dr. Yngve Larsson, who made important contributions to the city's future during twenty-two years as commissioner, spoke for most of his colleagues when he described his job:

I was, more or less, a political boss, perhaps not in a political party sense, but I was responsible to the city council. The city council is a political body and the boss, the political boss, ought not to mix in [with] the details of the office [in his case, the City Planning Department]. . . . The director must feel that he is responsible for the technical side of the work. With regard to the big ideas there was of course much debate between myself and the director.[30]

Or, as one of Larsson's successors said to a candidate for an administrative position: "I'll take care of the politics—you take care of the job." [31]

28. For a discussion of the "independence" of national-level administrators, see Thomas J. Anton, Claes Linde, and Anders Mellbourn, "Bureaucrats in Politics: A Profile of the Swedish Administrative Elite." Paper delivered at the Sixty-second Annual Meeting of the Society for the Advancement of Scandinavian Study, New York, May, 1972.

29. Klason, op. cit., p. 158.

30. Pass, op. cit., p. 199.

31. Interview, Direktör K-G. Paulsson.

POLITICS—ADMINISTRATION

The administrative heads also accept this politics-administration dichotomy willingly, adding only an occasional assertion of professionalism which strengthens their sense of independence. According to one *Direktör* who was interviewed recently, all chief administrators should operate with a three-part "code of honor." First, an administrator should always tell the truth, including the truth about his own uncertainties or lack of knowledge. Failure to speak honestly or attempts to conceal his own uncertainty ultimately produce a loss of confidence in the administrator and destroy his effectiveness. Second, an administrator should never allow his political sympathies or antipathies to color the picture he gives of present or future reality. An administrator is perfectly free to be as much of an active partisan as he likes outside the job. But if he ever becomes identified on the job as a centrist or a conservative or a communist, "then his possibilities of bringing the board he serves to a decision are considerably worsened, and he can no longer function as Direktör in any case." Third, "You work for the entire board. You do not work for the chairman (a commissioner), even though you may have strong sympathies for the political views he represents." [32]

Superficially, these are wholly conventional views: politicians will handle policies and partisanship, while administrators will administer and provide professionally neutral advice on policy matters, not to individual politicians, but to the entire board. Both sides of this relationship accept these platitudes, so in a sense they are in fact operative. What is hidden, however, is the extent to which administrators may dominate policy by shaping the points of view of commissioners. Joakim Garpe, for example, has argued that Stockholm is governed best, and the commissioners operate best, when each has "come to an agreement" with his administrators, based on full appreciation of each other's points of view. A good relationship with his administrator gives a commissioner access to expert information, and also permits him to *avoid disagreements* in board meetings. Careful formulation of agenda, anticipation of possible disagreements, and advance preparation of responses to possible conflicts enable a commissioner to exert considerable influence over his board's decision processes and policy products.

32. Quotations taken from interview transcript. Respondent in this case was promised anonymity. See note 28, above, for a description of the study from which this transcript was taken.

Moreover, when a commissioner offers a major proposal, advance preparation of supporting arguments can be persuasive, particularly if the administrative chief concurs. A good commissioner-administrator relationship, then, enables this little coalition to dominate board activities. A bad relationship, on the other hand, can produce public conflict and seriously impair the board's ability to reach decisions.[33] The development of such a situation would undermine confidence in the competence of both commissioner and administrator. Both parties therefore have powerful incentives for avoiding such conflict. In this effort an administrator necessarily develops close ties to the commissioner.

But on whose terms is this relationship built? Partisanship is rejected by the politicians as unworthy, and by the administrators as irrelevant. Yet there is a compelling need to rationalize choices and policies. Given that need, there is virtually no alternative to the terms propounded by the administrators. Over time, politicians thus learn the jargon of administrative specialization. From the practice of rationalizing choice, they form the habit of thinking in administrative terms: means-ends relationships, efficiency, functionality.

ADMINISTRATOR INFLUENCE

In this context, administrator influence in Stockholm politics means far more than control over information and expertise. Forced to seek nonembarrassing criteria of choice, but limited by their own multitude of responsibilities, city politicians move in the direction of least resistance by learning to think in administrative terms. The framework within which issues are posed and solutions offered is itself a product of administrative professionalism. Within such a framework some issues—i.e., the aesthetic quality of the city—are difficult to raise. Others, such as governmental elitism, never get raised at all. But the framework remains useful to commissioners in ways that can be best understood by looking at a commissioner's relationships with his fellow commissioners.

COMMISSIONERS' INTERACTIONS

Three norms guide the interactions among commissioners. The first is *independence:* each commissioner is expected to handle activities falling within his division without help or interference from other commissioners. Indeed, commissioners would be affronted at

33. Interview, former Commissioner Joakim Garpe.

the very suggestion that they needed assistance from their colleagues. The norm of independence is manifested in commissioner actions; it is reinforced, over time, by recruitment practices. While a commissioner is usually not able to select his own administrative heads, he can select a personal staff and, given sufficient tenure, he will eventually have a say in a considerable number of positions.

Most incumbent commissioners have had long tenure, with the result that "their" people are found in sensitive positions throughout the city bureaucracy. For that matter, most incumbent commissioners were themselves brought into city employment through such a favored relationship with a senior city official.[34] More often than not this recruitment pattern produces technically competent officials, but personal loyalty, rather than qualification *per se,* is the primary criterion of selection. Thus each of the city's "little monarchs" has his own cadre of "vassals" to provide an additional network of information and political support, if necessary. The structure is almost feudal in character, helping to maintain the independence of each commissioner from collegial interference.

The second norm is *consultation:* each commissioner is expected to inform and consult the appropriate colleague when he undertakes action that is related to that colleague's domain of responsibility. If this is not done, the city will often appear to be acting at cross purposes, or wastefully, or both. With so many city agencies and companies distributed among commissioners in no very rational pattern, it is inevitable that commissioners' paths will cross.[35] When they do, the consultation norm provides a useful counterweight to the norm of independence. The strength of the consultation norm is reflected in the Vårby affair, described earlier, when the entire coalition system was threatened by the failure of a planning commissioner to inform a real estate commissioner about a piece of land to be annexed to the city. No one disputed the desirability of the annexation, but even the leaders of the plot admitted a serious breach of accepted procedure. Perhaps it was this recognition that led one of them to argue later that "The most important quality a commissioner must have is the capacity to cooperate." [36]

There is a third major norm, more diffuse but nevertheless important: *protect the institution.* Commissioners recognize that they

34. See Kubu, *op. cit.,* pp. 52–100, for some evidence.
35. For example, see *ibid.,* pp. 253–255.
36. Interview, Commissioner Inge Hörlén.

occupy a very special place in the Stockholm system and are sensitive to the desirability of maintaining that special position. Structurally insulated from the most intense partisan conflicts, commissioners hesitate to criticize their colleagues publicly, and are very reluctant to do so in overly harsh terms. After all, these are men with whom they will have to live and work for some considerable time. That knowledge alone bars the bitterest forms of criticism, even in private.

LIMITING PUBLIC CONFLICT

A more important consideration is the potential impact of public conflict on the chosen status of commissioners. A serious conflict can cast doubt on the existence of an administratively "best" road to the city's interest. If a commissioner has difficulty rationalizing his position, conflict may suggest incompetence. Accordingly, commissioners find ways to overcome or live with their antagonisms, if they have any, toward colleagues.[37] They also provide occasional "cover" for colleagues who prove less able than expected. Above all they employ techniques that permit suppression or control of conflict.

Suppression of conflict is of course relatively easy in the Stockholm system, since there are so few channels in which it can arise. The absence of neighborhood or *ad hoc* pressure groups during most of the postwar period has meant that, unless a newspaper wanted to stir up a potentially divisive issue, the only settings in which conflict might arise have been the administrative boards. Here, a commissioner has a great advantage, for all proposals that arise must be submitted to the administration for evaluation and review. On ordinary matters the review itself—lengthy, detailed, and exhaustingly thorough—is a major mechanism for conflict suppression. If the administrator does his work well, what emerges will be a proposal so thoroughly reviewed that little opportunity for disagreement remains.

On less ordinary matters, referral to the administration gives a commissioner (with appropriate advice from the administrator) an opportunity to identify points of conflict and to negotiate agreement, if possible, even before any public report is issued from the adminis-

37. On one occasion Hjalmar Mehr became so angry at a colleague that he retracted the "dropping-of-title" that typically marks the boundary between formal and friendly relations in Sweden—henceforward he would address his colleague by title rather than the familiar *Du.* After further consideration, however, he changed his mind and wrote to his colleague that "I am 'Du' with many who are worse than 'Du' so I suppose you should get the same treatment." Kubu, *op. cit.,* p. 42.

tration. A commissioner who is a skillful enough negotiator, and who has a good enough "understanding" with his administrative chief, will be able to find areas of agreement informally, perhaps through telephone conversations with key people. Even potentially divisive proposals will then emerge into public view as finely tuned rationalizations of the obvious. A successful and competent commissioner will manage his various boards so that they provide the least possible evidence of public disagreement.

Naturally, all conflict cannot be suppressed. On those few issues where conflict arises, however, it can be controlled by agreement among commissioners. As was suggested earlier, the technique is ritualization: commissioners simply "agree to disagree" formally, without allowing the disagreement to affect their relationships on other issues.

Finally, there is a technique which neither suppresses nor controls present conflict, but instead helps prevent conflict. For want of a better term we shall call it the "hostage principle." In Stockholm politics it consists of implicating *all* local party leaders in decisions whose future consequences are uncertain. Usually these are decisions that set major policy or that represent major departures from existing policy. In some cases the hostages are institutionalized: in creating AB STRADA, for example, it was carefully specified that the board controlling the company's land-purchase operations would include the leaders of all local party organizations. Similarly, the party leaders are included on the boards of the city's housing companies, and of the newer development companies working in the suburbs. In other cases, "hostages" are held in *ad hoc* committees, of which the Greater County Council Committee, discussed earlier, is a good example.

Either form of the hostage principle can be a useful device for generating unity on major city policy issues. From another point of view, however, there is no institutionalized source of complaint should those policies fail. As we have seen, policies are often the manipulated product of a single clever party leader. Nevertheless the hostage principle leaves other party representatives without grounds to complain over later failures because they have been implicated from the beginning and presumably share responsibility. Used often enough, the hostage principle reduces the boundaries of serious partisan conflict to virtually meaningless proportions.

None of this can or should be taken to mean that conflict is either nonexistent or unimportant in city politics. Conflict aplenty exists, though it typically appears as conflict *between individual officials,* rather than between opposing governing principles.[39] Because even this conflict takes place informally, in bureaucratic rather than public settings—recall that meetings of administrative boards are not open to ordinary citizens—the public is seldom, if ever, part of the audience. Officials are thereby spared the necessity of giving a public account of their activities, and can thus continue to pretend that they are men of superior expertise, searching rationally for policies that will serve the best interests of the city, in a spirit of civic unanimity. It is not conflict that is absent but public *evidence* of conflict. That absence permits members of the governing elite to maintain their hold on power more easily, and to reach agreement more readily on appropriate solutions to public problems.[39]

But why should the elite care about retaining power or solving problems? A system that implicates all parties in virtually all major as well as minor decisions necessarily makes it impossible to assign credit for successful policies to either individual parties or individual politicians. Indeed, one of the more amusing recurring aspects of local politics is the effort made by the various parties at election time to find ingenious ways of establishing their claims as policy originators, in the face of other claims which always appear equally good. The satisfactions of political heroism are thus denied to city officials, no matter how they try. Nor can they claim significant influence over electoral outcomes, for they appreciate as well as anyone that national issues are dominant. Why, then, should they care? What satisfactions do they seek, and obtain?

In searching for an answer, let us recall that the Stockholm elite is a small group of men who have learned to share the same professional-administrative ideology, who feel independent, but who also work in settings that give them plentiful opportunities to observe and know each other's work, as well as opportunities to perform before those colleagues themselves. Because of overlapping responsibilities, everyone more or less knows what everyone else is doing. (This fact, incidentally, provides the best explanation for the general lack of corruption among local officials.) And because they share the same evaluative standards, these officials easily reach conclusions about who is and

38. But see below, Chapter VII, for evidence of change in this pattern.

39. There is abundant written evidence of policy conflict in the *Reports* (*Utlåtanden*) which form the bases for official Council action. Apart from officials themselves and a few reporters, however, it is doubtful that very many people ever see these documents.

is not performing competently. Given the intimacy of their knowledge about other actors, in fact, there is no way to avoid such conclusions.[40]

In such an environment the pressure to avoid error is high, since knowledge of error will be immediate and widespread among a critical audience. But the pressure to achieve something notable—beyond the mere avoidance of error—is even higher, partly because there are so few alternative methods for acquiring personal status, and partly because achievement will be clearly recognized among the small circle who count. Once recognized, of course, an official's capacity for achievement becomes a major political resource.

AN "ACHIEVING SOCIETY"

By freeing officials from local political constraints, filling them full of professional-administrative ideologies, and placing them in settings where they constantly perform for one another, the "system" structures a highly competitive "achieving society." Each official competes against all others for the system's principal political resource: *reputation.* Precisely because the group whose collective opinion establishes reputation is so small and so familiar, the highest reputations for achievement can never be based on knowledge and expertise alone. In such a system the roots of reputation must lie in an ability to maneuver people into desirable relationships: by dropping a hint here, suggesting an innuendo there, or offering a well-devised proposal at an opportune moment.

An appropriate concept might be "capacity," but that English term is far inferior to the Swedish *skicklighet.* The latter combines notions of expertise and capability with connotations of cunning and wisdom. It is a complicated concept, but no less complicated than the intricate, mostly invisible operations of the system itself—a system in which grounds for agreement are negotiated and communicated without apparent communication, commitments are always tentative and often broken even as they are affirmed, and individual achievement is always masked in collective responsibility. The Danes have a saying: "The Orient begins in Malmö!" Most observers of politics in modern Stockholm would probably agree.

40. It is difficult to overemphasize the extent to which Swedish politics is dominated by an elite that appears, to outsiders at least, to possess total familiarity. In part, this is due to family and educational linkages that may go back for decades. In part, too, it is due to the amount of public information that exists on government officials. As Swedes themselves say, it is a small country.

GAMES, ROLES, AND SYSTEM PERFORMANCE

Taking social structure into account gives us a rather different and more comprehensive view of individual actors and the policies they generated in postwar Stockholm. From a metropolitan perspective, certainly, it is easy enough to understand Stockholm's ability to dominate other area governments. By concentrating responsibility for specific policies in single individuals—Garpe in suburban housing, Mehr in land, for example—while giving them the full support of a unanimous group of party leaders and the resources of a large bureaucracy, the city virtually guaranteed some form of control over the divided and resource-poor suburbs. By keeping the same group of men in power for more than three decades, the party system and coalition tradition guaranteed a continuing interest in issues (such as metropolitan reform) that had achieved acceptance as important components of the urban political agenda. Finally, by freeing city and suburban politicians from localized political constraints, the nationalized electoral system encouraged policy proposals that largely ignored the interplay of local interests.

Freedom from electoral constraints was matched by insulation of political and administrative leaders from most partisan controversy, which reduced the power of partisanship in the shaping of policy. Ritualization of partisanship, coupled with the structurally guaranteed participation of independent professional administrators, created a policy environment in which professional values and techniques dominated the role conceptions of all members of the governing elite. This was and remains crucial, not only because of its impact on the *substance* of urban policy, but more importantly because, among a small and permanently interacting elite, professional ideologies helped to create a powerful *achievement* motivation. This is probably the most fundamental source of what was referred to earlier as the "pattern of opportunistic problem-solving."

Consider, in addition, what some awareness of social structure can tell us about actor "style" in the policy process. Hjalmar Mehr's organization and manipulation of the Greater County Council Committee, described earlier as "the politics of manipulation," is a good example. First an *ad hoc* committee (administrative board) is created, including the leaders of all local political parties (a coalition, using the "hostage" system). Next, Mehr's administrative chief was instructed to prepare a detailed agenda, complete with proposed actions, for circulation prior to the meeting.

After discussion, Mehr's proposals were accepted and later meetings followed precisely the same pattern: (1) thorough advance preparation by Mehr's administrative chiefs, including detailed research on agenda items and proposals for adaptation, (2) discussion, and (3) approval of Mehr's proposals (the "special" relationship in action).[41] When disagreement appeared, the committee was enlarged (providing more hostages), and the enlarged committee was subjected to the same procedures of agenda control, proposal presentation, and agreement. When further disagreement emerged, a final meeting was postponed for a weekend, so that Mehr and the other party leaders could "work things out," with the help of the top administrators. The conclusion expressed unanimous agreement on the major substantive points proposed by Mehr. It also permitted the bourgeois party representatives to publicly reaffirm a policy they had been promoting for years (ritualization).

Described as an independent sequence of discrete events, this process probably suggests individual cleverness. Yet what is it but a typical behavior pattern for Stockholm City Commissioners? Indeed, with some modification, the sequence is a prototype of relationships between a commissioner, his administrative chief, and his board. Surely Hjalmar Mehr's "success" in this case was due in no small measure to the fact that he had engaged in precisely the same kind of behavior hundreds of times previously in his career as commissioner. It demeans neither the stature nor the competence of individual City Commissioners, then, to suggest that there is a certain logic of behavior inherent in the structure of their relationships to colleagues. The pattern of constraints and incentives that defines that logic may not produce identical action in similar situations, but the range of variation is not large, even for such unusual individuals as Hjalmar Mehr. All commissioners are participants in a *system* of action, based upon a determinate social structure.

If the performance of Stockholm's political system is judged to have been a "success," therefore, a search for causes must begin with the political structures which represented desirable values and arranged behavior that achieved those values. Having described that system of behavior, it is now necessary to ask whether the pattern is unique to Sweden or whether it is somehow exportable, in whole or in part. As a variant of a classic question among students of comparative politics, the question is theoretically interesting. It also has sub-

41. See above, Chapter IV, for the details that are touched briefly here.

stantial practical significance: depending on how we answer, we have either very little or very much to learn from the Stockholm experience. The reader may have already drawn his own conclusions in this matter. My own effort to answer the question begins in the following chapter.

CHAPTER VI

CITY AND NATION:
THE CONTEXT OF URBAN
POLITICAL CHANGE

THE POSTWAR TRANSFORMATION of Stockholm from a "city" to an "urban region" forced area politicians to solve a number of problems commonly associated with urban growth. A housing shortage, stimulated by immigration from rural areas and aggravated by the city's own renewal policies, produced continuing political pressure. Population growth and housing construction required simultaneous expansion of water and sewer facilities, public schools, and a variety of other municipal services. All of this required coordination, both between the city and the suburbs and among the various suburban governments. As population grew and services expanded, still another factor—the private automobile—created wholly unanticipated demands for further expansion of public services. None of these problems was peculiar to Stockholm. Indeed, few cities in western Europe, the United States, or other urbanizing areas of the world have escaped them in the postwar era.[1]

Nor is the Stockholm solution to these various difficulties entirely unfamiliar to officials in other metropolitan regions. Until the late 1950s Stockholm followed an incremental approach to metropolitan policy, negotiating separate service contracts with individual municipalities. These "inter-jurisdictional agreements," to use the language of American metropolitan politics, structured city-suburban coopera-

1. See Peter Hall, *The World Cities* (New York: McGraw-Hill, 1966), for some examples.

164

tion in a variety of important service areas: water, sewers, education, health care, and others. Later, when the national government began supporting the city, it became possible to restructure metropolitan governmental institutions, using a foundation laid by an area-wide mass transportation agreement. There was nothing particularly novel or interesting about the new institutions, however. The metro structure finally achieved in 1971 had been discussed by Swedish politicians for more than three decades, and for even longer by writers concerned with the so-called "metropolitan problem." [2] Those who look to the Stockholm experience for some "new insights" or "innovative solutions" are thus destined to look in vain.

If neither its problems nor its solutions contribute much to our appreciation of the urban dilemma, why pay any attention to Stockholm at all? A common answer is that a variety of proposed solutions to urban problems have been *implemented* in the Stockholm region, even if their origins are elsewhere. Thus it may be instructive for officials of other regions to observe the application of solutions they have not yet attempted.[3] At the level of engineering or technology, certainly, this is a reasonable enough justification. Stockholm is a worthwhile place to visit for an urban engineer interested in how a subway tunnel was bored through a hill, or for a planner interested in the layout of an unusual shopping center, or for an architect concerned about locating an apartment complex to take advantage of the natural landscape. Observing such technological applications can reveal unanticipated difficulties and suggest improved methods of getting things done.

But moving beyond this simple, almost trivial, level of justification turns out to be extraordinarily complicated, for what lies beyond is a structure of social institutions specific to time and culture, and thus virtually impossible to transplant. Yet those who use the Stockholm experience as a basis for recommendations applicable to other political systems typically confuse the technological with the social, or ignore this vital distinction altogether. American observers, for example, often judge Stockholm development policies to have been a great "success," and attribute that success to the city's land-purchase policies. These observers then proceed from such conclusions to a seem-

2. See, for example, Arthur W. Bromage, *Introduction to Municipal Government and Administration* (New York: Appleton-Century-Crofts, Inc., 1957), pp. 88–106, or John C. Bollens and Henry J. Schmandt, *The Metropolis* (New York: Harper & Row, 2nd ed., 1970), pp. 27–46.

3. An intelligent example of this kind of thinking is Boyce Richardson, *The Future of Canadian Cities* (Toronto: New Press, 1972), pp. 50–65.

ingly obvious policy recommendation, namely that American cities should copy Stockholm's suburban land-purchase policies.[4]

Taken by itself, the technique of suburban land purchase appears to make sense; the difficulty is that the technique *cannot* be taken by itself. It was effective in the Stockholm region because (1) there was unanimous support from the city's political leaders, (2) the city had well-organized and competent building companies able to do something with the land acquired, (3) the national government gave both political and financial support, and (4) suburban governments increasingly came to appreciate the interest they had in working with the city building companies. Remove these related conditions and the technique fails, even in Stockholm, for it constitutes only one among many interrelated strands of social relations. Recommending only the technique, without the associated conditions that make it effective, is either ignorant or frivolous. But taking account of related conditions drastically changes the nature of the basic recommendation. If social relations are taken into account, the recommendation changes from: "buy land in the suburbs," to "change the political system so that a city can control the use of suburban land."

Recommendations that treat policy as mere technique, divorced from the social relations that motivate and sustain it, often become proposals for fundamental system change, whether or not the authors realize it. Authors are not always aware of the implications of their recommendations, of course, and it is precisely for this reason that studies of Stockholm or other major cities are relevant. Such studies permit us to accumulate more evidence concerning relationships between social conditions and public policy. For some time to come, the accumulation of such evidence will necessarily be inconclusive, in part because of insufficient information, and in part because of the extraordinary complexity of these relationships. While social conditions surely influence policy, they can hardly be said to *determine* policy—at least on the basis of information presently available.[5]

But complexity is more than a matter of "play" in the relationships between social structure and policy. It is also a question of which social structures help us explain and understand those relationships.

4. For an effort to combine such a recommendation with a sensible consideration of the problems involved, see Passow, *loc. cit.*

5. For a useful consideration of the social structure-policy relationship, in the context of an overall assessment of policy research, see Herbert Jacob and Michael Lipsky, "Outputs, Structure, and Power: An Assessment of Changes in the Study of State and Local Politics," *Journal of Politics*, Vol. 30 (1968), pp. 510–538.

The preceding discussion has argued the utility of seeking explanations in the game-related behavior of organizational elites, playing out political roles in the Stockholm region. Yet these players are more than members of a "Stockholm" elite. They are also Swedish citizens, educated in the same standards of conduct and evaluation as their countrymen, members of organizations which participate actively in national (and in some cases international) affairs, and members of a governing system with well-defined expectations for municipalities. The *latent role orientations* structured by these relationships must be understood before we attempt any final judgments on the relevance of the Stockholm experience. For appropriate evidence we can review the structure of relationships between local and national authorities, and re-study the processes of policy formulation already described.

STATE-CITY OR CITY-STATE?

No observer of politics in postwar Stockholm can be faulted for wondering why such extraordinary efforts have been made to avoid even the appearance of conflict in municipal affairs. Issues are not permitted to arise, except in "proper" channels. If a disagreement occurs, it is smothered in a time-consuming process of study and secret negotiations by a tiny elite. The products of such negotiations usually are heavily documented rationalizations of policies the entire elite has already accepted. Disagreements that remain are given a ritualized exposure but not seriously discussed, and they are never allowed to disrupt the process of agreement in other matters. Like a modern digital computer, the system works quietly, generates a vast output, and seems programmed to reject all formulations that fail to match pre-coded instructions for unanimity.

NATIONALIZATION OF LOCAL CONFLICT

But the issues over which ritualized conflict occurs do not disappear simply because Stockholm politicians are unable to resolve them. On the contrary, such issues are shifted to a higher level for ultimate resolution. Thus, one of the most important consequences of the Stockholm political process is the *nationalization of local conflict*. All issues involving serious (thus irresolvable) conflict are ritualized at the local level, and dealt with seriously by groups that include national-level officials. As we have seen, such issues have included—and have been dominated by—problems of housing, planning, and transportation. Accordingly, we can conclude that national officials have been at least as involved as local politicians in policies affecting the postwar development of the Stockholm region. It was neither unusual nor accidental that the Social Minister became directly involved in the Stockholm housing question, or that the Interior Minister intervened to resolve the problem of apartment distribution among area residents, or that the Prime Minister had a hand in the politics of land-acquisition around Stockholm. None of this was accidental, because the system itself can fairly be described as one in which local policy-making, as well as local conflict, is nationalized.

This suggests that local and national governmental levels are not viewed as separate structures, but as constituent units of the same structure. An obvious division of labor follows. Local officials, knowing that any major policy change will require participation by national officials, operate the municipality as an administrative arm of the national government. At this level officials deal primarily with problems on which policy is settled (i.e., there is no conflict) and pass other policy questions on to the national government through the technique of ritualization. National officials, in turn, may assume responsibility for local policy, but use conflict as the test for their intervention. If no conflict appears, national officials need not, and usually will not, intervene.

The local officials who spend countless hours negotiating agreements with their colleagues thus perform tasks that serve the interests of national officials as well as their own. In their continuing efforts to devise programs for local application, they help to determine the need for new national policy. Similarly, national officials perform a valuable service for local politicians by removing the "heat" of policy conflict from their shoulders. Both sides in this exchange have an incentive for avoiding conflict. The less local conflict, the less there is need for exertion by national officials, and therefore the greater the autonomy of local officials. This view may not tell us why so much effort is devoted to avoiding the appearance of conflict, but it suggests some functional interrelationships that surely help us understand that effort.

THE LOCAL POLICY OF THE NATIONAL GOVERNMENT

Clearly enough, the "nationalization" of local policy-making works well only if the national unit has a local policy. There are limits, after all, to the matters that can be passed upward as "policy" concerns. Since 1945 those limits have been under careful review by the national government, in active pursuit of a two-pronged policy. On one hand the responsibilities of local governments have been significantly broadened. Especially in the fields of housing, planning, and social welfare, activities previously dealt with by national authorities were gradually assigned to local units after 1946. As these activities were assumed and local bureaucracies built up, they were necessarily accompanied by new patterns of local-national communication to deal with the unavoidable problems of implementation. Appropriately enough, then, one reason why so much local policy has been nationalized is that so much national responsibility has been localized.[6]

The second, and perhaps more important, prong of national policy since 1945 has been structural rationalization. This policy has been noted briefly, but it deserves more consideration here for what it can tell us about citizen attitudes toward governmental activities. Concern with the adequacy of local government structure had been voiced as early as the mid-1930s, when depopulation of numerous rural municipalities undermined municipal ability to finance local welfare services, and even the public schools. The rural population decline continued apace after World War II, and led ultimately to a national inquiry on municipal boundaries which attempted to establish a criterion for appropriate municipal size.

The first result of this effort came on January 1, 1952, when, following legislation passed by the *Riksdag,* the number of Swedish municipalities was reduced from 2,500 to approximately 1,000. The goal was a population of at least 8,000 in each new municipality, since that was thought to be the minimum number capable of supporting essential welfare, education, and other municipal services. Boundary changes for the enlarged local units were based on careful studies of interaction patterns. New municipal units were intended to reflect living and operating social relationships, rather than mere geographic boundaries.[7]

This reform had barely gone into effect before complaints arose that the reform was inadequate. New local responsibilities and citizen demands, it was said, required even larger municipalities, with even better tax resources, and hence fewer municipalities. Accordingly, new municipal reform legislation was enacted in 1962, setting forth new criteria for "communal blocks" and establishing a new goal of

6. A useful review of these changing relationships, in English, is Per Langenfelt, *Local Government in Sweden* (Stockholm: The Swedish Institute, 1964).
7. See Per Langenfelt, *Principles for a New Division of Sweden's Municipalities* (Stockholm: The Swedish Institute, 1962), for more detail on reform criteria.

only 274 local governments, to be achieved by 1974. Thus, in little more than two decades, national legislation reduced Sweden's total number of local governments by a factor of 10—from 2,500 to just over 250! [8]

EMPHASIS ON PERFORMANCE CAPACITY

Originally the postwar reform was a response to local financial crises. Gradually, however, the reform effort came to emphasize performance capacity as the fundamental criterion of judgment for municipalities. Because only large and well-funded municipalities were considered capable of handling their increasing responsibilities, the small, poorly financed, and rural communes had to be replaced— and thousands of locally elected officials eliminated. Above all, Swedish municipalities had to provide public services. For that, a strong economic base was much more important than large numbers of local politicians.

This view became the basis for the Social Democratic party slogan, "Strong Society," and formed an important component of that party's drive to rationalize Sweden's "service democracy." [9] But in this case, as in so many others, the Social Democrats appear to have jumped on a rolling bandwagon: the great majority of local officials, including those who would lose their jobs, *supported* both the 1952 and the 1962 legislation eliminating so many municipalities.[10] Moreover, it was the municipalities' own national interest group, the Municipal League (*Kommunförbundet*), that both initiated and negotiated the reforms that were finally adopted.[11] For the Swedish local politician, *doing* a job proved more important than *having* a job. When a choice had to be made, it was function rather than status that won out.

The domination of performance capacity, rather than status, as the organizing principle for Swedish municipalities is entirely consistent with citizen orientations toward government. Although there is overwhelming evidence to support the proposition that Swedish citizens are quite uninterested in the question of who governs or how, it is equally clear that they are very much interested in what comes out of the governmental box in the form of municipal serv-

8. Sandalow, *loc. cit.*, pp. 770–774, provides a useful commentary on the process. See also Niemi, *op. cit.*, pp. 135–159.
9. See Chapter I, above.
10. Niemi, *op. cit.*, pp. 41, 163, provides supporting evidence.
11. *Ibid., passim.*

ices.[12] Earlier it was suggested that citizen focus on output rather than input has the effect of undermining the social significance of municipal boundaries. The combination of high demand for public service delivery and low interest in the structure of the delivery system characterizes the average Swede as primarily a *consumer of public services*. For Sven Svensson, what matters is not which governmental unit provides a service, but that the service be provided, at a high standard, and at the lowest possible cost.

These official and citizen orientations had a powerful impact on Stockholm regional development after 1945, when Hjalmar Mehr, Joakim Garpe, and other Social Democrats became well known for their almost brutal insistence on a city and region that "functions efficiently." For Mehr, the recent criticism of Skärholmen and other large housing estates built on land he and Garpe secured is either a product of political resentment among the bourgeois parties or an irrelevant romanticism that ignores the improvement in living conditions produced by the new housing estates. Recently an interviewer asked Mehr, in the context of the debate over Skärholmen, whether he thought it possible to combine the popular dream of the romantic city with an efficient and modern city. Consider his response:

> I think it is not impossible to combine them to a large extent. For what is it that one wishes to preserve of the "romantic" city? What was romantic about Lower Norrmalm? Vasastan? Kungsholmen? Lower Norrmalm's properties were rotten to the core, pitched up during periods of bull-market speculation by private contractors, who then fattened up their rental income. I am virtually the only one, among all those who discuss this matter, who has lived there the whole time. My mother moved just about every other year. Large, old-fashioned apartments with earth floors and rats in the yard and other hellishly bad conditions—in other words, buildings ripe for demolition. Romanticism is for those who already live well—and who seldom worry about how long poor people live in rotten housing. The kind of properties we had there [Lower Norrmalm] had no aesthetic, architectural or cultural value.[13]

These are tough words, and in them one can sense the kind of drive that led Mehr and his party colleagues to press vigorously for decent-quality housing, especially for poor people, for efficient transportation to and from the job, and for easy access to the service facilities necessary for everyday life in a metropolitan region. This drive for a region capable of functioning well and smoothly—what Mehr calls

12. Donald S. Connery evokes the Swedish demand for "more and better" in his *The Scandinavians* (New York: Simon and Schuster, 1966), pp. 281–301.
13. Quoted in Akerman, *op. cit.*, pp. 121–122.

"funktionsduglighet"—led to no major structural changes in the Stockholm region comparable to what the rest of the nation experienced, largely because it was possible to argue for so long that piecemeal agreements between the city and the suburbs made structural changes unnecessary.

THE ROYAL COMMISSION

By 1961, however, as the traffic problem became an issue, and the housing queue continued to grow, the national government created a Royal Commission to look into the structure of regional government once again. Naturally, Mehr was appointed to this Commission, along with Aronson, Garpe, and Agrenius from the city, and such illustrious suburban figures as Nils Eliasson and P. A. Sköldin. Creation of the Commission in October 1961 was a clear signal from the national government that it was preparing to take action. Appointment of these particular officials from the Stockholm region was a way of ensuring acceptance of whatever action was finally taken. A conflict had broken out that could not be resolved at the local level, and the Commission represented a step toward achievement of a *national* solution.[14]

All this suggests a somewhat different and enriched perspective on Hjalmar Mehr's activities before and after his speech of December 1963. By that time he had already invested two years in the work of a Royal Commission investigating precisely the problem he was now proposing to solve. To be sure, the Interior Ministry had made no threats and demanded no actions. Nevertheless it was clear that the Ministry was planning steps that would impose the same standards of performance on Stockholm that were being imposed on the rest of the country. Mehr supported those standards, and had participated actively in working them out. But the Royal Commission had significantly altered the conditions under which the standards could or would be applied in the Stockholm region. Now there was a good deal of additional pressure to act, or lose the initiative for action.

MEHR'S PROPOSAL

In this context, Mehr's December 1963 proposal can be viewed either as an attempt to forestall more drastic but imposed change, or as an effort to seize an opportunity for the incremental reform he then proposed. Depending on which view one takes, of course, Mehr

14. SOU 1964:56 reports the results of the Commission's work.

becomes either an opponent of change or a far-sighted visionary. And depending on which aspects of this complicated, three-sided relationship the observer chooses to emphasize, one can conclude that it was either national or local initiative that was fundamental to the reform that became effective on January 1, 1971. The complexities of these interrelationships are enormous; certainty is impossible.

But the quest for certainty is misdirected in any case. Judgments about Mehr's "real" motivations, or about the "real" initiators of reform, are less relevant to the Stockholm experience than the realization that local and national-level politicians were locked into an ongoing system of interaction, structured by common values concerning municipalities, and fueled by public problems that required public solutions. A year after Mehr's speech, the Royal Commission urged support for the "Greater County Council" solution. At that point, whether it was Mehr's plan or someone else's was far less relevant than the fact that a group of national and local "experts" had decided what to do about the Stockholm area problem.[15]

A NATIONAL-LOCAL CONTINUUM

To observe the significance of national-level actors in this activity is to observe only half of what is truly significant. If national officials assume a responsibility for local policy, so too do these local officials acknowledge the national significance of local action: they recognize a national interest and a national constituency to which they are directly connected. Psychologically, they are less "local" officials than they are "national officials entrusted with locally defined responsibilities."[16] Such an orientation weakens the relationship between local public office and localized constituencies at the same time that it legitimizes an appeal to the "national interest" in the resolution of disputes. Citizens who see themselves primarily as public service consumers are thus nicely complemented by local officials who see themselves primarily as branch managers of the corporation providing the services. In Sweden, the "community" is the state itself.

15. *Ibid.*, p. 14.
16. I once asked a suburban administrator what he would do if his "Board" rejected a proposal he had made. "Naturally I could not force them to agree with me," he replied. "But I have an obligation to the nation, as well as to this commune, and I would have to make clear to them that my professional judgment is not based solely on the problems of this municipality."

PATIENCE, RESTRAINT, AND ACCOMMODATION: THE LATENT NORMS OF POLICY-MAKING

If we now reconsider the processes of institutional change described earlier, in light of a continuous and direct involvement of national-level officials in local affairs, a number of questions become more pressing. It is clear, for example, that open national intervention has been decisive, as in the creation of a metropolitan authority for allocating access to new housing units. But less formal methods of intervention have been equally decisive. Examples include the 1956 national decision to support more housing, which led ultimately to city construction of vast housing estates in the suburbs; the decision to divert automobile tax revenue to mass transportation, which resolved the Stockholm transportation problem; and the 1961 Royal Commission study, which provided the foundation for Hjalmar Mehr's ultimately successful plan to create a Greater County Council.

INTERVENTION: SLOW, DELIBERATE, INDIRECT

Given this record, plus citizen-official agreement on appropriate criteria to evaluate municipalities, plus mounting evidence of a crisis in housing and transportation services, why did the national government not intervene earlier and "solve" the Stockholm problem once and for all? The "solution" finally achieved had been proposed as early as the 1920s and had been thoroughly analyzed—including comparisons with other possible solutions—during the late 1930s and early 1940s. The city pleaded for some form of national intervention in 1950, and the various plans previously proposed were debated during the 1950s. Yet the national government made no response to the city in 1950. Thereafter, its actions came one at a time, never approaching the radical restructuring of local governments which was ordered for other parts of Sweden. Why?

And why, when national intervention did come, was it so often indirect in style, almost apologetic in tone? Having finally decided that intervention was necessary to deal with the Stockholm structural problem, national officials did not propose legislation on the basis of a mountain of accumulated evidence and discussion. Instead the government appointed a commission, composed in good part of local officials, and asked for a report some time in the future (in this case three years later).[17] "You come to an agreement," the government ap-

17. The Commission appointed in October 1961 reported on November 26, 1964. *SOU 1964:56.*

peared to be saying, "so that we will not have to impose a decision."
Indeed, the government explicitly said as much in the process leading
to creation of the metropolitan housing allocation authority. After
thirteen years of unsuccessful effort, complete with voluminous research, the government created a commission whose reports, three
and five years later, viewed national policy as a last resort, acceptable
only if area municipalities failed to agree.[18] Such patterns are remi-
niscent of the elaborate procedures followed in Stockholm to avoid
conflict, or the refusal of city politicians to openly challenge their
counterparts in the suburbs. Let us explore these patterns further,
and investigate their relationship to the processes of system change.

THE LONG VIEW

First, it seems quite clear that problem-solving time perspectives
among Swedish public officials are extraordinarily lengthy, encompassing decades rather than years, or historical periods rather than
decades. The expectation of long tenure and the absence of localized public constraints encourage local officials to develop a "we can
wait" attitude which all but eliminates immediacy from the Swedish
sense of crisis. One consequence is that issues take a long time to
resolve—even those that are defined as being critical. Consider again
the lengthy and involved proceedings leading to the various partial
solutions to the housing "crisis," or recall the even better example of
the negotiator appointed by the national government to resolve the
metropolitan transportation "crisis." The appointment itself was
highly unusual, as was the assignment of a large office, a separate staff,
and the authority of the national government. With these resources,
and no other responsibilities, the negotiator labored for an entire
year to produce a city-county agreement. Afterward, he was widely
judged to have worked both quickly and well. Indeed, so *skickligt*
was his performance judged to be that he was awarded a major political prize: Directorship of the Swedish Post Office.[19] In Sweden, policy-
making simply cannot be rushed.

Viewing policy issues historically, rather than in a context of immediacy, permits officials to take the future into account as they make
decisions. The assistant director of AB STRADA, for example, was
asked not long ago how he determined which parcels of land should
be purchased by the city. "It is really very simple," he replied, pull-
ing down a large wall map of the Stockholm region. "You see here

18. *SOU 1965:51*, and *SOU 1967:1*, pp. 82–83.
19. Kubu, *Det politiska spelet . . .* , p. 176.

that we are blocked in the east by the archipelago, and in the west by Lake Mälaren, so the only direction in which we can buy land is either to the north or to the south, and that is where we buy, taking account of the size of the parcel, its situation, the neighboring property and the existence or nonexistence of city land in the same vicinity." Not satisfied, the interviewer continued by asking what such purchases were for, and how the city could justify the purchase of land situated as much as 50 kilometers away from the city's boundaries. With great patience at such an obvious absence of comprehension, the STRADA official explained:

It is true that we are now buying land far from the city, and it is true that we have no specific plans for much of this land. But you must understand that the city has grown enormously over the past fifty years, and we have no reason to believe that it will not continue to expand. Therefore, we buy land where we can. We may not need it next year, or five years from now, or even twenty years from now. But we know that someday we will have use for the land, so we buy it.[20]

To properly interpret these remarks the reader should bear in mind that the governing board of AB STRADA—that is, the officials who set policy and who approve all purchases—is composed of the leaders of all the major party groups in Stockholm. These men, like the administrators with whom they work so closely, are as concerned about the future as they are about the present. For them it is the historical judgment, yet to be made, that really counts, not the immediate resolution of crisis.

RESTRAINT

A second significant aspect of these behavior patterns is *restraint,* i.e., the refusal to advocate or take extreme actions. The system's very structure suggests a kind of restraint, of course, for the allocation of political positions in proportion to party electoral strength means that the name of the Stockholm political game is not "winner take all," but "winner take his share." Nothing in law prevents a winning coalition from allocating all positions of importance to its own members, but it is simply not done: all organized groups are assumed to deserve representation in proportion to their strength.[21] In bargain-

20. Interview, Assistant Director Sven Jönsson.
21. Bertil Ohlin, Professor of Economics and former leader of the Liberal party once remarked to me that he could not see why Americans tolerated a system in which a 51 per cent majority allowed the winning party to dispose of 100 per cent of the available political offices. "We would not think of doing that here," he said.

ing, too, the politicians clearly follow the assumption that nobody should be totally left out. Thus every effort is made to cut up the cake so that everyone gets a piece, whether it is a suburban agreement whereby the city trades its organization skills for access to suburban apartments, a city agreement under which contractors trade their financial resources for a guaranteed piece of the construction pie, or an intergovernmental agreement for the city to furnish transit services in return for a county financial commitment. "Everyone's entitled" seems to be the motto of a system in which there are seldom any big winners, but *never* any total losers.

MASKING COERCION: PRESERVING STATUS

Over time, this system creates an expectation that no interest will ever be sacrificed—or, that if sacrificial action becomes necessary, ways will be found to soften the blow. One easy softener is time itself: a great many actions are postponed simply because there seems no easy way to take them without doing obvious harm to one interest or another. More common, and far more confusing, is *symbolic masking of coercive action*. All local politicians understood, for example, that failure to produce more housing through city-suburban contracts during the early 1960s would result in some form of national assumption of local housing responsibilities, but no one ever said so publicly. Instead, in speeches and voluminous public documents, local officials repeatedly—and ritually—congratulated themselves on the "voluntary" cooperation they had achieved.[22] Similarly, all parties to the 1964 transportation agreement praised the wisdom of both the city and county governments, whose voluntary agreement created an historic policy breakthrough.[23] Everyone understood that the iron fist of national insistence was at work, but the velvet glove of local voluntarism provided the public cover for national coercion.

Before dismissing such behavior as poorly informed or disingenuous, we do well to inquire into its significance for, plainly, the names people use in thinking about their activities are not inconsequential. At a very obvious level, insistence on retaining the concept of "volun-

22. In Järfälla, for example, this process began even before the first contract with Stockholm was signed. The commune's closeness to Stockholm, wrote a local politician in 1960, "means that it must do its share in supplying housing for Greater Stockholm." See *Järfälla-Bygden*, 1960, and Jonason, *op. cit.*

23. See Kubu, *Det politiska spelet* . . . , pp. 171–176, for another view of these negotiations. A more congratulatory, but nevertheless useful, discussion is *KSL: Public Transport in Greater Stockholm* (Stockholm: Information Department of KSL, 1969).

tary" agreement for what in fact were coerced agreements represented an effort to reaffirm the value, and maintain the status, of existing local governments. With as little popular and official commitment to those units as was clearly evident in the postwar thrust of national policy, it was highly unlikely that anyone else would defend their continued independence—even if that independence was largely a myth.

But that is the point. Preserving the myth of local independence accomplished two things. First, it traditionalized the new, defining new municipal responsibilities as products of the old tradition of local strength. Second, it permitted local officials to mask their surrender in appeals to administrative rationality and the public interest. When it became clear that the national government was determined to increase housing production, and was prepared to support Stockholm in its thrust toward a suburban solution, local officials who had spent a decade opposing the city began to see the world differently. Their speeches and public statements began to be filled with a sense of the urgency of the city's housing problem, and with their own assumption of responsibility: "We must do our share to provide housing for those who need it." [24] "Voluntary" acceptance of what they realized they could not avoid permitted suburban officials to stay within the tradition of the Swedish "expert" administrator, who sees his duty, and does it in the best and most efficient way.

Naturally there are less obvious levels of understanding behavior designed to mask reality and preserve status. We can begin to appreciate some of these subtleties by asking whose status such behavior seeks to preserve. Obviously, if Swedish citizens are as distant from their municipalities as the evidence suggests, then citizens have little stake in local boundaries. Those who have a stake are local officials. Thus it seems reasonable to conclude that *elite status* is what is being defended by the facade of metropolitan voluntarism.

THE 1971 CHANGES

A reconsideration of the institutional changes achieved on January 1, 1971, suggests that the defenders did their job well. Not only were no municipalities lost as a consequence of the new metro, but the new structure made possible eight more "little monarchs" to govern the Stockholm region. Although the city lost over one-third of its employees, it nevertheless retained the same number of City Com-

24. See note 22, above.

missioners (nine).[25] Meanwhile the county, with several thousand new employees and a variety of new functions, decided that it would need eight "County Commissioners." To avoid invidious comparisons, these new officials would have to receive the same salary and perquisites as their city counterparts (Skr 135,000 per year).[26]

Clearly enough, the pattern of commissioner-dominated politics that has characterized Stockholm was also envisioned for the new metro. This suggests that the change in regional politics has been structural and organizational, but not motivational. The increment of rationality achieved by attaching a few regional functions to a regional tax base is precisely that: incremental. But the same values of professionalism-performance will be sought in the same way by the same men, except that there are now seventeen instead of nine. Thus the politics of institutional change in Stockholm has been very much a politics of status-generation and status-enhancement. Municipal responsibilities have been commandeered and rearranged, but no municipal status has been sacrificed.[27]

ACCOMMODATION: AVOIDING OPEN CONFLICT

There is an obvious contradiction between this multiplication of opportunities for status-enhancement on the one hand, and concern for professionalism-performance on the other. Area politicians seldom attempt to rationalize this contradiction, largely because they prefer *accommodation*—even to an obviously "less efficient" system—over activities that might lead to open conflict. The preference for accommodation has emerged repeatedly as a powerful theme in these pages: in the reluctance of national and city officials to push suburban bosses into policy positions, or in the relative ease with which a strongly advocated position is accepted by former opponents of that position, or in the elaborate rituals designed to mask the existence of conflict. Moreover, we know from other studies that the Swedish official elite perceives the world in terms that encourage accommodation.[28] All

25. The reasoning behind this decision is available in "Rapport från arbetsgruppen om antalet Borgarråd och rotelindelningen" (Stockholm: Självstyrelseutredningen, 1970), pp. 34ff. Mimeographed.

26. *Dagens Nyheter*, January 26, 1971, reports on amusing sidelights to the question of county commissioner salaries.

27. It should be pointed out, here, however, that several Stockholm area municipalities—including Danderyd-Djursholm—were combined on January 1, 1971, as a result of national reform legislation.

28. See Anton, Linde, and Mellbourn, "Bureaucrats in Politics . . . ," *op. cit.*, pp. 30–32, for a description of Swedish officials as people who have "a marked

this makes clear that area politicians very much prefer harmonious interpersonal relationships, and will go to considerable lengths to achieve such relationships.

If one asks why such emphasis is placed on social harmony, the first answer—at least for the Stockholm politician—must be that failure to achieve it is politically dangerous. Given citizen discomfort with open conflict, strong public criticism of official behavior can destroy political careers. Recent Swedish political history is replete with cases of national figures who leave office in the wake of criticism they were unable to manage.[29] More to the point, many Stockholm area politicians have had similar experiences. Garpe, for example, is known to have felt personally aggrieved by criticism levelled against him during the debate over the 1962 city plan, for which he had major responsibility. Though he wanted to resign immediately, he stayed on until 1964, precisely to avoid the appearance of being hounded from office.[30]

Even Hjalmar Mehr, veteran of many hard campaigns in which he gave as much criticism as he received, left office in 1971 after a year of struggle over a group of large elm trees in a downtown park, capped by a summer in which he felt compelled to call out the police to quell a disturbance at the site. Mehr's departure from City Hall may have been entirely coincidental, or due to totally unrelated political factors,[31] but a system that judges politicians in good part by their ability to avoid *any* conflicts—let alone breakdowns in public order—suggests obvious conclusions to be drawn from events such as the elm tree conflict. In an order-conscious society, attacks can in fact destroy political careers. That is a major reason why such attacks are undertaken neither lightly nor often. It also helps to explain why public political discourse in Sweden is so restrained, masking even

tendency to particularize their perceptions of the world." This tendency, it is then argued, encourages agreement rather than conflict.

29. For example, Jarl Hjalmarsson, former Conservative party leader, whose criticism of the Soviet Union damaged his ability to continue to lead the party, or more recently Sven Widén, who was unable to maintain his leadership of the Liberal party after strong criticism during the 1968 election campaign.

30. Kubu, *Det politiska spelet* . . . , p. 256. The Social Democrats in general, and Garpe in particular, were severely criticized during the 1962 campaign for having destroyed too much in their drive to renew the city.

31. In 1971 Mehr was offered, and accepted, the Governorship of Stockholm County. Given the prestige of this position, and given also his hospitalization for overwork in early 1971, he clearly had a number of powerful incentives for accepting the position. Interestingly enough, he was succeeded as Finance Commissioner by his brother-in-law, Albert Aronson.

substantial criticism in phrases that sound like praise, and smothering political debate in highly ritualized assertions of mutual good will.[32] In Stockholm politics, to accommodate is to survive.

LATENT ROLE ORIENTATIONS
AND THE POLITICS OF CHANGE

The complexity of policy-making behavior in urban Stockholm suggests how difficult it would be to use the Stockholm experience as a model for solving the problems of other urban regions. It is not that Stockholm's problems are unique, nor are Stockholm's solutions uninteresting. But the most important aspect of the Stockholm experience is inherently the most difficult to transfer: the social system through which policy is generated and problems are resolved.

Again and again city administrators, steeped in professionalism and well versed in the latest policy innovations in other parts of the world, have identified problems, researched alternative solutions, and presented area politicians with plans for solving them. Again and again, those plans have been held up while the politicians grew accustomed to them, came to appreciate their social and political implications, and finally "agreed" to changes that often were radically different from the *status quo*. Although administrative expertise clearly led the way toward defining system goals, none of those goals would have had the slightest impact in the absence of highly developed political skills among area public officials. To seriously offer the Stockholm experience as a model, then, we would have to urge that other urban regions not only copy the Stockholm technology, but that they copy Stockholm's problem-solving procedures as well. In short, we would be urging other regions to copy the politics of Stockholm.

Copy their politics! Is that possible, and would it be desirable? To be sure, there are some aspects of Stockholm area politics that can be instructive to other regions. One example is the commitment of area politicians to the values of efficiency in function and equality in service distribution, which guided their pursuit of solutions to specific problems and provided the necessary value framework for settling disagreements. A second example is the development of organizational and administrative capacity by the city in fields such as housing and mass transit. This resource, along with city control over large land

32. For a more detailed discussion of the conflict over the elm trees, see below, Chapter VII.

reserves in the suburbs, laid the foundation for city-suburban bargaining.

Similarly, the structural combination of independent political authority, and group support for such authority in Stockholm city administration, may be said to have contributed greatly to regional political achievements. Nor can we avoid mention of the open and permanent participation of the national government in regional affairs, which provided both pressure to act and financial assistance to speed action. Each of these gross characteristics—of value, structure, national integration—helps to "explain" Stockholm's success. Together they offer some insight into what might be done to achieve similar success elsewhere.

But even limited insights of this kind are questionable if they fail to take contextual factors into account. Though seldom directly observable in specific actions, latent role orientations provide both assumptions and evaluative standards which structure the way problems are defined and solutions sought. A citizenry that discounts the political and social value of governmental units in favor of their service-production value provides an ideal foil for officials interested in pursuing administrative efficiency and functionality. Planned institutional change is hardly surprising when officials can confidently look ahead to a tenure of a decade or more in office, free from any form of citizen agitation that could possibly force them to act in haste. Moreover, agreement among men who see themselves as quite independent is made easier, if not guaranteed, by the political and personal costs of failing to agree—in a society whose citizens place such high value on social harmony. To the extent that latent orientations limit policy-making, transfer of problem-solving technology from one national system to another will indeed be limited.

All this would be a lesson of stunning banality, were it not for our inability to learn it. By treating policy as mere technique (and vice versa), or by focusing primarily on "a decision," scholars repeatedly obscure the sociopolitical preconditions associated with policies and policy-making.[33] Yet if the Stockholm experience shows anything, it shows the absolute necessity of understanding the social foundations on which advanced urban technology rests: we do not understand city planning in the Stockholm region unless we understand the poli-

33. Robert R. Alford has made an interesting effort to bring together these various perspectives in his "Explanatory Variables in the Comparative Study of Urban Administration and Politics," in Robert T. Daland, ed., *Comparative Urban Research* (Beverly Hills, California: Sage Publications, 1969), pp. 272–324.

tics of housing there, nor do we understand the new metropolitan transit system unless we understand the curious relationship of a Swedish citizen to his elected local representatives. If this seems obvious in the Stockholm case, it should be overwhelming in considering policy-making for American cities, where environments are more complex and political structures are far less organized. Many nevertheless persist in the assumption—or is it a hope—that the problems of American cities will be susceptible to one or another form of technological "breakthrough": a new computer system, a method of producing low-cost housing through mass-production techniques, a PPBS system for management, a "new idea" imported from Stockholm or some other foreign city.

If the preceding argument is correct, these assumptions (or hopes) are bound to be frustrated. Techniques that "work" in one region may have entirely different consequences in another, depending on peculiar characteristics of the problem, no less than the mix of local political traditions and values. The Stockholm experience, therefore, will give us no clear-cut answers to questions posed in different regions. Nevertheless, it may help in other ways. Instead of asking whether Stockholm can offer *solutions* to other metropolitan regions, let us conclude by asking whether there is anything in the range of *problems* Stockholm has dealt with that can assist other regions. This may seem a less dramatic inquiry but, as we shall see, it has ramifications of no little consequence.

CHAPTER VII

TOWARD THE NEW POLITICS
OF METROPOLITAN GOVERNANCE

STOCKHOLM is only one among a large number of urban regions that have attempted to restructure their governmental machinery in the past quarter century. Throughout Europe and North America problems created by urban growth—inadequate housing, the need for expanded public services, congested transportation systems, etc.—have created political pressures to reorganize existing structures of local government, or to replace such structures with institutions better suited to the management of urban development. Scholars have begun to notice these efforts at institutional reform, with promising results.[1]

Although general conclusions must await the completion of further studies, it is not too early to begin the analysis of common issues.[2] Accordingly, after a brief review of the postwar Stockholm experience, this chapter assesses the political issues dealt with by Stockholm

1. For a review of the American experience, see Thomas M. Scott, "Metropolitan Governmental Reorganization Proposals," *Western Political Quarterly*, Vol. XXI (1968), pp. 252–261. For an interesting review of reform efforts in Vancouver, which also manages to review the Canadian experience in general, see Paul Tennant and David Zirnhelt, "Metropolitan Government in Vancouver: The Strategy of Gentle Imposition," *Canadian Public Administration*, Vol. 16 (1973), pp. 124–138. For a review that focuses on the European experience, see Annmarie Hauck Walsh, *The Urban Challenge to Government: An International Comparison of Thirteen Cities* (New York: Praeger, 1969).

2. Donald L. Foley offers the beginnings of such analysis in his *Governing the London Region* (Berkeley: University of California Press, 1972), pp. 180–189. Oliver P. Williams attempts to place such an analysis within a general framework in his valuable little book, *Metropolitan Political Analysis* (New York: The Free Press, 1971), pp. 97–110.

area politicians that seem unavoidable in other contexts—particularly the American context. A reconsideration of concepts used to examine issues follows, and a modest reformulation of concepts is suggested as a more useful analytic tool. The reformulated concepts are then used to structure some speculations about the future of Stockholm's new metropolitan government.

COMPONENTS OF PERFORMANCE

In some ways, the Stockholm experience in the postwar era deserves to be regarded as "deviant." Compared to European cities such as London or Berlin, Stockholm suffered no wartime damage to property and little of the psychological or political trauma associated with such damage. Compared to American cities such as Chicago, Detroit, or Philadelphia, Stockholm experienced no postwar influx of people of different race, nationality or culture.

Class distinctions, important as they were in city politics, were nevertheless distinctions *among Swedes,* who attended the same schools, read the same newspapers, listened to the same three radio stations and watched the same television channel.[3] For all these reasons, a persuasive case can be made that the "load" of problems to be dealt with by the regional political system after 1945 was relatively light, compared to other major cities. Certainly the harassed officials of many American cities would agree with a conclusion recently offered by a Canadian Minister that "Sweden is an easy country to govern. . . ."[4]

From a strictly Swedish perspective, too, the Stockholm experience was different. National standards of performance capacity began to be applied to Swedish municipalities in 1952; almost two decades more were required before the same standards began to be seriously applied in the Stockholm region. To a large extent this lag in the application of national standards must be attributed to the city bureaucracy. Because of its size and resources, the city administrative corps was able to induce suburban governments into service agreements that blunted the thrust of national intervention. And because of their sophisticated competence, city administrative politicians were often able to outwit and outmaneuver national officials who might otherwise have succeeded in substituting national for regional

3. By 1971, a second television channel had begun operation.
4. Boyce Richardson, *The Future of Canadian Cities* (Toronto: New Press, 1972), p. 52.

decisions.[5] Stockholm was not able to avoid imposition of national standards indefinitely, nor did it wish to avoid those standards. Their application, however, took place on terms defined largely by regional rather than national politicians.

There is a final important "difference": Stockholm has been more successful than most other urban regions in managing urban growth. Consider the manner in which the region has accommodated almost one-half million new postwar residents. Physically, the worst slums of central Stockholm have been eliminated, an entirely new core area has been constructed, and tens of thousands of new dwelling units have been built in both the city and its surrounding suburbs. An entirely new subway system linking the city to almost all of these new residential areas has been constructed, and continues even now to expand.

Annual housing production in the region increased dramatically after 1955, reaching a peak of more than 20,000 units in the late 1960s before stabilizing at a lower level. Meanwhile, housing quality —as measured either by space or equipment—has been greatly improved.[6] Significantly, these results have been achieved without destroying the environment. It remains possible to walk for miles through woodland or along unspoiled shores—and still be in the heart of Stockholm! Whether or not Stockholm's problems have been somehow less pressing than those of other cities, it seems incontestable that, at least in these respects, the region has been governed with great skill.

The more important structural and motivational components of that skill deserve to be emphasized:

A Passive Population: Except for the formality of voting, citizen interest, knowledge, and involvement in policy-making was minimal, freeing regional political leaders from pressure to act in haste, or without sufficient information.

Elite Concentration: Political influence was centered in a handful of city and suburban politicians, whose command of important governmental resources meant that agreement among them was the equivalent of a metropolitan public policy.

5. I base this judgment on the maneuvers of Hjalmar Mehr and his colleagues, though I realize a contrary case can easily be made.
6. For this evidence, see *Skiss 1966 till regionplan för stockholmstrakten* (Stockholm: Stockholmtraktens regionplankontor, 1967), pp. 80–81.

Elite Stability: Virtually all members of the Stockholm elite had been engaged in regional politics for at least a decade, and sometimes two or three decades. They could *plan* because they expected to be in office long enough to implement their intentions; they could *coordinate* because they could communicate easily with colleagues they already knew, or soon came to know; they could *act* because they had accumulated a great deal of experience in the art of decision; they could *adjust* because they were in office long enough to observe consequences of prior decisions.

National-Local Integration: The joint participation of national and regional officials in the resolution of metropolitan policy problems provided additional resources and incentives which repeatedly shaped metropolitan policy outcomes.

Elite Ideologies: Because of background and training, members of the regional elite operated in terms of a common set of commitments: to *professionalism* (the most effective solution should be sought), to *equalitarianism* (no solution should benefit one group more than another), to *realism* (solutions will be paid for by someone, thus cost is always an appropriate criterion of judgment).

Elite Opportunism: The settings in which members of the elite interacted, coupled with ideological commitments, structured their pursuit of competence and innovation in dealing with regional problems.

It should be added that these components of the Stockholm urban development game changed far less than did the physical and demographic face of the Stockholm region. To be sure, the formal structure of authority was gradually altered as city and suburban politicians became integrated into a more centralized structure. But even as this process was taking place, development decisions continued to be made by a tiny, stable, and professionalized elite, according to shared ideologies, without significant public interference. In short, the game was dominated by veterans, who knew how to keep their jobs, and how to produce.

Unfortunately, knowledge of the components of Stockholm's management "success" leads to no obvious recommendations for other urban regions. Techniques that work in Stockholm may be totally inapplicable in other political systems, with different traditions and public preferences. American readers who resist this conclusion can perform a simple mental experiment that might help to establish its validity: imagine the fate of a proposal, made in any major American city, to establish publicly owned and publicly financed housing companies. Similarly, the political characteristics associated with "success" in Stockholm may have different consequences elsewhere. The Stockholm experience, for example, suggests that citizen passivity encouraged good urban design, but think of Detroit or Los Angeles, where citizens are hardly less passive. The Stockholm experience suggests that elite stability promotes effective urban planning, but consider Chicago, another city notable for the stability of its governors.[7] These examples imply that we do not now know enough about cause and effect relationships in urban governance. They also suggest that comparisons among cities, on a scale yet to be imagined, would be necessary to identify such relationships.[8]

ISSUES OF REFORM

Meanwhile, efforts to reform institutions of urban governance continue, without a knowledge base sufficient to offer unambiguous guidelines for change. This may be unfortunate, but it is also the typical predicament faced by authorities responsible for the design of public policy.[9] In this situation it does not seem unreasonable to derive whatever we can from the Stockholm experience. Although the Stockholm experience cannot give us ready-made solutions to problems, surely it can help us to achieve a better insight into the nature of those problems. However "different" Stockholm may be, it remains an "exploding metropolis," that has been forced to deal with developmental problems, through institutions that reflect a democratic heritage. If we focus on politics, rather than on program technologies, several real political issues stand out:

1. The Purposes of "Municipal" Government. Should a political system have "local" governments? If so, what purposes should they serve? These two questions structure an issue well illustrated by the Stockholm experience—and one likely to become increasingly important. In democratic societies answers to the first question are

7. Probably the best evocation of "planning" in Chicago is Martin Meyerson and Edward C. Banfield, Politics, Planning and the Public Interest (Glencoe: The Free Press, 1955). For other cities in America, see Edward C. Banfield and James Q. Wilson, City Politics (Cambridge: Harvard University Press, 1966).

8. For a recent consideration of this problem, see Robert C. Fried, "Comparative Urban Performance." Working Paper No. 1, European Urban Research, UCLA, 1973. Mimeographed.

9. Donald A. Schon makes this point very effectively in his Beyond the Stable State (New York: W. W. Norton & Co., 1971), pp. 201–237.

likely to repeat the justifications contained in Hjalmar Mehr's speech of December 1963: local government is necessary because it trains people in the exercise of democratic responsibilities and because, in the long run, it will be more effective than centralized government alone. The fact that Mehr raised the issue at all was significant, for it implied his recognition that the issue could not be regarded as settled. In the Swedish context, of course, the issue was far from settled. More than a thousand local governments had been eliminated at the time Mehr spoke, and hundreds more were in the process of being eliminated because of performance failures. Mehr's statement provided symbolic support for participation, in a context heavily biased toward performance.

In the American context the participation-performance scale is tipped the other way. Americans not only accept the desirability of local government, but they seem willing to tolerate an enormous number of such governments, presumably because they afford opportunities for participation. Americans view efficient provision of public services as only one among several legitimate purposes of local government—and not the most important one at that.[10] Among the purposes that seem more important in metropolitan areas is protection of status and privilege. To provide protection against industry, or poor people, or people of a different race or nationality, a municipality need not have a good tax base, nor a well-trained cadre of officials. All that is required is political commitment and control.

Democratic participation thus becomes a device that uses municipal boundaries to separate one group or class from another.[11] Given the power of these motivations in the racially and socially heterogeneous metropolitan areas of the United States, use of the municipality to protect status and privilege will inevitably be incompatible with workable metropolitan solutions to public problems. To the extent that metropolitan solutions come to be seen as useful alternatives in the future, the issue of legitimate municipal purposes will become even more pronounced.

Stockholm area politicians confronted this problem openly during the period 1945–1970. They resolved it without destroying existing municipalities, although a number of important municipal functions

10. Oliver P. Williams makes this point in an especially interesting way in his *Metropolitan Political Analysis* (New York: The Free Press, 1971), pp. 36–49.
11. A good summary of evidence on this point is Bernard J. Frieden, *Metropolitan America: Challenge to Federalism* (Washington: Advisory Commission on Intergovernmental Relations, 1966), Ch. 11.

were transferred to a new metropolitan institution. There is nothing particularly innovative about the Stockholm solution, but the willingness of area politicians to be flexible in thinking about municipal purposes suggests that Americans, too, might profitably reexamine their assumptions about the purposes of local government. Democratic participation is a legitimate enough justification for local government, yet a great many studies demonstrate that American local government is seldom very democratic, at least in its present variety of forms.[12]

Protection of status and privilege is a more dubious conception of municipal purpose, but even if it is accepted as legitimate, evidence is accumulating that municipalities are less and less able to offer such protection. State and federal courts are imposing higher level standards on local units in education, taxation, and a variety of service activities.[13] The growing trend toward corporate participation in land and community development means that many of our localities are literally under siege by large oil corporations, national insurance companies, the major automobile corporations, the conglomerates, or the new giant firms which specialize in land development.[14] Against organizations of such size and resources, American municipalities are seldom a good match.[15] Finally, the provision of adequate public services of even the simplest kind has fallen victim to declining revenues, especially in America's largest cities.[16]

These developments lead inexorably to a single conclusion: the problem of municipal purpose will not go away. Citizen response to the problem has begun to be expressed in reluctance to continue financing localized public activities, and a similar interest in higher level intervention.[17] Those with the greatest stake in the values of local institutions—municipal officials—would do well to heed the ex-

12. Two "classics" (among many studies) that support this point are Floyd Hunter, *Community Power Structure* (Chapel Hill: The University of North Carolina Press, 1953), and Robert A. Dahl, *Who Governs?* (New Haven: Yale University Press, 1961).

13. *Serrano v. Priest*, 5 Cal 3rd, 584 (1971).

14. A good study of these activities is yet to be written, but see *Urban and Rural America: Policies for Future Growth* (Washington: Advisory Commission on Intergovernmental Relations, 1968), pp. 79–82, for some preliminary evidence.

15. For a more comprehensive review of local government structure and resources, see Douglas Commission, *Report*, pp. 323–416.

16. *Ibid.*, p. 355ff.

17. Both citizens and officials have expressed this interest: the former in defeating millage and bonding proposals, the latter in the steady demand for more state and federal financial assistance.

ample of their Swedish counterparts: developments that seem inevitable may nevertheless be influenced by "choosing" to participate in them.

2. *Governmental Conflicts of Interest.* If a political system chooses to have a system of local governments, it is necessarily creating governmental conflicts of interest. Such conflicts will occur not because local officials are mean-spirited or irrational, but rather because there will always be some issues on which the interests of one community conflict with the interests of others. Location, size, wealth (however measured), and characteristics of municipal populations are matters which tend to cause even the most carefully conceived governmental programs to have a differential impact. Moreover, governmental organizations are like other kinds of organizations: once established, they quickly develop a vested interest in their own continuation, however well or badly they serve their manifest goals. For all these reasons, municipalities are likely to conflict with one another frequently, and this is especially true in metropolitan regions.

In Stockholm, for example, questions that involved direct conflicts of interest between area municipalities included control over the allocation of apartments to renters, the ownership of land, representation on regional bodies, the assignments of costs for transit facilities, and the allocation of national funding for roadways. Stockholm politicians ultimately were able to resolve most of these conflicts, in large measure because they had developed the habit of identifying the interests of all parties as clearly and as openly as they could.

By contrast, American metropolitan politicians quite commonly fail to achieve clear statements of municipal interests. Participants are often either too arrogant (cities) or too fearful (suburbs) to admit the legitimacy of views different from their own. Observers, on the other hand, often retain such a naive belief in "the one best solution" that alternative solutions are quickly branded as products of ignorance, racism, or other assorted evils.[18] The Stockholm experience, however, makes clear that such conflicts are neither illegitimate nor the result of evil intentions; they are in fact endemic to systems in which real authority is dispersed. The Stockholm experience suggests, too, that resolution of metropolitan conflicts may be encouraged by a common determination to identify the interests at stake, define them carefully, and deal with them as legitimate matters of political bargaining.

18. In this connection, see Scott Greer, *Metropolitics* (New York: John Wiley, 1963), pp. 1–18.

3. Conflict Resolution by Appeal to Higher Authority. If the preceding argument is valid, there are bound to be many conflicts among municipalities in metropolitan areas that cannot be resolved by local officials. Unless higher authority intervenes—that is, unless higher levels adopt policy positions aimed at coordinating municipal activities—intermunicipal coordination cannot be achieved. The Swedish experience gives special emphasis to this point, precisely because elimination of 90 per cent of local governments in Sweden was *supported* by a majority of local officials.

Yet even in an environment in which local officials can agree to eliminate their own jobs, politicians in the nation's major metropolitan area could not agree on a method for allocating dwelling units. Moreover they reached agreement in other controversial areas only when the national government exercised its coercive "persuasion." Higher level intervention, of course, assumes the existence of a higher level policy. Imposing that policy is clearly a delicate matter in systems that take pride in the strength of their local governments. The very strength of those governments, however, implies a need for a higher level mechanism to alleviate unavoidable conflict.[19]

4. Views of Appropriate "Public" Responsibilities. Most large American cities suffer from housing shortages and dilapidation of existing housing units. As the "ticky-tacky" houses constructed during the postwar suburban housing boom pass into their third and fourth decades of existence, moreover, we can expect the housing problem to assume a decidedly suburban character. Yet, compared to Stockholm, American urban governments are confined to a secondary and poorly financed role in the production of new units. Limitations on the housing responsibilities of public authorities reflect the general American reluctance to seek public solutions to problems if there is any possibility for private solutions. Put another way, the scope of governmental activity accepted as legitimate is distinctly broader in Sweden and Stockholm than it is in the United States. Whereas public policy imagery in Sweden has come to emphasize community-defined living standards, guaranteed for all citizens, American imagery continues to stress freedom from community standards, individual initiative, and the chance to "strike it rich."

There is some question whether American reluctance to rely on

19. This would seem to be particularly true where there is no tradition of attachment to a more encompassing polity, as there is in Sweden. Could local officials in the United States be encouraged to develop attachments to the state systems in which they operate? If so, how?

public solutions represents principle, or simply a convenient rationale for the protection of propertied interests.[20] There is little doubt, on the other hand, that acceptance of a more active governmental role in Stockholm gives to that system a variety of political advantages. The existence of publicly owned and operated housing companies, for example, not only encouraged a high volume of housing construction but, equally important, gave Stockholm resources that could be used in bargaining with other governments. In return for access to badly needed land, the city was able to trade its financial and management resources, both of which were lacking in the suburbs. More bargains could be arranged, in short, because there was more to bargain with. The obvious cost of a larger role for public authority is higher taxes—indeed, Swedish taxes are now regarded as the highest in any "western" nation.[21] Yet as urban regions continue to expand, and as social relations within them continue to become more complex, expansion of public authority seems unavoidable. Will Americans find some ingenious way to avoid the "unavoidable"? Or will they move toward a more active governmental role in their urban regions, and if so, how? These are real issues, of serious consequence. They deserve sustained political attention.

Finally, there is another, more diffuse, issue which can be derived from the Stockholm experience: the issue is public and official attitudes toward governmental experimentation. No public institution, designed by humans to serve human purposes, is set in concrete. As social conditions change, institutions either change to meet new conditions, or become less and less relevant. In the United States, a comparatively new nation, official resistance to institutional change is often so great that crisis seems our most effective change mechanism. In Sweden, an old society, officials seem far more experimental. If an institutional arrangement breaks down, an adjustment is made. If observation reveals continuing problems, other adjustments are made, and the process of observation, evaluation, and adjustment repeats itself.

20. In the housing area, for example, there has been no reluctance to distribute public benefits to those who appear to need it least. The Douglas Commission (see note 15, above) has demonstrated that FHA programs have benefited the middle classes primarily, and Henry Aaron has shown that some $7 billion in annual tax write-offs are enjoyed by mortgage holders, mostly in the middle- and upper-income brackets. See Henry Aaron, *Shelter and Subsidies* (Washington: The Brookings Institution, 1972), p. 162.

21. For basic information, see *Taxes in Sweden* (Stockholm: The Swedish Institute, 1973).

There is no need to pretend that these processes characterize all of Swedish government, all of the time, or even that these processes are always effective. The point is that institutional experimentation is widely practiced by Swedish public authorities, in ways that permit them to combine a conservative *rate* of changing, with an essentially continuous *process* of change. It is as though the highway markers guiding those who steer Swedish institutional vehicles all carry the same instruction: "Drive slowly, but keep moving."

IMAGES OF CHANGE, LANGUAGE OF STABILITY

Scholars have only recently begun to appreciate the difficulties of understanding systems whose processes result in continuous self-transformation.[22] The most obvious difficulty, of course, is conceptual: the categories of thought we use to describe and analyse these processes seem both limited and limiting.

THE DECISION-MAKING CONCEPT

Consider the difficulties involved in applying the concept of decision-making to the Stockholm experience. What "decision" would we want to select for detailed analysis, and on what grounds?

If our goal is to understand creation of the new metropolitan government, we could plausibly choose Hjalmar Mehr's speech of December 1963, which laid out a plan not very different from the institutional structures actually created in 1971. But we might also choose, with equal plausibility, the transportation agreement of October 1963, which Mehr interpreted as a signal to go ahead, or the *Lex Bollmora* of December 1958, or even the decision to create a "foreign minister" for Stockholm in December 1954. Retrospectively, each of these events can be seen to be related to the new Metro, though in rather different ways.

Yet the "decision-making" approach would have us choose one as crucial and deal with the others, if at all, as part of a "situation," or perhaps as "background." Short of perfect knowledge, such a judgment is bound to be arbitrary and thus bound to influence conclusions for essentially arbitrary reasons. Moreover, as the events of October–December 1963 make clear, the *relatedness* of events is often their most important quality. Attempting to slice out a single event

22. The pioneering work in political analysis, of course, was Karl Deutsch, *The Nerves of Government* (New York: The Free Press of Glencoe, 1963). But see Schon, *op. cit.*, for an interesting recent statement.

from a number of closely interrelated events is bound to be not only arbitrary, but misleading.

Suppose, however, that we have selected one of these events as the decision to be analyzed. What aspects of the event do we examine? The decision-making schema suggests that we first identify the relevant actors, then investigate their perceptions, and finally analyze their *goals* with regard to the situation. The decision can then be "explained" by reference to the goals that motivated whatever action took place.

This disarmingly simple formulation conceals two problems. The first is that goals are seldom formulated with enough precision to give such statements explanatory power. Confronted with a situation demanding action, politicians may find that they have no clear-cut goals regarding that situation. They may proceed to develop a goal or goals, only to find that further situational developments require that earlier formulations be changed. Thus, anything but a routine decision is likely to generate goal statements that are ambiguous, that change over time, and that result as much from a process of interaction as from the intentions of a single individual.

Between December 1963 and January 1971 several important changes were made in Hjalmar Mehr's plan for a metropolitan government. Mehr's original goals clearly were not achieved, but how do we then explain the final outcome? To retain "goals" as an explanation we might simply assert that original intentions were changed. But how do we then account for those changes? Obviously a number of other factors are relevant, among them interorganizational communication patterns, organizational self-preservation, and competition for power. Within the decision-making framework, however, it is difficult to take such factors into account.[23]

The second problem is the individualistic and rationalistic bias of decision-making analysis. Focusing on individual actors necessarily neglects the structures in which they operate.[24] Similarly, explaining actions in terms of intentions—what Allison has aptly called the "rational actor" model—assumes that other kinds of explanations are

23. For similar arguments see Sir Geoffrey Vickers, *The Art of Judgment* (New York: Basic Books, Inc., 1965), pp. 13–35, and Raymond A. Bauer, "The Study of Policy Formation: An Introduction," in Raymond A. Bauer and Kenneth J. Gergen, eds., *The Study of Policy Formation* (New York: The Free Press, 1968), pp. 1–26.

24. *Ibid.* Victor A. Thompson also makes this point effectively in his *Modern Organization* (New York: Alfred A. Knopf, 1961), pp. 3–9.

less worthy of attention.[25] These assumptions make it difficult to account for a variety of political behaviors. Hjalmar Mehr was *in favor of* a metropolitan governmental solution in the late 1940s, *against* it in the mid-1950s, and *for* it again in the early 1960s. Presumably, no reader of the preceding material would argue that Mehr became less rational over time, or that his intentions were subject to wild fluctuations. Mehr's calculations, like those of any sensible politician, were necessarily shaped in part by situations that changed over time. To understand his behavior, it is clearly necessary to place it within a *context* and a *structure,* no less than a framework of presumed rationality.

THE CONCEPT OF PLANNING

Equally serious problems plague the related concept of planning. Earlier definitions of the concept laid primary emphasis on the plan, whose existence would somehow guide land-use decisions. Later, discussions of planning came to emphasize the processes of devising and implementing methods for controlling future development. In this form, the definition of planning seems identical to *rational decision-making,* that is, a style of making decisions in which objectives are clearly specified, alternative methods of achieving those objectives are developed, along with the consequences (in costs and benefits) of each alternative, and a choice made based on greatest achievement at least cost.[26]

As an ideal, this image of public officials pursuing rationality on behalf of the public interest has motivated the creation of "planning" agencies in communities all over the world. As a description of reality, however, the "rational process" model seems no more useful than the "rational actor" model. To be sure, the Stockholm Area Regional Planning Board labored long and hard—after overcoming early organizational difficulties—to produce a regional plan approved by area governments in 1958 and by the national government in 1960. But we have seen that the process of organizing the work of the board was itself intensely political, and we have also noted that many of the most important prescriptions derived from that plan—for example, the location of new suburban housing—were not followed.

25. Graham T. Allison, *Essence of Decision* (Boston: Little, Brown and Company, 1971), pp. 10–38.

26. For a penetrating analysis of this ideal, in the context of the development of planning ideologies, see Alan A. Altshuler, *The City Planning Process* (Ithaca: Cornell University Press, 1965), esp. pp. 299–405.

The board's activities did generate a good deal of information useful in forecasting, and the process of preparing a plan did bring area politicians together socially and psychologically, but those benefits were primarily political. Moreover, the board was involved only peripherally in later activities that were crucial to area development: gaining control of suburban land and coordination of mass transit facilities. These activities, too, were governed by political rather than rational planning considerations. Objectives could seldom be defined with great precision; as often as not, "alternative" courses of action were simply unavailable; choices were responses to opportunity rather than efforts to maximize some criterion of value.

THE CONCEPT OF "POLICY-MAKING"

The concept of "policy-making" resolves some, but not all, of these difficulties. Because policy is conceived as a series of similar decisions, rather than a single one, we are forced to extend our analysis through time. Extension through time, in turn, normally forces us to consider the actions of many individuals, rather than a few, and thus requires a modification of analytic focus. Roles and organizations (or players and games) become more appropriate concepts, precisely because they suggest the continuation of action and purpose through time, regardless of individual identity. These concepts permit us to relate individual behavior to social structures and allow us to examine structural interrelationships in the search for origins of policy.

Indeed, these concepts give so much emphasis to continuity and stability that they may well impede the analysis of change.[27] An analyst who sets out to find repetitive patterns of behavior will find them, in part because he will have purposely overlooked evidence suggesting nonrepetitive actions. To examine change, without destroying conclusions (based on assumptions) about continuity and stability, it often seems expedient to return to the analysis of a single, "crucial," decision. Analytically, we wind up chasing our tails—or so it would seem.

END-STATE

What each of these concepts shares with the others is *an implicit vision of an end-state*, after which no further action takes place. We say that a decision is "made," a goal is "achieved," a plan is "devel-

27. For a consideration of the problem, in a relevant context, see William Mitchell, *Sociological Analysis and Politics: The Theories of Talcott Parsons* (Englewood Cliffs, N.J.: Prentice-Hall, Inc., 1967), pp. 145–192.

oped," or a policy is "stated." The verbs themselves imply that a sequence of activities has come to an end, that whatever preceded the end-state is no longer of interest, and that nothing follows except continuation of the end-state condition. These are largely artificial images, imposed by the words used, but they seem consequential nonetheless. The implicit messages contained in these kinds of words may not be unrelated to the curious aversion scholars show toward problems of program implementation. With few exceptions, such problems are avoided in favor of what may appear to be the more dramatic activities that precede a choice of program. And surely these images reflect a widespread need to believe in what Donald A. Schon calls the "stable state," that is, "the unchangeability, the constancy of central aspects of our lives, or belief that we can attain such a constancy." [28]

A DETERMINISTIC ENVIRONMENT

At the other end of the process envisioned by these standard concepts, meanwhile, is a peculiarly *deterministic environment,* which sets the parameters within which decisions or policies are made, but which itself seems strangely impervious to human action. Studies of planning or policy-making typically begin by delineating a "problem" in terms of environmental characteristics assumed to have an objective reality: a "housing shortage" as measured by the following figures, population "overcrowding" as seen in the following table, and so on. Orientations and actions focused on this "problem" are then portrayed as preliminaries to some decision or policy tailored to the "problem" through the vehicle of actor intentions or goals.

Since the typical study stops at this point, it is never clear that the environment is affected by the action portrayed. The implication, however, is that the "problem" is resolved by the action. Since a problem is by definition "unusual," the further implication is that problem resolution returns the environment to a previously existing, "normal," condition. Over the life-time of a typical decisional analysis, then, the environment remains unchanged, yet it seems to both initiate and set parameters for the action described. Whether or not people need to believe in it, a stable state is what scholars typically describe.

28. Schon, *op. cit.,* p. 9.

THE IMAGE OF THE REACTIVE POLITICIAN

There is a third characteristic common to our standard concepts of public choice: *the image of the reactive politician*. The problems that initiate action and the limitations on what can be done are both somewhere "out there," in the environment. Political action reacts to environmental problems through observation and analysis designed to produce solutions. But even when such reactive action is successful, the result is no more than restoration of the environment to a preexistent state. From time to time, changes in the forms of political action may occur (i.e., governmental reorganization). Such changes, however, do no more than improve the ameliorative capacity of human action. Real environmental change remains beyond the reach of actors, as it remains beyond the view of analysts.

MANAGING THE ENVIRONMENT

To some extent, of course, these observations about the implicit meanings of common concepts of public choice represent a caricature of what analysts themselves mean to say. Nevertheless, the caricature may be valuable, for it clearly suggests that currently popular concepts are quite inhospitable to the analysis of change, or to the behavior of politicians involved in change. Practicing politicians, for example, understand the importance of *managing the environment,* and those who are successful manage the environment very well. Yet current styles of analysis imply that the opposite relationship is more likely to be true. Was there not, after all, a flood of people to the Stockholm region after 1945, creating an environment in which rapid population growth was inevitable? Was there not, as a consequence, an environmentally generated housing shortage that forced Stockholm politicians to act? And did not their actions produce so many dwelling units, concentrated in so few places, that it became "necessary" to deal with the transportation problem?

From a process point of view, the best answer to such questions is another: "Who says so?" Postwar Stockholm was unquestionably a powerful magnet for individuals seeking better jobs at higher rates of pay. Projections of population growth for a specific period of time, however, were always subject to uncertainty, and thus to manipulation. Through appropriate manipulation, a presumption of inevitable future growth could be established among regional and national policy-makers. Once established, that presumption could feed upon itself, motivating decisions (i.e., increased housing quotas for Stockholm) that ensured the validity of the original presumption.[29]

Similarly, the length of the housing queue has always been partly a function of rules that define who can, and who cannot, be registered. Rules that permit the registration of young people, single people, or people seeking improvement over perfectly adequate current accommodations are rules that clearly help to maintain a lengthy queue. A lengthy queue, in turn, helps to maintain an image of "shortage" in housing, which politicians may find useful.[30] And finally, if it is in fact true that concentrated housing developments created traffic congestion, then certainly it is appropriate to ask why area politicians insisted on repeatedly building such developments.[31] The problems of the Stockholm environment, in short, were not "just there." Many of them were created by politicians who possessed a sophisticated appreciation of the art of agenda-setting.

A FAR MORE ACTIVE ROLE

These considerations suggest a far more active role for political leaders than is implied by conventional analytic modes. Indeed, they suggest that much of what is recognized, after the fact, as part of a political environment has achieved that status through acts of political will: issues and problems, it turns out, have to be *defined* by someone. (One might add here that solutions, too, have to be defined. Hjalmar Mehr's constant repetition of the Greater County Council idea, at a time when no one else seemed to care about it, is a classic example.) Managing the agenda of public issues thus becomes the

29. Interviews with commissioners involved in these processes made clear that conflict over what estimates to use were common, both among themselves, and between themselves and the planning staffs.

30. I do not mean to discount the severe discomfort experienced by many Stockholmers who were—and are—forced to wait for years to obtain housing. These discomforts and official responses to them have been thoroughly aired, for example, in *SOU 1967:1*. It is clear, on the other hand, that the figures generated to demonstrate "shortage" have been quite ambiguous, and that the politicians have found no reason to attempt any clarification of that ambiguity.

31. The "norm" that no apartment should be more than 500 meters away from a subway station has been the rationale used by planners. See Kell Aström, *City Planning in Sweden* (Stockholm: The Swedish Institute, 1967), p. 55. For the politicians, economic calculations regarding the number of people required to support a subway system led to the same conclusion. See, for example, Anders Nordberg, "Utbyggnaden av tunnelbanenätet." Anförand av utredningschefen hos generalplanberedningen, den 30 juni 1965. Mimeographed. Nevertheless, such developments were certain to generate "problems" for politicians to "solve" at some later point, and the politicians knew it.

crucial component of managing the environment. Successful agenda-control requires the ability to anticipate what elite and mass publics can be persuaded to accept as issues. It also requires the capacity to learn: every political act rearranges existing relationships to some extent, thus creating somewhat different opportunities and incentives for further action. Both of these qualities imply a third: a sense of timing well enough developed to move issues on and off the agenda.

Managing the environment through management of the agenda of public issues are concepts that carry us some distance away from more conventional notions about decision-making. Accordingly, the implicit messages contained within this language are quite different. The world is more relativistic, incapable of yielding "objective" answers to political questions, politicians are more active, and public choice less determined by unyielding external constraints. In this context it is the agenda of public choice—what it contains and how it changes—that is of first importance, not "a decision," or even "a policy." Insofar as decisions are explained, the explanation takes the form of locating a decision on the agenda, and identifying the relationships that constitute the forces that have given it an agenda position. Since both agenda and relationships are in continual flux, there is no end-state envisioned: the emphasis is on process, operating in a context, through time. Change, rather than stability, is normal.[32]

METRO: NEW GOVERNMENT, NEW AGENDA, NEW POLITICS

Sensible assessment of the operation and impact of Stockholm's new metropolitan government, the Greater County Council, must await further experience. It seems clear even now, however, that the new government will shortly rival the City of Stockholm for metropolitan influence. Metro now controls important service activities such as mass transportation and hospitals, a housing agency is active, and assumption of further metropolitan responsibilities is made possible by a far-sighted charter. With direct access to a metropolitan tax base, and the ability to influence "visible" policies such as the recent $10 monthly fee for unlimited use of mass transit facilities,[33] it is perfectly predictable that the new government will soon be per-

32. In addition to the work of Deutsch, Vickers, Bauer, and Schon, cited above, this formulation is built on other work cited in my "Administration 'Blowin' in the Wind'," *Public Administration Review*, Vol. XXIX (1969), pp. 309–316.

33. The so-called "månadskort," or monthly ticket, is of course heavily subsidized from tax revenues.

ceived as powerful, and that competition for leadership positions within it will be keen. Metro seems destined to play an increasingly important role in Stockholm regional government.

To view Metro as a "decision" that "resolved" an issue once and for all, however, would be as misleading as it is analytically primitive. Metro created new positions and rearranged the formal rules of the game somewhat, but older political forces continue to operate. Metro, it should be recalled, retained an existing system of local governments. It thereby retained the potential for intermunicipal conflict, particularly city-suburban conflict.

WELFARE PROBLEMS

The ancient city-suburban conflict surfaced again in 1971 as suburban politicians, ever weary of their municipal big brother, circulated a study documenting the increasing concentration of welfare recipients in the suburbs.[34] Welfare increases had become a problem for reasons that had nothing to do with city-suburban relations: foreign trade deficits, rapid inflation, and rising unemployment combined to create a serious problem for the entire nation in 1970–71. But suburban welfare cases seemed to be concentrated in the rental units constructed and managed by the City of Stockholm! The greater the number of city-owned apartments in a suburban jurisdiction, the larger the number of welfare cases there.[35] Indeed, much of the welfare cost increase experienced by suburban municipalities was devoted to rental assistance for persons unable to meet their monthly obligations to the city companies. Despite a remarkable—by American standards—program of city rental subsidies to suburban units,[36] suburban taxpayers seemed to be in a position of not only subsidizing the poor, but subsidizing city companies as well. In view of the long record of past suburban efforts to avoid exactly this result, the welfare

34. "Socialhjälpskotsnadernas utveckling i Stockholms förortskommuner" (Stockholm: Stockholms förortskommuners samarbetsnämd, October 1970). Mimeographed.

35. Because of data inadequacies this relationship could not be conclusively established, nor could causes be identified. But the relationship seems present on a scatter-diagram. *Ibid.*, Bilaga 6.

36. Because costs of the metropolitan housing queue administration are apportioned according to tax resources, Stockholm pays almost two-thirds of the bill. See *Utlåtande nr 256, 1967* for the constitution and figures, as of that time. More recently, the city has begun contributing to a metropolitan rental subsidy fund, assuming a similar burden. The city is paying, and getting it back. But then, so are the suburbs.

problem could only aggravate city-suburban relations. That strain, in turn, was bound to affect the activities of Metro.

DEVELOPMENT AND THE "GREEN WAVE"

Meanwhile, the national government had begun a shift in its position regarding the Stockholm region that was certain to create a somewhat different set of problems. In 1964, not long after the national government announced that the former military exercise area, *Järvafältet,* would become available for development, Stockholm and four neighboring municipalities reached an agreement to jointly develop the area.[37] By 1970 development was in full swing, with massive planning and financial commitments made, and massive construction under way: this last remaining open area was to be developed as a series of neighborhoods providing housing for an additional 100,000 Stockholmers.

By that time, however, the national government was beginning to feel the effects of trade deficits and inflation, as well as the beginnings of what has come to be known as the "green wave," that is, hostility toward the size of the city, toward the congestion and stress of the city, and toward the idea of future growth of the city. Accordingly, in 1971 the government announced its intention to decentralize the national government structure by moving many large offices to smaller municipalities in other parts of Sweden.[38] The municipal consortium, with financial troubles of its own, responded by rethinking its overall plan for developing the *Järva* area: planning for portions of the project was stopped and several construction projects were slowed down. A whole series of arrangements had come unstuck, including plans for the kind of subway system to be developed for the area. Metro, as well as the municipal consortium, was affected, in ways that would require sustained attention for a considerable time.

If nothing else, these developments suggest that older relationships between city and suburb, and between national and regional governments, will continue to require observation if future development is

37. *Utlåtande nr 118, 1966.*
38. Swedes have always had a fondness for nature and a desire to enjoy its rewards of openness and solitude. In this sense the so-called "green wave" is nothing new, though directing it *against* the city may be new. For a nice evocation of nature loving in Sweden, see Donald S. Connery, *The Scandinavians* (New York: Simon and Schuster, 1966), pp. 302–318. Recently the city has joined forces with officials from the new Metro to protest national policy. See *Dagens Nyheter,* March 24, 1973, for an example.

to be understood. How Metro affects the future will depend in part on how its officials play the game. But it is also conceivable that the game itself is changing in ways that Metro may not be in a position to affect. Agenda management, in particular, may have become a far more difficult task.

Consider, for example, the so-called "green wave" mentioned above. For years, the large numbers of people streaming into Stockholm had justified greater housing production, the idea of economy had justified large-scale and concentrated construction in order to reduce unit costs, and the idea of functionality had justified the co-ordination of transit and service facilities. Growth, economy, and functionality made up an agenda that was accepted by the tiny elite that counted, and could be adroitly managed through timely release of housing statistics and other information. Beginning in the late 1960s, however, the wave of protests sweeping the world came to Stockholm in the form of neighborhood groups (called *byalag*) formed to protest various official actions that threatened neighborhood stability. In September 1968, when the new and well-publicized suburb of *Skärholmen* was opened, the leading Stockholm (and Swedish) newspaper greeted it with a headline that read "Tear Skärholmen Down!" That headline symbolized the beginning of a long and effective alliance between neighborhood groups and the media.

The lengthy and often bitter public debate that followed gradually expanded its focus from *Skärholmen* to another, allegedly worse, new development called *Tensta* (located in *Järvafeltet*), and from there to the overall system of planning itself. In the 1970 Stockholm election, the Center party, whose basic constituency until recently had been farmers, captured 11 per cent of the city vote on the strength of a platform that thoroughly denounced further growth and called for decentralizing the city. This was not only an unprecedented total vote for the Center party, it was also enough to give the party one of the nine City Commissioner positions. In summary the context was: protest against basic planning policies and ideologies, the growth of an entirely new political infrastructure based on neighborhood rather than party interests, and real evidence of the political power of anti-urban sentiment.

THE BATTLE OF THE ELMS

In this context the city announced its intention to cut down an attractive stand of elm trees in a downtown park. According to city officials, the trees had to be eliminated in order to make way for a new subway station. The elm tree issue had in fact been simmering for a year. Months earlier, after the usual progress through at least three City Boards (each of which approved the decision to cut), the City Council had voted to cut down the trees. An audience made up largely of young people observed this event and greeted the decision with hisses, banners, and paper airplanes aimed at city councilmen— a sequence of events that was not only unprecedented, but probably unique in Stockholm history! More rational protests were also made in a review process that ultimately involved Prime Minister Palme, who also approved the decision. Only after the national government indicated approval did the city announce its intention to proceed.

Instead of sailing paper airplanes, the protesters this time organized an encampment in and around the trees. Hammocks were strung among the branches, tents and other paraphernalia required by a large crowd were placed around the base of the trees, and the protesters vowed to stay as long as necessary to prevent the city from acting. Meanwhile, professional architects and planners issued critiques of city plans and alternative plans of their own, showing how a new subway station could be built without destroying the trees. In the midst of all this, gangs of motorcycle toughs decided that the protesters were a perfect target for violent sport. When some preliminary battering of heads showed the situation to be potentially murderous, Mehr asked for sufficient police intervention to maintain peace. In addition, the decision to cut the trees down was temporarily suspended to allow still another committee to review the situation. Months later, the city announced quietly that the trees would be allowed to stand: it was now possible to design a subway station that did not require that the elm trees be destroyed.[39]

What was at stake in this dispute, of course, was the agenda for future political concern. Neighborhood groups had attempted to agitate a variety of other issues previously, but the elm trees proved to be a far better focal point for drama that could be publicized by the media. Media publicity provided a variety of images—from well-rationalized presentations of alternative solutions to extraordinarily defensive statements by city politicians—suggesting that the politicians had already lost control of the agenda.

Had they not already lost control, these events would never have become an "issue," for the decision to cut down the trees was a classic example of how the game was supposed to be played. The

39. This summary is taken from *Dagens Nyheter*, March–May 1971.

process had taken a great deal of time, several different city decision-making bodies had been involved, a variety of organized interests were represented on those bodies, appeals were considered all the way up to the Prime Minister himself, and a great effort was made to "rationalize" the decision in terms of a larger plan for expanding the metropolitan subway network to accommodate citizens and institutions (such as the University of Stockholm) in need of transit service.

Neither the protesters nor the media were prepared to respond to images drawn from the old political agenda. When the politicians talked about ways of accommodating increased traffic caused by growth, the protesters responded by challenging the desirability of growth. When the politicians pointed to the increased costs that would be incurred if their plan were not followed, the protesters replied that the environmental cost of removing the trees would be incalculable. When the politicians talked about their efforts to design a facility that would meet the service and transportation needs of commuters, the protesters attacked the politicians' failure to consider alternative conceptions of service and transportation needs. The politicians were using the language of economy and functionality, but the protesters had something different in mind—an "Alternative City." [40]

NEW PRIORITIES . . . AND BROADER PARTICIPATION

The "victory" of the anti-city forces in the elm tree battle legitimized an entirely different order of priorities for future city policies. It may also have signalled an important broadening of participation in the formation of those policies. During the battle, plans and arguments put forward by various city "experts" were repeatedly shown to be inconsistent, misconceived, or inaccurate. Expertise thus became less compelling as support for a policy position, and experts themselves were shown to be not really different from other political figures with axes to grind. Conversely, the political power of conviction, unadorned by weighty studies, suddenly became apparent. These results of the elm tree affair added stature to neighborhood groups and encouraged greater political participation by "average" citizens. A new style of participation, emphasizing expressiveness and determination more than preparation and rationality, also may have achieved some legitimacy. If so, the events of Spring 1971 will have

40. "Alternative City" is the name of one of the new neighborhood groups in Stockholm.

marked not only the emergence of a different political agenda, but a stage of broader citizen political participation as well.

It is easy enough to argue that these kinds of changes in citizen values and orientations are temporary adjustments, soon to be replaced (if not already replaced) by a return to older, more stable, attitudes. The American experience makes clear that municipal reform is extraordinarily difficult to sustain, and it has recently been seen how sensitive "participation" is to fluctuations in the economic climate.[41] Yet there is reason to doubt a return to some presumed "stability" of public orientations.[42] We know that the activists in Stockholm neighborhood groups have tended to be young, middle-class, and well educated.[43] Unlike their older countrymen, these groups have attended schools in which the curriculum emphasizes participation in decision-making. Having experienced a major political success, they can be expected to maintain their pressure for changed political priorities.[44] We know, too, that the Stockholm population has recently begun to reflect cultural, as well as class, differences, as immigrants from various countries have become more numerous.[45] Anticipation, so essential for successful agenda-management, is bound to be more difficult in these circumstances.

Finally, we know that the opportunity for significant public policy error has become greater, as the scale of public undertakings has increased. Arranging financing, construction, and administrative commitments for developments large enough to accommodate as many as 100,000 people is bound to be enormously complex under the best of conditions. If conditions are less than optimal, or if they change in unexpected ways, error seems unavoidable: *Skärholmen,* designed to provide residences for 40,000 people and a shopping center for 180,000 people, opened without a fire station! Among a docile people such misfortune is likely to provoke little comment. Among people

41. For an excellent study of reform and its difficulties, see James Reichley, *The Art of Government* (New York: Fund for the Republic, 1959).

42. I use the phrase "presumed stability" here because, if the preceding argument is sound, orientations are likely to be far less stable than scholars have thought them to be.

43. Häggroth, *op. cit.,* pp. 30–35.

44. In an unpublished paper, Christopher Wheeler of Beloit College has argued that these educational changes presage major behavioral changes in the future. See his "The Decline of Deference: Participation v. Effectiveness in Swedish Politics." Mimeographed.

45. There are now some 300,000 foreign immigrants in Sweden—enough to constitute settlements of foreign language and culture in Swedish cities.

interested in more participation, however, such events are likely to produce a dynamic of criticism and response which can move in unforeseen directions.

A NEW AGENDA

The Stockholm Greater County Council has thus begun its life at a time when many assumptions central to the old urban development game are no longer to be taken for granted. A new political agenda, as potent as it is vague, has replaced the comfortable trilogy of growth, economy, and functionality. Citizens appear to be more aware and more active. Opportunities for governmental error seem greater, and awareness of the variety of orientations that now exist among citizen groups seems less than at any time in the postwar period. Plainly enough, it will no longer be easy to manage the environment. Metro is now part of that environment, of course, with a capacity to shape it that has hardly been tested as yet. But Metro is no "solution," nor did it result from "a decision." Merto grew out of a process of political change, and will itself be effective to the extent that it can further that process with some intelligence.

A MESSAGE OF FIRST IMPORTANCE

Stockholm Metro thus represents little more than a promise to "do better," in a context defined by old antagonisms as well as new hopes. To citizens of San Francisco, Toronto, Detroit, or London, however, Stockholm represents performance, no less than promise. To them, the continuing experiment that is Stockholm contains a message of first importance: mid-twentieth-century cities need not be dangerous and decaying relics of a former age; efficient function need not destroy beauty and liveability; in this age, on this earth, a group of men entrusted with the future of their urban environment have behaved responsibly, and with a measure of success that the rest of the world can envy, if not emulate. For giving us that message, the politicians of Stockholm deserve our respect, as well as our attention.

PROGRESS AND REGIONAL COOPERATION
by HJALMAR MEHR

Excerpts from State of the City Address.
Delivered to the Stockholm City Council, December 5, 1963.

OUR GREATEST problem at present is coordination with the County. This is our most serious problem because it comprehends an entire complex of massive special problems such as housing, transportation, medical care, education, and many more. Virtually no large question can now be planned by Stockholm for the long-term future without taking into account the kind of solution that is tenable from a Greater Stockholm point of view.

This process has now gone so far that, as a practical matter, one cannot discuss any such problem today without causing a debate to flare up regarding the administrative forms for Greater Stockholm cooperation. A new Greater Stockholm concept and a new Greater Stockholm atmosphere continues to develop. Let me point out two factors. The first is our fundamental commonality of interests. Business, industry, the labor market, cultural life, entertainment and recreation in reality function as a unity, and it thereby follows that fundamental questions such as housing, employment, the road network, mass transportation, medical care, education and social institutions are also to a considerable extent common problems. It is thus logical and natural that Greater Stockholm should replace Stockholm as the subject of development. The second factor that is hastening the process is the continuing emigration caused by shortages of land and housing in Stockholm. The new residents in neighboring communes are largely the children of the middle-aged generation of Stockholmers. Many seek to move out after they marry in order to find housing, but they retain their jobs in Stockholm. They feel themselves to be Stockholmers, they regard our trolleys and subways as theirs, our social and cultural institutions as theirs, and they have, naturally enough, considerably less sensitivity for administrative boundaries than the old county residents.

The debate on administrative forms is becoming more and more intensive, and occasionally inflamed. And a reasoned debate on complicated questions of social organization, with implications for a large number of special problems, can hardly profit from too high a temperature.

Paradoxically enough, and fortunately enough, the debate has not become *politically* inflamed. The political parties are conscious of the unusually difficult and intricate character of the administrative question and are playing a waiting game. Nevertheless, I believe that the ripening process among the public has come so far that it may be time to move the positions still another step forward. That the administrative integration process has *systematically* advanced during the past few years seems indisputable, even if it has taken place voluntarily. I will shortly return to this point.

But I note as a great opportunity that all party groups, on both sides of the City boundary, view the problem with a certain cold-bloodedness. I believe that, in the main, these views are grounded on realization of the hard realities. A great deal is at stake for both citizens and municipalities. Too rapid or insufficiently thought-through steps can easily cause administrative unpreparedness—indeed, absolute chaos in certain respects—for one does not create an extensive new community apparatus in one step. Moreover, significant tax increases on both sides of the boundary can result from precipitate action. Hasty action can even lead to poorer service, worse access to hospital beds or places in the schools, not only during a transfer period, but for years into the future. Where one commune may win in reduced waiting time in the housing queue, another may lose; where one patient may win in waiting time for a hospital place, another may lose. Within a commune one may be unhappy with train or bus schedules but still be unprepared to pay large contributions in support of increased service, which for practical reasons cannot begin for a long time. And those who already have housing may not be prepared to offer anything for persons in another commune who do not have housing. In short, a more forceful coordination can bring about major dislocations in the lives of a great many people. The so-called "inertia" of local officials, or their much-discussed "village politics," clearly is built upon substantial political foundations.

The truth, of course, is that the large and difficult problem of "Metropolitan Areas," that is, regional administrative coordination, can hardly be said to have been solved in a functionally acceptable way anywhere in the world. Toronto, and more recently Greater London, are usually cited, but in London and its environs the problem is far from solved, while in Toronto there are many critical voices. And ask Copenhagen, which became fully built long before Stockholm! The reality, in others words, is that virtually all growing metropolitan cities are fighting a difficult fight with the coordination problem. We should bear that in mind when attacking local officials, the national government, and others. The problem is exceedingly difficult, not least in democratically governed countries, where drastic interference with strong opinions is not so easy to accomplish.

In general, how have the Riksdag, other national authorities, county authorities, and the County Council reacted to Stockholm's efforts on various occasions—one as recently as 1950—to promote administrative coordination?

Not more than a few years ago the Riksdag deleted the largest portion of our national grant for regional planning, arguing that it was pretty much unnecessary. Only a few years ago national authorities rejected on principle our proposal for equal grants to subways and highways. Just a year or so ago the cities—especially the large cities— received only a fraction of what they should have received—and what the country areas did receive. The State Railways still has virtually a total stop on new investments for traffic in Greater Stockholm.

No, the iron-hard realities of the urbanization process, with its revolutionary consequences for both rural and settled areas, have not been obvious to so many people for such a long time. As Chairman of the League of Municipalities I have found it to be one of my most urgent responsibilities to utilize the League's collective power to disseminate information on urbanization and its consequences for our nation. Our era's greatest population movement—from the country to settled areas—needs and must receive more effective mechanisms for community finance and administration, for investments in community development, and for more effective guidance of the urbanization process.

It is of little use, now, to blame institutions, parties or persons for what has happened; instead we must successively adjust our operations to new conditions. The political parties, the communes and the national government all must be prepared to do business without the burdensome weight of earlier conceptions, in order to methodically work out professionally correct solutions to the many development problems of the region.

THE SINGLE METROPOLITAN MUNICIPALITY

Before I discuss concrete coordination problems, I want to touch
upon, but put aside, the repeatedly suggested idea that we might
solve the developmental and constitutional problems of the capital
city region by combining all of the communes in Greater Stockholm
into *one* commune.

The single metropolitan municipality is often presented as an ideal
solution, which at one stroke would solve all problems, create apartments, coordinate the traffic system into a well-oiled and streamlined
machine, do away with all overcrowded areas, and cause all bottlenecks to disappear. Naturally the picture is not painted in quite that
way. But when traffic difficulties become evident, when housing production slows down, when the shortages of hospital beds comes into
the limelight, or when school places are insufficient, then the single
metropolitan municipality stands out as the great solution. I do not
caricature: newspaper clippings are piling up in heaps, like the criticisms levied against local officials, particularly those in the county,
for their unwillingness to voluntarily give up their municipal independence.

It is always tempting to say that if we only had a single municipality we could solve our problems more easily and more quickly. And
it is clear that the "law of large numbers" has a good deal to offer.
Rationalization into larger units is a popular solution today in business, industry, finance, transportation. Great changes are also taking
place in community life: the labor market, health insurance, pension
benefits, highway activities, police work are a few examples where the
influence of laymen has disappeared or been limited and where larger
units have been accepted because they have brought about lower
costs and higher effectivity.

But are the large units always best? Stockholm is a region which
today has roughly 1.2 million inhabitants, and which in 15 to 20
years should have in the neighborhood of 1.5 million, and by the end
of the century perhaps 1.7 million, which will be close to one-fifth of
the country's total population. If the Gothenburg and Malmö regions
also become single municipalities, then our perspective becomes
quite overpowering. Why stop there? Why not combine all communes into three, two or perhaps *one* commune—that is, transfer
municipal responsibilities up to the national government.

Let me refrain from predicting the future, however, although I
realize that municipal boundaries are as unlikely to be everlasting as

are other administrative forms, including national boundaries caught in tides generated by the great powers.

Let me focus instead on another fundamental question, namely the question of municipal self-government.

When one is prepared to do away with close to 30 independent communes, with energetic, capable, purposeful local administrations, with their own development programs, their own party groups, their own interest organizations, their own independently operating citizen groups, one should consider the implications carefully. Has local self-government no worth of its own? For my own part I say that it does. In depth, breadth and significance, municipal self-government in our nation is unique, with its total sovereignty over essential community responsibilities. It trains women and men in responsibility; it anchors social consciousness and individual governing capacity in the citizenry; it is one of the cornerstones of Swedish democracy.

It is understandable that the communes in the county defend themselves against being sucked into the so-called giant Stockholm's maelstrom. Local officials regard themselves as bearers of a great and essential social ideal, not as narrow-minded town politicians, as they are sometimes called.

And why has local self-government suddenly become so worn-out? It is genuinely disturbing to see the ease with which central ways-of-thinking are broken apart.

What is the cause? I will not now deal with the deeper motives in this connection. That can wait for another time. *The immediate reason* is the alleged failure of voluntary cooperation. Has voluntary cooperation failed, then? I believe that judgment to be unjustified. In the first place, voluntary cooperation has been the only practical approach possible. A proclamation from Stockholm of a singly metropolitan municipality would have immediately destroyed all bridges to our neighbors, poisoned the atmosphere, and hindered virtually every form of voluntary cooperation for solutions to common problems.

In the second place, a number of concrete results have now been achieved through voluntary cooperation. These results have involved housing, sewers, water supply, highways, medical care, high schools, and trade schools. We have come so far in medical care that a good basis has been laid for a common construction program projected at over a billion crowns. In that area we have a common planning staff. Common interests have also been satisfied in national government activities affecting municipalities. The principles for future road construction have been successfully adjusted between the municipalities and the national government. But success breeds no complaints, and in all these areas where things are working well there is silence.

Another essential factor is that through this patient work in a variety of common organizations a totally new spirit of understanding, respect and trust has developed. I cannot over-emphasize the unusual significance of the Greater Stockholm Division, and the personal contributions that have made in function successfully.

Stockholm views its neighbors as equally responsible and legitimate partners. Our neighbors view Stockholm as a municipality whose leaders seek intelligent and correct solutions that serve the best interests of citizens throughout the region, regardless of municipal boundaries. They know in particular that we do not seek any dominance or hold any quasi-imperialistic views. This is a sentiment of real political significance. If we now raise the question of developing cooperation even further through legislation, everyone knows that this is a reasonable and positive suggestion, not an effort to undermine or overwhelm smaller units. In the same spirit I begin, in the discussion to come, from the following position: *that a regional solution to vital problems of coordination can be won with preservation of independent and active municipalities.* Obviously I ignore here the changes that may come as a result of the national program of municipal boundary reform.

Which areas of community responsibility require far-sighted developmental policies for a future in which urban concentration will continue?

Let me begin with transportation.

TRANSPORTATION

When housing and industrial construction is spread out over larger and larger areas the need for transportation facilities grows. Supplying those facilities obviously is no longer a responsibility of one or another municipality but is instead a regional problem, which demands a far-reaching coordination. In last year's address, I stated a clear desire for a solution based on a triangular coordination of national, city, and county efforts. It is probable that Greater Stockholm's inner traffic must be built upon the skeleton provided by mass transportation facilities. The nature of the problem suggests that transportation construction should be coordinated with housing and job development as much as possible. The ultimate goal, in my view, ought to be a Greater Stockholm joint transportation company.

During the past year the coordination idea has progressed. One may say that we have taken our most decisive step toward Greater Stockholm through the *de facto* decision on a third subway line, whose future service area will be largely outside of our jurisdiction. In connection with this we have reached an agreement to extend the subway network beyond the City's boundaries. The agreement involves the subway for Järvafältet through Solna and Sundbyberg. We have arranged a contract with Lidingö for dividing the costs of extending the subway to Ropsten, near the Lidingö boundary. The northeast suburbs have agreed to a study which assumes national participation in the provision of traffic service for that area. It is particularly important that the County Council has expressed a positive interest in common solutions to mass transportation problems. With that we leave the proposition that these are municipal responsibilities. To suitably round off these developments I note that the Communications Minister, after involved consideration and discussions with us and representatives of the County has decided to appoint a negotiator to seek out a form of coordination for Greater Stockholm transportation.

This progress in the transportation question signifies the beginning of a new era, but I emphasize, only a beginning. Large and difficult problems remain. Cooperation will mean very large financial contributions from the three parties for further road construction, railway investments, and development of the subway system. This is likely to mean changes in our fare system, adjustment of traffic routes, and a variety of other changes that in the long run will be beneficial, but during the transfer period will be difficult. *It is crucial for a solution to the problem that the County be prepared to adopt and accept the consequences of a regional perspective and that the national government consciously participate in solving this great urban problem with increased participation in investments.*

THE HOUSING QUESTION

Just as everyone must admit that the traffic problem is being resolved, so must everyone undoubtedly feel unhappy with the housing problem—the queue is growing. This general unhappiness is seeking an outlet and right now it is the suburban municipalities that are bearing the blame. Their portions of the housing action program have not been fulfilled, it is said, thus providing a clear manifestation of the deficiencies of voluntary cooperation.

Let me first substantiate that a certain amount of slack has occurred in the second housing action program for the 1962–1966 period. Neither last year nor this year will we reach the designated volume of production. The county municipalities have fallen behind somewhat, and it is problematic whether the slack can be made up.

The causes of the slackening are many. A shortage of capital for secondary investments (schools, roads, water and sewer, etc.) has restrained many communes from proceeding with more energy. In other communes, such as Solna, construction has been delayed because of unsolved land problems with the national government which, contrary to earlier expectations, chose to set aside a great deal of land for national institutions. In other communes difficult negotiations over land have once again put a brake on planning, as have unresolved highway problems in which agreement has not been reached with the national government. A significant cause of slowdown has been confusion over the goals of local development-planning. It is also likely that, after the unusual strain experienced in carrying through the first action program—a great success for voluntary cooperation—a certain amount of understandable weariness has overtaken suburban planning agencies. At the same time, area municipalities have come up against a shortage of capital. I remind you that the municipality of Huddinge practically went into bankruptcy hardly two years ago and, like other communes, was then criticized for having built too much without guarantees for the necessary capital.

Is this slowdown in and of itself sufficient ground to declare these communes finished? On the first of January 1946 the 18 larger communes in the county had roughly 165,000 inhabitants. On the first of January 1964 around 370,000 people lived there. That is an increase of over 100 per cent. Is it, then, fair to talk now about a "failure"? Ten years ago these communes built fewer than 3,000 apartments per year. In 1962 they built 9,200 apartments. The first housing action program increased housing construction in the region from 10,000 apartments per year to 14,000, at a time when Stockholm's own construction within its boundaries sank (because of land shortages) from 7,000 to 4,000 per year.

The new action program for 1962–66 was approved by the suburban communes with strong pressure from Stockholm, but also with some resistance because the suburbs recognize their difficulties—

bottlenecks in land acquisition, city plans, capital, roads, specialists, work-force, etc. We pressed our demands up to the limits of their capacity. Now they are being blamed. In the name of fairness, however, let us bear in mind what they have accomplished.

It is sometimes suggested that the national government could produce better results than the municipalities, building ideal housing in lightning-fast time, following the English model. The English "lightning-fast" pace is slow enough compared to the pace in Järfälla, Huddinge, Solna and Täby—to say nothing of Vällingby, Farsta and Sätra-Vårby. But we have a national example, Märsta, where the national government initiated development, and where the commune has in fact had great difficulties with capital, plans, and everything else that has bothered other municipalities.

A month ago I mentioned a rapid ripening process. Whereas Stockholmers quite recently thought that our own outer city area was dreadfully far away and uncomfortable, and that everyone should be permitted to live within the tolls,* now that psychological distance has been overcome. And do not forget that, when the Greater Stockholm Commissioner raised the idea of *Lex Bollmora,* it was greeted with hard opposition from a variety of sources. There was no reason for us to take the risks involved in building in other municipalities, it was said. The municipality of Tyresö was positive, but many within our own city were negative. *Where was the extra-parliamentary support to allow us to build outside our own boundaries then?*

In discussing the housing problem I have been primarily defensive until now, only reviewing our experience in order to do justice to our friends in the county who undertook a difficult municipal activity without receiving appropriate recognition for their work. Let me now take a more comprehensive view of the housing question. As far as Stockholm is concerned, it is clear that the Sätra-Vårby acquisition must be given our undivided attention. The timetable we established is being met. The first residents have moved in only 25 months after the City Council's decision to purchase Sätra. *The first 800 apartments will be ready this year. Next year 4,000 more will be ready. In 1965 and 1966 we will have 4,000 and 4,800 apartments ready for occupancy. If we take housing construction in other parts of the city*

* In its earlier history, the City of Stockholm levied a charge on persons entering and leaving the city. Toll gates were established for this purpose, and these gates came to define the limits of the residential city considered desirable. Although the tolls have been done away with, their names still designate neighborhoods.

into account, we will reach an annual production of 6,000 to 7,000 apartments in the next few years. On October 31, 1961, 5,100 apartments were under construction; this year the figure is 7,600—the highest figure since 1959. We see an increase for all of Greater Stockholm. *On October 31, 1963 construction was under way on 18,360 apartments, around 2,000 more than the comparable figure from last year.*

Our goal—already agreed to by the Liberal Party and, I am convinced, accepted by the other parties—it is to speed the development of Järvafältet and to exert as much pressure on the national government as we can contribute to that end. It is already clear that the first 50,000 "room units" of the 150,000 room units contained in the new disposition plan for the area (of which 71,000 are in Stockholm) can be started relatively soon: Sundbyberg is already under way with some 10,000 units, and I saw in the papers that Solna has arranged a competition already for its planned construction in the Ulriksdal area. What all this means from the point of view of our timetable I don't know. For our part, the location of 35,000 of our room units south of Enköpingsvägen means that we hope to be able to organize land preparations there at a pace that will permit us to continue with Järva construction when the action at Sätra-Vårby begins to wind up.

I remind you also that, in addition to the 6 to 7,000 annual apartments Stockholm will be building in the next few years, we must add the agreements we have reached with our neighbors for construction in their communes—Tyresö, Järfälla, Salem, Nacka. Altogether, those agreements will produce some 6,000 apartments to be divided among Stockholmers during the next 3 to 4 years. New agreements are possible. I call your attention to the preliminary agreement that has been reached that may allocate 10 per cent of newly constructed units to a common pool.

The new housing action program calls for 75,000 apartments during the period 1962–66, or an average of 15,000 per year, with a successive increase from 14,000 in the first year to 16,000 in the last year. Since Vårby was incorporated we have been able to increase the 5-year program by 5,000 apartments, planned for the latter portions of that period. This should mean an increase in annual production to around 18,000 apartments by the middle of the 1960s. Even with our recent slackening taken into account, most signs suggest that, for the period as a whole, it will be possible to achieve the goals of the action program, among other reasons because the Stockholm portion will be larger than the sharply limited contribution the Real Estate Board previously had in mind.

IS THE HOUSING PROGRAM ENOUGH?

But even if it thus should be possible to recover the slack, one can ask whether our projected housing production is sufficient. The answer depends on, among other things, economic developments and further increases in our standard of living. Housing demand is a function of the general economy and the welfare of individual citizens. If Stockholmers had been satisfied with 1945 space standards, but we had built as much as we have, *we would have not thousands, but tens-of-thousands of empty apartments today.* Our statisticians calculate that Greater Stockholm will have some 1.7 million inhabitants by the turn of the century. That is not more than a good 36 years away, which is to say that we hope that our children and possibly some of those present—although certainly none of the over-stressed Commissioners—will be able to experience that time. If the space standards we now enjoy remain the same—hardly a safe assumption! —we would need to build an additional 150,000 apartments. But if the thinning-out—that is, the increase in living standards expressed in demands for more space—continues, we will need to build more than twice as many new apartments: certainly more than 300,000, possibly more than 400,000. And I have not even taken account of the need to replace buildings torn down because of old age, of which there will surely be a great many over a 36-year period.

With full appreciation of the fragility of all prognoses it is nevertheless obvious that we will need many more dwelling units than we have calculated up to now. This may appear paradoxical against the background of factual difficulties we have experienced in achieving current programs. But the conclusion is inescapable: if we want to solve the housing problem in the Greater Stockholm region we must continue to increase construction and increase it more than we have so far dared to imagine. *I conclude that we must set higher goals for ourselves in order to more quickly reach a higher figure, perhaps 20,000 apartments per year or more.*

Is this realistic, when municipalities now have such great difficulties in achieving their present volume? It is at precisely this point that all of my reasoning about regional planning and a more comprehensive structure comes into view. When one suggests that a single municipality would immediately create possibilities for a totally different and more embracing housing program one is really suggesting that Stockholm should take over. I believe that we ought to be very careful with such opinions. Stockholm cannot simply eliminate the other communes and in one step assume responsibility for all planning and execution. Many communes have perfectly good planning agencies of their own, their own building companies, and even their own land; other communes have good planning agencies but neither land nor their own building agencies. Certain communes build themselves. Others deal with private consortiums or HSB or with Riksbyggen, or a combined operation. One does not simply displace these working arrangements or destroy these independent, and for the most part highly effective, agencies without consequences. I think it is totally out of the question to solve the problem of development planning and coordination through a one-shot dose of some patent medicine. But I do think that we can and must take certain definite steps toward coordination, methodically and purposefully. I will return shortly to the question of forms for coordination.

THE AVAILABILITY OF CAPITAL

If we succeed in solving the problem of creating some metropolitan apparatus for increasing housing production, the next question is: Will the national government support an increased production of housing in the Greater Stockholm region? If so, it will be necessary to put aside economic resources, in the form of a portion of the national investment program, dedicated to this purpose. Everyone knows that virtually all communes in the Stockholm area, including Stockholm itself, are having extraordinary difficulties in securing capital. All of them have high tax rates. One cannot ask these communes, in this situation, to throw themselves into such an audacious undertaking without providing guarantees for the required capital.

Such guarantees must include not only national housing loans, but also resources for necessary land acquisition, schools, water, sewers, roads, social and other institutions—in other words, everything that follows from housing development.

What we in the governing bodies of the City and County must request, therefore, is national economic policies sufficiently urban in orientation so that this region, which annually accounts for roughly half of the national population increase, is guaranteed sufficient capital to support a far-sighted and functional development of the region. Despite its heavy tax load, Stockholm alone requires loans of some 300 million crowns per year. The County is said to require more than 200 million crowns. A comprehensive over-view of investment needs is lacking at the moment, but it is necessary to have. Current national economic planning cannot be said to meet these needs adequately. Even here, however, rapid change is taking place, and I will unreservedly state that the government, through its initiatives in traffic, housing and other questions, seems conscious of the accelerated pace of urbanization, and its consequences.

I hope that the national authorities—the government and the Riksdag—take account of the local sector in their budget policies. That sector undoubtedly will require more capital. A deficit in the national budget will lead to an increased need for national credit, probably at the expense of the municipalities, no less than business. If the need for increased capital produced by population concentration is to be met, it is of the utmost importance that Finance Minister Sträng's budget policies receive the support of the Riksdag—as little national borrowing as possible!

THE REGIONAL SOLUTION—
THE GREATER COUNTY COUNCIL

Around the world municipal self-government continues to be drained of its content, indeed, more or less totally eliminated. If one wishes, even here, to protest this development but at the same time do so in a realistic way, one must in part follow the path proposed by the national government, namely create capable and financially powerful municipalities. But it will also be necessary to transfer responsibilities that have exceeded municipal resources up to a regional level, that is to say, increase functional capacity.

It is obvious, of course, that certain *common* problems can be solved better in a large unit, on a larger scale. The question then is whether to allow those responsibilities to be handled by regional units of the *national* administration, that is, a bureaucratic governing model—with no offense to the national administration intended—or to retain representative government—popular control in the form of local self-government.

For regional responsibilities wise fathers and lawmakers have given us the County Council, a second-level municipal parliament, which now deals primarily with medical care responsibilities but which, in my view, should assume other regional responsibilities. Since the process of urbanization has advanced the furthest here in our large region, it is only natural that the problem of larger responsibilities and greater authority has first come to attention here.

For Stockholm to combine with the county municipalities in a Greater County Council would mean that the primary communes would be retained but that in certain common inter-municipal responsibilities that common county commune—the Greater County Council, County Parliament—would assume responsibility.

One can seldom copy foreign models exactly, but I think that a close enough parallel can be found in Switzerland, where the *municipalities* have a large area of responsibility but where, at the same time, the *cantons*—with their own parliamentary system—carry out essential functions of a common nature. Special legislation to achieve such a system for our region would not be unusual, provided that it did not generally destroy current county competence. Stockholm City already has its own legislation, its own legally fixed organization for social care, child care, etc. Our great size always has motivated special legislation for the administration of Stockholm. A County Parliament form would obviously be very similar to existing municipalities, since it is assumed that their all-round work responsibilities would continue.

The responsibilities for a Greater County Council, which I would like to sketch out as I now see them, would be 1) *regional planning;* 2) *coordination and support for municipal housing construction;* 3) *common planning of water-supply and sewer systems;* 4) *mass transportation in cooperation with the national government;* 5) *medical care;* 6) *planning of school operations above the grammar-school level.*

I am aware that other responsibilities can be discussed. I am also convinced that what I have proposed cannot be arranged into a Greater County Council in one step or without further considerations. For these various sub-problems it will certainly be necessary to think in terms of transfer phases of differing time-periods.

But from Stockholm's point of view, we and representatives of both the County and the suburbs ought to be prepared to look into the question of a common county parliament, its responsibilities, its demarcation, and its construction. A Royal Commission is now investigating county structure and national administrative organization in our three largest cities. I believe it would be of great value if the capital city and the county could agree on a common proposal on how we would want to structure regional cooperation among municipalities. Such a proposal would provide a secure basis for the Royal Commission, whose recommendations must precede a national decision.

COORDINATION OF DEVELOPMENT PLANNING

I have already proposed that we set a target of 20,000 or more new apartments per year in Greater Stockholm. Such a target, however, assumes a simultaneous strengthening of administrative resources and an increased coordination of development planning. To attempt this through some sort of single municipality would represent, at the present moment, a dismantling of our planning apparatus; the Greater County Council does not yet exist and it will require a significant amount of time before it will have anything that can be called a functionally capable administration. For the moment, therefore, we should proceed in other ways. But even this can be done systematically, so as to produce increased efficiency. I would like to see the following model followed. At present we have an excellent regional plan and a splendid regional planning office, which is following up and further developing the plan. Similarly we have, in the Greater Stockholm Planning Board, not only a concrete housing program, but also a well-practiced technique for extending that program on the basis of new goals. *In my view, this Planning Board ought to be the center for coordination of development planning in the region until further notice, and it should be strengthened by adding the expertise that is required. I do not mean that we should attempt to build up a giant company, but rather that a capacity for more effective planning and implementation for different communities ought to be developed within existing agencies.*

I want to point out some examples of what I mean.

In Tyresö and Salem, our own company, "Swedish Housing," is now using its technical and administrative capabilities to plan and direct a comprehensive development. *This agency has a significant flexibility and can be placed at the disposal of still other municipalities, if they so desire.* I want to emphasize that this is not a question of placing more construction work in this company's hands, but rather of developing an administration capable of the advance planning required before construction. In Järfälla the Stockholm company "Homes of Stockholm" is being used, and in certain other communes HSB and Riksbyggen are operating in a similar way. Experience demonstrates that effective cooperation is more likely when such communes have access to agencies with this kind of technical capacity. . . .

For today I will not delve further into all of the practical problems of coordination. For example, one of the essential conditions for increasing housing construction is access to large numbers of workers. The supply of workers required by a more intensive development must be made available to the region. We anticipate a positive response from national authorities—in particular the Labor Market Board.

The essential condition for dealing with practical problems is that we have a common understanding of the nature of our problems, namely the need for an increased coordination of development planning in the region and the need for guidelines to implement planning goals.

Finally, I will emphasize that twin national initiatives provide support for regional development planning: the National Housing Board's directives for local 5-year development plans, and the Interior Minister's directive on a common, eventually obligatory, housing queue administration.

SUMMARY

The proposal for a negotiating program regarding regional problems that I have laid out obviously contains no final plans, but should be seen as a basis of discussion between the affected parties. The program can be summarized in the following points.

1. MUNICIPAL ACTIVITIES MUST BE ADJUSTED TO THE DEMANDS OF DEVELOPMENT. PRIMARY MUNICIPALITIES IN GREATER STOCKHOLM SHOULD REMAIN, BUT A BINDING FORM OF COOPERATION SHOULD BE DEVISED TO DEAL WITH REGIONAL PROBLEMS.
2. TO THAT END WE SHOULD CONSIDER A UNIFICATION OF THE CAPITAL CITY AND THE ENTIRE COUNTY IN A COMMON GREATER COUNTY COUNCIL, WITH THE FOLLOWING MAIN RESPONSIBILITIES:
    a. Regional Planning.
    b. Medical Care.
    c. Coordination of and Support for Municipal Housing Development.
    d. Planning of Water Supply and Sewer Systems.
    e. Mass Transportation in Cooperation with the National Government.
    f. Planning of School Operations Above the Grammar School Level.
3. HOUSING PRODUCTION SHOULD BE INCREASED TO AN ANNUAL FIGURE OF AT LEAST 20,000 APARTMENTS, AS QUICKLY AS POSSIBLE.
4. DEVELOPMENT OF JÄRVAFÄLTET SHOULD BE COORDINATED UNDER

THE DIRECTION OF A COMMON PLANNING AND NEGOTIATING AGENCY FOR THE FIVE AFFECTED MUNICIPALITIES, AND THIS AGENCY OUGHT TO BE ESTABLISHED IMMEDIATELY.

5. AS WE AWAIT THE GREATER COUNTY COUNCIL, DEVELOPMENT PLANNING FOR THE CITY AND COUNTY SHOULD BE EXPANDED WITH THE GREATER STOCKHOLM PLANNING BOARD PROVIDING LEADERSHIP, UTILIZING EXISTING AGENCIES THAT CAN BE PLACED AT THE DISPOSAL OF AREA MUNICIPALITIES.

6. DURING THIS WAITING PERIOD, TOO, EFFORTS TO ACHIEVE COORDINATION OF MASS TRANSPORTATION SHOULD BE FOLLOWED UP BY THE CITY, COUNTY, AND NATIONAL GOVERNMENTS.

7. THE CITY AND COUNTY TOGETHER SHOULD URGE NATIONAL AUTHORITIES TO PROVIDE GUARANTEES FOR THE SUPPLY OF CAPITAL NECESSARY FOR HOUSING, SECONDARY INVESTMENTS, AND LONG-RANGE COMMUNITY PLANNING.

An initiative to adjust administrative forms to demands of the time and needs of the situation, coming from supporters of municipal self-government, is an expression of municipal vitality and capacity. I invite everyone to cooperate.

APPENDIX TABLE 1

Number of Registrants for Housing
City and Suburbs

Year	Stockholm	Suburbs	Total	
1948	22,733			
1950	40,428			
1952	59,311			
1954	76,450			
1956	94,130			
1958	108,520	35,557	144,077	
1960	106,910	40,644	147,554	
1962	103,555	43,744	147,299	(est.)
1964	122,600	46,854	169,454	
1966	122,360	58,384	180,744	
1968	101,379	67,683	169,062	
1970	111,278	74,120	185,398	

Sources: Compiled from the statistical yearbooks published annually by the City of Stockholm. Since no one seems to have put together these figures in one place, however, we have had to estimate, for example, in the 1962 figures. These figures, accordingly, should not be taken as fully accurate, though they do give an accurate presentation of both the general number of registrants and the rate of change in the number of registrants.

226

APPENDIX TABLE 2

Age of Dwelling Units, in Per Cent, by Municipality, Metropolitan
Stockholm—Date of Construction

Municipality	Before 1901	1901–50	1951–60	1961–65	Total apartments
City of Stockholm	10.4	64.1	19.2	5.7	328,596
Sundbyberg	2.1	62.7	21.5	13.3	10,905
Solna	3.9	45.3	35.0	14.6	20,914
Stocksund	3.4	79.8	10.0	6.1	1,582
Djursholm	9.4	64.4	11.6	12.8	2,261
Danderyd	0.7	35.1	31.6	30.9	5,059
Järfälla	1.0	14.3	33.5	51.1	11,639
Sollentuna	1.2	44.3	28.2	26.0	10,440
Täby	1.0	26.0	38.8	32.3	9,679
Upplands-Väsby	4.4	25.4	29.7	37.4	4,138
Märsta	5.3	11.7	21.4	56.7	4,584
Lidingö	1.6	45.5	33.5	16.5	11,387
Boo	4.4	57.4	19.4	15.1	2,523
Nacka	4.3	43.7	29.0	21.4	8,136
Saltsjöbaden	8.3	49.6	16.4	25.5	1,938
Tyresö	0.6	18.1	17.0	62.6	4,970
Österhaninge	4.9	20.1	27.5	45.9	5,389
Huddinge	1.0	37.0	27.1	33.6	14,417
Botkyrka	3.1	30.7	44.6	18.9	5,321
Inner suburbs	2.6	37.8	29.7	28.3	135,282
Vallentuna	13.0	26.6	32.7	25.0	2,289
Österåker	7.5	30.9	27.5	32.2	2,849
Vaxholm	18.4	35.7	9.4	24.2	1,583
Värmdö	18.0	48.9	13.6	16.3	748
Gustavsberg	14.3	46.8	29.6	17.5	2,298
Västerhaninge	6.1	19.7	35.1	36.9	3,253
Grödinge	17.7	38.7	20.0	22.1	750
Salem	8.1	51.4	7.6	32.1	1,034
Ekerö	29.6	34.3	11.5	23.7	1,742
Färingsö	20.7	51.3	15.8	8.9	1,207
Outer suburbs	13.8	34.9	22.6	26.0	17,753
Greater Stockholm Total	8.3	55.7	22.2	12.8	481,631

Source: City of Stockholm Statistical Office, *Housing in Greater Stockholm*, Part IV, pp. 63–64.

APPENDIX TABLE 3

Condition of Dwelling Units, by Municipality, Metropolitan Stockholm

Municipality	Excellent	Good	Poor or unfit
City of Stockholm	77.3	12.1	10.4
Sundbyberg	84.1	11.6	3.6
Solna	82.1	8.4	9.1
Stocksund	89.6	7.4	2.7
Djursholm	85.6	10.1	3.8
Danderyd	93.3	3.8	1.9
Järfälla	94.5	2.0	3.4
Sollentuna	86.9	6.5	6.5
Täby	86.7	3.0	9.6
Upplands-Väsby	78.8	9.3	10.9
Märsta	86.5	3.5	7.7
Lidingö	86.0	8.8	4.4
Boo	60.8	7.4	31.8
Nacka	79.0	6.5	14.3
Saltsjöbaden	78.3	8.9	12.5
Tyresö	91.6	2.2	5.9
Österhaninge	82.1	3.4	13.4
Huddinge	83.9	3.3	11.8
Botkyrka	79.5	6.8	12.4
Inner suburbs	84.8	6.2	8.4
Vallentuna	70.6	5.9	22.8
Österåker	70.4	6.1	22.7
Vaxholm	67.2	10.7	19.3
Värmdö	44.9	7.5	44.8
Gustavsberg	63.8	13.2	21.5
Västerhaninge	83.9	3.7	11.5
Grödinge	71.6	6.5	21.6
Salem	56.1	16.6	27.1
Ekerö	59.2	11.2	29.4
Färingsö	48.8	11.0	38.1
Outer suburbs	67.3	8.5	23.1
Greater Stockholm Total	79.0	10.3	10.3

Source: City of Stockholm Statistical Office, *Housing in Greater Stockholm*, Part IV, pp. 49–60.

Note: The above ratings are based on Stockholm's "quality group ratings." These rate apartments in terms of the presence of running water, sewer connections, indoor toilet, central heating, separate bath or shower, gas or electric stove with oven, and refrigerator. "Excellent" ratings are awarded to apartments possessing all of these facilities or those which lack only the last two; "good" ratings are given to apartments lacking the final three facilities; "poor or unfit" labels are given to those which lack any combination of the first four. We have applied words to these 3 categories. Stockholm identifies them only by number.

ARBETARKOMMUN   Workers Union. Locally organized units of the Swedish Social Democratic party. Although these are primarily party organizations, designed to get out the vote for Social Democratic candidates, they also promote a variety of other social activities and thus contribute to the organizational strength and solidarity of the party.

ÅRSBOK   Yearbook. A common title, particularly for official governmental reports of various kinds.

BORGARRÅD   City Commissioner. This term is used in Stockholm for the nine members of the Board of Commissioners. Commissioners are typically drawn from the leadership of the city's major political parties, and meet twice each week as a group to coordinate city political activities. Since each commissioner also is given administrative responsibility for several administrative agencies, the position gives incumbents extraordinary resources for political action.

BORGARRÅDSBEREDNINGEN   The Commissioners Conference. Twice weekly, the nine City Commissioners meet together to discuss the affairs of their respective administrative agencies, determine which reports to forward to the Central Executive Board for transmission to the Council, and coordinate the political activities of their respective party groups. The conference is thus both an important decision-making body and an essential mechanism of communication.

BOSTAD   Residence or dwelling.

BYALAG   Neighborhood Group. In the past few years a number of civic action groups have been organized in and around Stockholm. The old Swedish word for village—"by"—provides the root concept for these groups, as well as a foundation for their protests against large bureaucracies, too-rapid urban growth, and other manifestations of a market-dominated urban system.

CROWN   The basic unit of Swedish currency, the crown, was valued at just under 20 cents during the 1960s.

DAGENS NYHETER   The major morning newspaper in Stockholm, and
in Sweden. A distinctly "high-brow" newspaper, with editorials and
features that are indistinguishable from articles in professional jour-
nals, the paper is aimed at, and shapes the perceptions of, the highly
educated corps of officials who constitute so much of the Stockholm
population. Thus, in addition to providing news, the paper is an important source of opinions among the elite and a major vehicle of communication among them. It is also an active political participant in
shaping local issues.

DEPARTEMENT   Ministry. Ministries in the Swedish governmental system are responsible for budgeting and policy planning, but not for general administration. Thus, Sweden gets by with only twelve ministries,
called "department." Responsibilities of these agencies are indicated
by the prefix, thus Inrikesdepartement refers to the Ministry of the Interior, Finansdepartement to the Ministry of Finance, and so on.

GREATER STOCKHOLM PLANNING BOARD   By agreement of city and
county officials, this agency was created in 1956 to inventory the land
available for housing construction in the Stockholm region. Its report
led to the first metropolitan housing plan, and its later activities helped
to coordinate the expansion of housing construction that took place in
the 1960s.

HSB   One of the two major housing cooperative organizations in
Sweden, HSB was a major actor in the development of new housing
estates in postwar Stockholm. Local HSB branches in the city and the
suburban municipalities gave its representatives access to local politicians, while its interest—and ability to fund, from member contribution—in new housing construction gave it especially close relations with
builders in the area.

KOMMUN (COMMUNE)   Municipality. This is the official legal term,
used for local authorities of all sizes. The somewhat more colloquial
term, stad, connotes an urban municipality, or city. Until recently, stad
was also used in official titles or communications (e.g., stadsfulmäktige,
or city council), but that usage is now replaced by the term kommun.

KOMMUNBLOCK   The term used to refer to the new municipal units
created by combining several existing municipalities into a new whole.
The process of reducing the number of municipalities in Sweden from
some 3,000 to 274 was begun in 1952 and was scheduled to be completed by July 1, 1974.

KOMMUNFÖRBUNDET   The League of Municipalities. Similar to leagues
or associations of municipalities in American states, this is the national
organization that represents municipal interests in Parliament and
other policy-making arenas, provides technical assistance to Swedish
municipalities, and provides a forum for the exchange of information
among Swedish local officials.

GLOSSARY

231

LÄN   County, or region. For governmental purposes, Sweden is divided into twenty-five regional administrative units, each of which carries out governmental functions under the control of elected officials. The national government also organizes many of its functions (including supervision of local governments) by county, and these activities are supervised by an official appointed by the national authorities. This official is called Landshövding, or County Governor.

LANDSHÖVDING   County Governor, or Provincial Governor. The highest administrative representative of the central government in each of Sweden's twenty-five counties (or provinces) is the County Governor. These positions carry extraordinary prestige, and typically go to former parliamentarians or other political figures to whom the government feels some obligation.

LANDSTING   County Council. Each of Sweden's twenty-five county governments is directed by an elected legislative body, which determines policy for the activities carried out by county units. Traditionally those activities have been largely confined to health care, hospitals, and minor educational programs.

REGIONAL PLANNING ASSOCIATION   This organization was created by order of the national government in 1949 in order to stimulate a regional approach to area problems among governments of the Stockholm region. Although hostility between the city and suburban governments hindered association activities in the early years, a regional plan was produced in 1958, and again in 1966. More significantly, the organization provided a locus for discussion and ultimate resolution of many area-wide problems during these years. In 1971, the Association became an arm of the metropolitan government for the Greater Stockholm Area.

RIKSDAG   Parliament. Formerly a two-chamber legislative body, the Swedish Parliament became a single-chamber body on January 1, 1971. The second election to this new body, held in September 1973, produced an exactly even division of seats between the parties of the "left" and the "right": each side received 175 seats in the 350-seat chamber.

ROTLAR   Division. Administratively, Stockholm groups its operating agencies into nine divisions, called rotlar, each headed by a commissioner. From time to time, the number of divisions is changed to deal with changing responsibilities.

ROYAL COMMISSION   The principal vehicle through which governmental activities are evaluated and new policies developed is the Swedish Royal Commission. In any given year, some 50 to 75 such commissions will be active, each of them composed of members of Parliament, governmental administrators, representatives of the relevant interest groups, and citizens. Commission proposals and the research and/or deliberative activities that support proposals are published in the SOU series, easily accessible by year and number (e.g., SOU 1971:48). These reports contain the best social research done in Sweden.

STADSFULLMÄKTIGE   City Council. Local legislative bodies are also referred to as *kommunfullmäktige,* a more generic term.

STADSKOLLEGEIT   Central Executive Board. In Stockholm, formal responsibility for organizing and facilitating the work of the City Council is assigned to a Central Executive Board of twelve members, chosen from each of the parties. In keeping with this responsibility, the Board is empowered to oversee the administration of city affairs, and to make proposals to the Council for dealing with administrative, as well as policy, problems.

STOCKHOLM SUBURBS COOPERATIVE ASSOCIATION   Created in 1947 as a vehicle to oppose encroachment on suburban territory, this suburban organization gradually became dormant as city-suburban cooperation increased. The organization still exists, however, and in the early 1970s was again used as a vehicle for suburban criticism of city policies.

STORLANDSTING   Greater County Council. The new legislative body for the Stockholm region came into existence on January 1, 1971. Like other county councils in Sweden, it is elected; unlike other councils, however, its responsibilities include metropolitan planning, operation of the metropolitan transportation system, regional water and sewer services, housing and secondary education—all in addition to the more traditional county functions of health care and minor educational programs. The new body is in fact a truly metropolitan government with county-wide taxing, as well as service, responsibility.

STRADA *AB*   A private company, totally owned and operated by the City of Stockholm, and used since 1956 to purchase land for city use. Because the company is legally a private corporation, its business need not be conducted in public; yet because it is under the control of city officials, its activities can be directed to publicly-determined ends.

SWEDISH HOUSING, INC.   In 1947 the City of Stockholm created a private stock company, totally controlled by city officials, to plan, construct, and manage new housing in the Stockholm area. This company, one of seven created by the city, was chiefly responsible for the development of the first of the postwar new suburbs, Vällingby, and later became the largest and most aggressive of the city housing companies.

UTLÅTANDE(N)   Report(s). Summaries of deliberations of council committees or administrative boards are typically issued in the form of reports, addressed to the City Council, and available to the public at large. Bound and numbered volumes of these reports are available annually, and constitute an extraordinarily valuable source of information about Stockholm politics and policies.

INDEX

Aaron, Henry, 193n
AB STRADA: land acquisition by, 31, 68; and Sätra acquisition, 78–79
Administrators: dominance in city politics, 48–49, 136–139; relationships to politicians, 143–145; ability to define issues, 147; independence, 152–153; views of responsibilities, 154–155
Agrenius, Gösta, City Commissioner, 150–151
Ahlberg, C. F., Regional Planning Director, 62n
Akerman, Nordal, 139n, 171n
Alesch, Daniel J., 34n
Alford, Robert R., 182n
Allison, Graham T., 196n
Alternative City, 206n
Altshuler, Alan A., 196n
Anton, Thomas J., 8n, 16n, 18n, 30n, 46n, 65n, 75n, 135n, 153n, 179–180n
APF, 28n
Aronson, Albert, 32n; positions held, 68; involvement in Lex Bollmora, 70–73
Åström, Kell, 200n
Åstrom, Torsten, 18n
Avoidance Structures, in local government, 30–32

Banfield, Edward C., 7n, 188n
Battle of the Elms, 204–206
Bauer, Raymond A., 9n, 195n
Berg, Gustaf, 36, 51; death, 101
Berglund, Helge, 35n, 36, 50n
Bergquist, Sven-Runo, 20n
Birgersson, Bengt Owe, 18n
Bjerlöw, Torsten, 24n
Björk, Kaj, 134n
Board, Joseph B., Jr., 25n
Board of Commissioners: description, 34; prestige, 34–35; growth of power, 36; expansion of, 53
Bollens, John C., 165n
Bollmora: Lex Bollmora, 69–73; application to Järfälla, 75–77

Bolmgren, Tomas, 23n
Bonjean, Charles M., 8n
Botkyrka, 57, 73; joint Stockholm Company, 93
Bredäng, 97
Bromage, Arthur W., 165n

Calmfors, Hans, 34n, 143n, 147n
Center party, support, 24
Citizens: orientations to local government, 20–23, 171, 206–208; privatization, 22–23; and local government organizations, 30–32; and Stockholm politics, 139; and local politicians, 142
Clark, Terry N., 8n
Communist party, support, 24
Community: citizen attachment to, 17–19; citizen participation in, 20–23
Conflict: individual orientations to, 23; between city and suburbs, 40–41, 43–45, 85; and governmental performance, 134–135; suppression by city commissioners, 157–159, 167; nationalization of local conflict, 167–168; avoidance by governments, 174–175; and political accommodation, 179–180; as function of dispersed authority, 191; resolution by higher authority, 192
Connery, Donald S., 171n, 203n
Cunningham, Richard D., 49n

Dahl, Robert A., 16n, 32n, 190n
Dahlberg, Gun-Britt, 17n, 28n
Daland, Robert T., 182n
Danderyd, 17n
Decision-making: and land use, 7; as concept, 8; and community politics, 8, 20–23; criticized, 8–9; and social structure, 9–10; and political culture, 16–23; and local government, 25; as applied to Stockholm experience, 194–196
Deutsch, Karl, 194n
Djursholm, 17n

233